D1223601

PRAISE FOR *ROCKY GRAZIANO*

"Jeffrey Sussman brings Rocky Graziano to life not only inside the ring but also—and more important to this reader—outside of it. Graziano's personality and his personal life, his postfight career as a television comedian with Martha Raye and as a television pitchman, and his giving nature to others less fortunate are what make this an outstanding biography."—**J Russell Peltz, boxing promoter, International Boxing Hall of Fame, class of 2004**

"Sussman tells Graziano's story like no other ever written. I learned things about Rocky I never knew before. I could not put it down! This book is a must-read for all, not just boxing fans."—**Bill Calogero, boxing historian and host of the *Talkin' Boxing with Billy C TV & Radio Program***

"Rocky Graziano was one of the most exciting and interesting boxers of the 20th century. Jeffrey Sussman has captured this man and this time period in a fascinating story. Every punch that Rocky threw from his young years through his championship years and into his old age is presented in riveting excitement. Once you start this book, you will not put it down."—**Bruce Silverglade, owner of Gleason's Gym**

"The rebellious knockout artist Rocky Graziano made a dramatic comeback in 1956 with Robert Wise's award-winning film *Somebody Up There Likes Me*. Now, 61 years later, Graziano is making what should be a second award-winning comeback with Jeffrey Sussman's *Rocky Graziano: Fists, Fame, and Fortune*. Graziano's life was colorful and turbulent, and it is chronicled here in exciting detail. Sussman captures it all. This is a must-read!"—**Peter W. Wood, author of *Confessions of a Fighter* and *A Clenched Fist: The Making of a Golden Gloves Champion***

"Jeffrey Sussman's writing on Rocky Graziano breathes life into a legendary fighter who has been largely forgotten in some quarters. Graziano's unlikely rise from thief to middleweight champion of the world and television star is beautifully realized. I thoroughly enjoyed it."—**John J. Raspanti, coauthor of *Intimate Warfare: The True Story of the Arturo Gatti and Micky Ward Boxing Trilogy***

"Boxing aficionado Jeffrey Sussman has done it again! Sussman tells the story of a hero from the late 1940s and 1950s in *Rocky Graziano: Fists, Fame, and Fortune*, discussing the appeal of boxing as a road to stardom."—**Steven R. Maggi, host/executive producer of the radio show *Vegas Never Sleeps***

[signature] 7/18/78

ROCKY GRAZIANO

ROCKY GRAZIANO

Fists, Fame, and Fortune

Jeffrey Sussman

HALF HOLLOW HILLS
COMMUNITY LIBRARY
55 Vanderbilt Parkway
Dix Hills, NY 11746

ROWMAN & LITTLEFIELD
Lanham • Boulder • New York • London

Published by Rowman & Littlefield
A wholly owned subsidiary of The Rowman & Littlefield Publishing Group, Inc.
4501 Forbes Boulevard, Suite 200, Lanham, Maryland 20706
www.rowman.com

Unit A, Whitacre Mews, 26-34 Stannary Street, London SE11 4AB

Copyright © 2018 by Jeffrey Sussman

All rights reserved. No part of this book may be reproduced in any form or by any electronic or mechanical means, including information storage and retrieval systems, without written permission from the publisher, except by a reviewer who may quote passages in a review.

British Library Cataloguing in Publication Information Available

Library of Congress Cataloging-in-Publication Data

Names: Sussman, Jeffrey, author.
Title: Rocky Graziano : fists, fame, and fortune / Jeffrey Sussman.
Description: Lanham, Maryland : Rowman & Littlefield, [2018] | Includes bibliographical references and index.
Identifiers: LCCN 2017035354 (print) | LCCN 2017047004 (ebook) | ISBN 9781538102626 (electronic) | ISBN 9781538102619 (hardback : alk. paper)
Subjects: LCSH: Graziano, Rocky, 1922–1990. | Boxers (Sports)—United States—Biography.
Classification: LCC GV1132.G62 (ebook) | LCC GV1132.G62 S87 2018 (print) | DDC 796.83092 [B] —dc23
LC record available at https://lccn.loc.gov/2017035354

♾ ™ The paper used in this publication meets the minimum requirements of American National Standard for Information Sciences Permanence of Paper for Printed Library Materials, ANSI/NISO Z39.48-1992.

Printed in the United States of America

To my wife, Barbara

CONTENTS

ACKNOWLEDGMENTS

For his indefatigable assistance in locating magazine and newspaper articles, I am grateful to Steven Spataro, chief reference librarian of the East Hampton Library, an institution of almost unlimited resources.

For her confidence in my ability to continue writing a series of books about world-famous boxers and her incisive and helpful comments about the manuscript, I am indebted to my editor, Christen Karniski.

My wife Barbara read my manuscript and pointed out spelling errors that not even my spell-checker flagged. For her diligence, I am grateful.

Sheila Levine, one of publishing's preeminent attorneys, provided me with invaluable and timely advice.

I am indebted to Rocky Graziano's autobiography, *Somebody Up There Likes Me*, for providing me with essential details of his childhood, his courtship with Norma Unger, and his numerous boxing matches, leading to the middleweight championship of the world.

INTRODUCTION

In the cool dimness of St. Patrick's Cathedral in New York City, I sat in a pew and waited for the funeral of Rocky Graziano, one of the most colorful boxing champions of the late 1940s and early 1950s. After having read his autobiography, *Somebody Up There Likes Me*, in 1955, I had made the Rock one of the heroes of my rebellious youth.

A few days before the funeral, I had read in the *New York Times* that the Rock had died of cardiopulmonary failure at New York Hospital. He was 71 years old. Memories of my youth came flooding back. I wanted to recapture the excitement I had felt as a 12-year-old.

I had been too young to see the Rock's fights, but I had been excited by not only his autobiography, but also the movie based on the book. During my aspiring delinquency when I was a teenager, the Rock's anti-authoritarian life stirred my admiration: While stationed at Fort Dix in the U.S. Army, Rock had flattened an officer with one punch, after the officer had challenged him. As a wild kid, he had spent time in Catholic protectories and reformatories with his boyhood pal, Jake LaMotta, aka the "Raging Bull." Rock's father, "Fighting Nick Bob," a failed boxer, had put the gloves on his son's tiny fists when the boy was barely out of diapers. He forced the toddler to box with his older brother Joey. Born into that young boy's brain was the language of fists, of hard-hitting fists, of fists that knew no mercy. The young boy's modus operandi was don't yell, don't argue, don't whine or complain: A punch ends with a strong exclamation mark. Your fist is your calling card. If you want it, you can punch your way to get it. If someone challenges you, a quick left jab followed by a hard right cross will deflate the challenge. That was the boy and the young man on the mean streets of the Lower East Side of New York City.

Yet, as he matured, he became a charming, friendly, and witty raconteur, beloved by everyone who knew him. He was generous to those in need, especially old boxers who lived on the edge of poverty. For example, one day at Stillman's Gym, located at Eighth Avenue and 49 Street, Rocky spotted a former fighter, still young but now blind, for whom Stillman's Gym had become a place for nostalgic reminiscing. The man was unable to make a living. Rocky took up a collection from other boxers, as well as trainers and managers who would congregate at the gym, his big-boned hands wrapped around mostly 10s, 20s, and a few 50s. After someone would offer $10 or $20, Rocky would ask if they could do a little better, give a little more to help out one of their own. He strode over to the former fighter and stuffed the bills into the man's breast pocket. He told him to come back to the gym every month.

I briefly got to meet Rocky when I was in my early 20s. Drenched in sweat, I climbed out of a hot, humid subway one summer evening in 1963. There, in Forest Hills, Queens, on the grounds of the Parker Towers apartment complex, was the Rock walking a small, white poodle. I was momentarily surprised to see this tough guy with such a small bundle of fluff who would not be expected to protect his master. Rocky being Rocky, however, he would wind up protecting the dog. Still, it was not the kind of dog I would have imagined Rocky walking. He had seemed like a German shepherd, rottweiler, or Doberman pinscher kind of guy to me. And there he was in Forest Hills, Queens, a primarily middle-class Jewish neighborhood of large apartment buildings. I had no idea he had taken up residence there; I approached him, just to make sure it was really him. I could see the pushed-in bridge of his nose and the slightly bulbous tip. When I was sure it was him, I waved and called out, "Hey Rock. How you doin'?"

"I'm walking the big guy," he said. "If I don't get him upstairs and give him a biscuit, he could take a bite out of my ankle."

I laughed, waved, and said, "Nice to see you. You're one of the great ones."

"I'll tell my wife. Thanks pal," he responded, heading toward one of the apartment buildings.

With a smile on my face, I walked with a bounce in my step for the next five blocks to my apartment. I never saw him again. I later learned he was living on the East Side of Manhattan, a more upscale neighborhood than Forest Hills, and a lifetime away from the Lower East Side.

And now it was May 1990. There, in St. Pat's, I replayed in my mind the movie version of *Somebody Up There Likes Me*. I thought Paul Newman had been a convincing Rocky Graziano: sullen, exuberant, pugnacious, naïve, often wrongheaded, and bighearted. He had mastered Rocky's "Noo Yawk" accent and way of walking, bouncing on his heels, moving with quick, jerky motions, walking fast paced with no place to go. I was surprised to learn that, if he hadn't died in a car accident, James Dean had been scheduled to play the part. The blond, Nordic-looking Dean seemed inappropriate for a son of Italy. Newman was just right: dark and brooding. A second surprise: Rocky had married a Jewish woman named Norma Unger. When I mentioned it to a boxing pal, he said Rocky had a Jewish manager and a Jewish trainer. He may have felt safe around Jews after growing up in his father's small, violent tenement apartment. Rocky's father, a failed middleweight and a successful drunk, could be brutal and carelessly sadistic to his youngest son. I wondered if Rocky and Norma had raised their two daughters, Audrey and Roxie, as Jews. In ways not often defined, Rocky had been escaping from his childhood his entire life.

After his boxing career ended, Rock appeared in a short-lived television series with Henny Youngman called *The Henny and Rocky Show*, but it was his regular appearances on the successful *Martha Raye Show* where I got to see him almost every week. He went into the living rooms of millions of people, who were won over by his elemental charm, good-guy humor, and self-deprecating jokes. Asked how he got his role on *The Martha Raye Show*, he told W. C. Heinz, "The producers were sitting around and one of them said, 'Why not get a stupid guy like Rocky Graziano?' And then one of them said, 'Let's get Graziano.'"[1] About his education, he said, "I quit school in the sixth grade because of pneumonia. Not because I had it, but because I couldn't spell it."[2] Regarding his juvenile delinquency, Rock described his modus operandi, saying, "We stole everything that began with an 'a'—a piece of fruit, a bicycle, a watch, anything that was not nailed down."[3]

Years later, rather than watching those early television shows, I turned to YouTube, where I was able to view many of Rock's most impressive bouts. As a boxer, he was a brawler, not a scientific fighter. He would swing wildly with both fists. He would take three or four punches just so he could get inside another fighter's defenses and deliver his famous right-handed knockout punch. His trainer, Whitey Bimstein, commented that Rocky was a difficult fighter to train. He went on instinct. He was always rebellious about taking lessons from anyone. All a trainer could do was get him into the best possible condition and let him fight unfettered by training. Once in the ring, facing an opponent, Rocky was fueled by anger and a relentless will to win. He was a force of nature, a hurricane of pugnacity, a cyclone of fury. He let loose with a rampage of punches that never quit. He treated each opponent as if he were a life-threatening enemy. He could only survive by fighting like a demon. Yet, after a fight, outside the ring, Rocky's anger evaporated, and he felt respect and kinship for his former opponents. After all, they had the courage to engage in one of the most brutal sports.

His three fights with Tony Zale were like gladiatorial combats, they were that brutal. Sportswriters claimed those fights were the most vicious, the bloodiest they had ever witnessed. It was during the second one, when the Rock knocked out Zale in the sixth round, that Rock earned the middleweight championship. Upon his return to New York from Chicago, he was like a Goliath-slaying David. In his East Side and Brooklyn neighborhoods, he was celebrated, a conquering hero returning from battle. Congratulations, in the form of telegrams and phone calls, poured in from movie and television stars, popular singers, and even the president of the United States. Rocky felt he had finally proven his worth to his mother and father, and to himself. It was only Norma who had never doubted him. For her, Rocky had always been a hero.

Later, Rocky had wanted to fight the inimitable Sugar Ray Robinson, the most talented middleweight champion of the twentieth century. What an accomplishment it would be to beat the man who stood at the top of the middleweight pyramid. To test oneself against Sugar Ray Robinson and win would be the greatest pugilistic accomplishment for Rocky. Thus, in 1952, at age 33, the Rock fought Sugar Ray. It was the brawler versus the elegant stylist, the wild-swinging aggressor versus the strategic puncher whose aim was like that of a sharpshooter. As expected, the Rock was the aggressor, and Ray was the dazzling and graceful counterpuncher. Rock was 5-foot-7, with a reach of 68½ inches; Robinson was 5-foot-11 and had a reach of 72 inches.

Although he was knocked out in round three, Rock landed a number of hard blows that stunned Ray. "I've met many tough fighters in my long career," Ray said, "but no one ever stung me more than Rocky did." Rocky had thrown the hardest punches Sugar had ever withstood. Yet, the Rock lost, was knocked out, and although it was humiliating for him, he earned more respect for engaging Sugar Ray than if he had avoided the fight. In a joint television interview on a sports program years later, the two men exhibited nothing but admiration and friendship for one another. They laughed and complimented one another; they acted like pals at a reunion reliving the best moments they had shared. Rocky had only one fight after that and then retired. His overall record was impressive: 67 wins, 52 knockouts, 10 losses, and 6 draws.

As I sat in St. Pat's, I heard former middleweight champ Vito Antuofermo say, "Rocky was what a fighter should be. He was tough, could hit like a mule, and had all the guts in the world." When I was 12, that's what had stirred my imagination, that's what I admired of the tough young man. And now he was gone, along with my youth, but not my youthful respect for one of the most colorful boxers of all time. I left the church but not the past.

I've written a biography of one of the most celebrated pugilists, a man who not only put gold into the golden age of boxing, but also polished that gold and made it shine with his colorful personality and skills as a great and fearless brawler. It is my intention to introduce this extraordinary man to a new generation of fight fans, rekindle the memories of those who witnessed his bouts and were thrilled by his victories, and honor a man who first entered the life of a young boy and has remained a fascinating and beloved figure for decades thereafter.

I

THE BAD BOY DID IT!

There he was, an angry, frightened three-year-old. Little Tommy Rocco. He wore a pair of boxing gloves that had been slipped onto his small hands by his father, Nick Barbella, once known as Fighting Nick Bob. Nick had been a pugilistic loser, compiling an undistinguished record of defeats and some wins against mediocre opponents. He couldn't make a living as a professional boxer and finally gave up the dreams of pugilistic glory for the demeaning work of unloading cargo ships on the Brooklyn docks. If he missed morning shape-up on the docks, he and his family went hungry. Indeed, they often went hungry. During the winter months, the family subsisted on sauceless macaroni; in the summer, they ate whatever would grow out of the ground and clams that could be dug out of the sand at local beaches. Coal stolen by young Rocky, sent out as if by a Fagin-like father, was dumped into a potbelly stove, which supplied heat to their miserable abode.

When Nick worked, he would spend most of his meager salary on wine, which he drank until his brain swarmed with anger at the losses he felt he had unjustly suffered and the wins that had not been duly celebrated. Bitterness was the constant taste in his mouth. He had two targets for his revenge against failure, against dreams destroyed, against his miserable life. He would nail his two sons to the cross of his failed ambitions. He would especially take it out on little Rocco.

One can imagine Nick yelling at Rocco to clench his fists. And Rocco's small fists would not defy the old guy, for Nick could deliver a stinging slap to the side of little Rocco's head. Thus, Rocco would fiercely clench his fists until his fingernails dug into the palms of his hands. The big boxing gloves looked like large, brown mushrooms at the ends of short, thin stems, those thin unmuscled arms. The gloves, made for adult boxers, were the only toys sadistically handed down by Nick in the poverty-stricken Barbella home.

Opposite little Rocco stood his older brother Joey. He was six, a head taller, and his father's favorite, for he would obligingly do as he was told, never argued, never talked back. To disobey would result in not only a slap to the head, but also a jolt to the brain, having been called a candy ass, a pussy, a loser. He was told to fight, and he fought. It was better to beat up his younger brother than soak in a bath of humiliation. So, the fight would go on. Joey would throw punch after punch, going after his little brother with the determination of a terrier. And so the older boy would pummel his younger sibling, hitting him with lefts and rights, jabs and upper cuts, blows to the gut and head. The old man, slurring his words, cheered on the beating.

Rocco's small, clenched fists could barely fold his gloves into larger fists. When he landed a blow, it was more of a slap than a punch. Yet, he wouldn't back down. He would swing wildly and with all the strength his small body could muster. Anger and fear fueled his flying fists. Although bigger and stronger than his little brother, Joey knew that if he gave up, walked away, called it quits, his brother would keep swinging at him like a banshee, at least until Nick pulled him off. Once the fighting started, a switch was thrown in Rocco; currents of anger, violence, revenge, humiliation, and fear shot though his body and would not dissipate, would not cool, would not cease. For the rest of Rocco's professional life, a referee would have to flip the switch off. It would end, and Rocco would either be drained and forlorn or pumped up and proud of his performance. For many years, Rocco dreamed night after night of pummeling his father, pummeling his brother, bloodying their faces, breaking their noses, knocking out their front teeth. Bred in the bones and psyche of Thomas Rocco Barbella was the anger of the viciously treated victim. W. H. Auden wrote, "Those to whom evil is done, do evil in return." And for much of his young life, Rocco was determined to spew that evil and anger onto targets of opportunity, most of whom were innocent of any offense. And then, as an angry young man, Rocco met the substitute father who would treat him with love, respect, kindness, and understanding, and

Rocco Barbella emerged as world middleweight boxing champion Rocky Graziano. This is his story, from thug to chump to champ.

Rocco was born on New Year's Day in 1919, on Rivington Street, on the Lower East Side of Manhattan. It was a street of Italian immigrants, and one could hear their voices all along the street—mothers calling to their children, children calling to their friends, fathers home from low-paying jobs as laborers yelling for their kids to get upstairs for dinner. Many of those families were from Naples or small towns not far from Naples.

Like many children in that neighborhood, Rocco was brought into the world by a midwife. His mother moaned on an old mattress in a back bedroom of their railroad flat, an apartment in which one room led into another without the presence of hallways. Rocco's father barely celebrated the new arrival; instead, he shot dice and drank beer in a front room with his boxing pals, all of whom were out of work.

Rivington Street did not contain the family for long. Looking for cheaper quarters, the family moved to Brooklyn. Whether they skipped out of paying the rent is unknown, although such maneuvers were commonplace among many poor families.

There, a young Rocco found the streets to be a school for young tough guys. Anything you wanted you got by being tough, tougher than the next guy, tougher than you ever imagined you could be. Toughness was the rule of the street. You want it, you gotta take it. If you don't, someone else will.

As he grew, Rocco became increasingly restless, increasingly wild. He had an internal fire and a hungry ego that needed to be fed by tough-guy action; he had no need for a conscience; it would have crippled his activities, made him a victim, set him up to be bullied. Remorse was not part of his emotional equipment. He could no more reflect on his restlessness, his wildness, his cruelty than he could imagine a future of success, peace, harmony, and a loving family. He was virtually illiterate and saw nothing of value in an education. He didn't care what teachers had to say; he disregarded the warnings of truant officers. He was a wild child, a child of the streets, and he knew how to satisfy his immediate needs with his fists. The streets were his universe and his university.

If asked about attending school, he would have said it was a waste of time. Sitting still was to be enslaved. Roaming the streets, looking for trouble, that was the life young Rocco chose without knowing why he had chosen it. Scrawny, wiry, tough, the redheaded Rocco had the lean, hungry look of one on the make, of a cat prowling alleys, looking for its next meal, its next victim. Rocco would spot another kid eating a bologna or salami sandwich, or a hot dog, and pounce, grabbing the food out of the kid's hands. Rocco moved so quickly, his victim barely had time to register the missing food. Don't wait to defend yourself; instead go on the offense. Rocco would throw a hard right to the kid's face, another to his belly, and a third to the face again. All the while, his left hand kept a tight grip on the stolen food. He would leave his victim bloodied and crying, bereft and humiliated.

Rocco's mother couldn't control him. His father's beatings with a leather strap only served to further inflame the youngster's anger. His mother bewailed the state of her home, the delinquency of her youngest boy. Her sadness descended into depression. The depression was like a thick, dark cloud that slowly descended on her, then engulfed her. She became a secretive drinker. It was her escape, but it also weighed down the ever-heavier sense of defeat. As days and nights of drinking increased, she began talking to herself, babbling incoherently. Then hysterical comments and screeching laughter erupted from her mouth. She screamed and yelled, she cursed and cried. When Nick couldn't end her crying, couldn't figure out what the hell had gone wrong, he took her to King's County Hospital. There, she was diagnosed as having a nervous breakdown.

For his mother, Rocco had only feelings of affection and warmth. She had never tormented her adorable little redheaded boy. He was the sunshine in the darkness of her existence. But she despaired of his delinquency. It darkened her mood, set her on a course of endless worry. When his mother was taken away, Rocco's anger and confusion were wound tightly together like a pair of pythons, each trying the squeeze the life out of the other. Would he sit still for a while and try to understand his confusion or give in to his anger and return to the streets?

He cursed the fate of his family. His mother's removal to the hospital served to confirm his opinion that life was filled with unrelenting cruelties. His response was to drive his fists against the ugly face of authority, to stick his thumbs in its eyes, to kick it in the groin, to never give in. Anger would be his badge of courage.

With his mother locked up, his home was dominated by his father and brother. Unable to tolerate them, he slept on benches, on front stoops, in abandoned cellars, and occasionally at the apartment of one of his friends' parents. When he did return home, there would be his father instructing Joey on how to be the next world champ. Nick would be demonstrating the perfect left jab, the power of a right cross. He would show Joey how to weave and feint. Rocco wanted to flatten both of them and then take off on an endless run on the beach.

The angry young man's fury was fired by an ever-higher grade of high-octane fuel. He was a menace on the mean streets of his Brooklyn neighborhood. He still refused to attend school, and a truant officer came to his house. He was put on probation, and his father gave him a few hard slaps across the face, accusing his son of being nothing but a bum and a hoodlum. He felt he could no longer beat any sense into his wayward boy, so he sent Rocco to live with his grandparents on the Lower East Side of Manhattan. Maybe they would have more success in controlling him.

His grandparents treated Rocco with love and affection. They fed him nourishing meals. He had his own bedroom; he wouldn't have to share it with anyone. They made him attend school, which he did only sporadically. Although his home life had improved, his sense of the world hadn't. He was still a menace to anyone who got in his way. Bump up against him on a sidewalk and he would push you onto the street. It didn't matter how big you were. Rocky was fueled by fury, and that fury knew no caution.

If you had a sled or a bicycle he wanted, he simply took it. If you resisted or complained, you got a hard fist crashing against your soft nose, soft mouth, or small chin. Blood and bruises were your reward for resistance. Rocco had now become Rocky. His new pals called him Rocky Bob, an echo of Nick Bob. And that young Rocky was as unrepentantly angry—angry at the world, angry at his mother, angry at his father and brother, angry at his poverty—as he had ever been. He would take his revenge against the world.

While living with his parents in a cold-water railroad flat in a Brooklyn tenement, it had been Rocky's job to steal coal from local coal sellers and dump the stolen chunks and bricks into the family's potbelly stove, which stood in the center of the kitchen; it was the only source of heat for four tiny rooms. At his grandparent's apartment, no such larceny was necessary. It didn't matter: he would find other things to steal.

In the summer, the top floor of the railroad flat occupied by the Barbella family was stiflingly hot, a virtual furnace where the air was so thick with humidity it was hard to breathe. The family spent hours on the tar-papered roof, known as "Tar Beach." The bedroom Rocky shared with his brother and sister at least had a fire escape, a poor family's version of a terrace or balcony. In his grandparent's apartment, he enjoyed the luxury of having his own bedroom. In Brooklyn, to help put food on the family's table, Rocky was sent off to nearby beaches to dig for clams. It was the family's only source of protein. At his grandparents' apartment, he enjoyed food that was bought from a local grocer, a fishmonger, a butcher, and a bakery. Rocky didn't feel he was on easy street, but he did feel as if he had moved from mean streets to less mean ones.

The Lower East Side was still a tough neighborhood; there were gangs of street thugs and Mafia social clubs. You still had to be tough to survive. Rocco felt he was a born fighter, trained by Fighting Nick Bob and his own encounters on the streets. He knew the rules of the streets: fight or be bullied, survive or die. It was up to you. As he wrote about one of his fights in *Somebody Up There Likes Me*, "Thumb in his eyes, knee in his groin; if I have to fight dirty, I will fight dirty."[1]

It wasn't fighting that got Rocco into trouble with the law; it was stealing. He and his gang of five thugs stole whatever wasn't nailed down and could be resold. They also stole suits, shirts, hats, and shoes so they could imitate the attire of such cinematic gangsters as George Raft. They stole watches, clocks, and radios, anything that could be fenced. It wasn't a great deal of money: a few bucks here, a few bucks there. It was just enough to keep the gang in food. None of them went to school. Life was lived on the streets, on the rooftops of their tenements, and briefly in the premises of burgled stores.

It was inevitable. It happened. Rocco was arrested. He was tried and convicted in family court. He was sent to a Catholic protectory. There, he proved himself by beating up the head of a gang. He was eventually released and returned to his street ways. He was caught and sent back. He escaped and felt like the toughest tough guy who ever broke out of the slammer and was on the lam from the cops, the FBI, and the courts. It turned out, however, that he was wanted only by the local truant officer. Dreams of gangster grandeur evaporated in the daylight of reality. Yet, Rocco continued stealing and fighting. As he got older, he was sentenced to serve time in prisons that were not as comfortable as the Catholic protectories. Escape would not be so easy. Rocco was on a steep downward spiral.

His mother was desperate to save her son; but she was helpless to convert him from career criminal to upstanding citizen. One day, upon his return from incarceration, he snuck into the bedroom he had shared with his brother Joey. There, he waited behind a door for his brother's arrival. As soon as Joey entered the room, Rocco let fly with fists filled with years of anger and revenge. He knocked Joey to the floor and nearly stomped him. Revenge taken, Rocco took off on a run. He ran and ran and ran until he could run no longer.

Where was his life taking him?

In later years, one of his mob ended up doing a long prison stretch in Sing Sing; another was sentenced to death in the electric chair at the same miserable prison. Was Rocco's life on a similar trajectory?

Rocco met another tough guy, a kid named Terry Young, who wanted to be a professional boxer. That's where the money and glory were. The two became fast friends and often went to the local Boys Club together. There, Rocco would watch Terry hit the speed bag and the body bag, skip rope, and shadowbox. Terry was a skillful boxer who thought he might have a chance to make it big as a pro. To Rocco, it looked like fun, but not if you were forced to do it. Rocco could not handle being told what to do, when to do it, and how to do it. He did it his way, and if anyone objected, they had better watch out. Training looked like a lot of work, requiring much self-discipline, a quality for which Rocco had nothing but contempt. Nevertheless, Terry convinced Rocco to enter the club's boxing competition. They had only been sparring with one another, but then Rocco delivered a stinging blow to Terry's chin that sent him flat on his back. Rather than express anger, Terry stared upward from his supine position for a few moments. Nodding his head, Terry said, "You're a real fighter!"[2]

Without saying a word, Rocco briefly nodded in agreement and opened his mind to a new possibility. Rocco entered the tournament, sized up his opponent as being more passive than aggressive, and knocked him out with a fast flurry of wild lefts and rights. Shortly after the fight, feeling contempt for his former opponent and executing the values of his gang, Rocco proceeded to go through the pockets of his beaten adversaries' pants. While withdrawing a few coins, he was caught and banned from the club. It was a humiliating end to a triumph. To make matters worse, the boy who Rocco had knocked out went on to win the club championship, a championship that could have been Rocco's.

And so, Rocco's initiation into the career of a boxer ended before he could pay his dues. Now his days were filled with more street fights, more thefts, more delusions of rising to the top of the rackets, of being one of the kingpins, the feared men of the underworld. Yet, Terry kept urging Rocco to return to boxing; that's where his future was. It was a vision that Rocco couldn't share with his friend. Unable or unwilling to explain what had happened to him, Rocco laughed at Terry's ambitions for him. He treated Terry as a naïve dreamer. Still, the seed of a boxing career had been surreptitiously planted in Rocco's psyche. While too embarrassed and angry to return to the Boys Club, Rocco found refuge at the Red Range Athletic Club. It served more as a hangout for Rocco's gang than a place to pursue an amateur boxing career.

And then Rocco's seemingly ongoing career as hoodlum and minor criminal was interrupted by yet another arrest. Rather than school diplomas, Rocco was acquiring a resume that listed Catholic protectories, reform schools, Rikers Island, and the Tombs jail, New York City's most forbidding prison.

Just as Rocco's days seemed to be filled with nothing but darkness and grime, Terry Young arrived on the scene again. He presented a new opportunity for Rocco: Calling him Rocky, his gang name being Rocky Bob, Terry told him Joe Giuliani, an aspiring boxer, was sick and could not compete in the New York City Amateur Athletic Union (AAU) boxing tournament. Terry urged Rocky to take Joe's place. He told Rocky he was a top welterweight and would surely win. Having experienced the power of Rocky's right fist, Terry knew it would deliver Rocky's winning ticket to the championship. The boys continued to argue, Rocky treating the idea of boxing as something less than a joke, while Terry kept urging Rocky to use his talents to become an amateur champ.

The day ended with neither side convincing the other. But the seeds of doubt had been planted in Rocky's mind. Would he continue to be a thug, a chump in the world of straight guys? Or would he turn his life around and become someone? It was hard for Rocky to shatter his self-made image as a gangster prodigy. He had contempt for the straight world; yet, if he could earn its respect, it would make his mother proud. It would also show up his father. After all, it would not be Joey who would be getting into the ring to make a name for himself. It would be the once-disgraced son of a failed boxer and a distraught mother.

The next day, a contemplative Rocky met Terry in front of the Boys Club. Terry introduced him to Constantine (Cus) D'Amato, a trainer par excellence. He had been training Joe and was willing to train the young, rebellious Rocky. Having watched Rocky's lack of technique, D'Amato explained to him that he must learn to jab with his left fist. He couldn't just keep throwing his right, as powerful as it was. He needed to learn defensive maneuvers. He couldn't just charge, bull-like, against his opponent, throwing rights and a few wild lefts, and expect to win. The fight was scheduled to take place in the Broadway Arena in Brooklyn. As much as D'Amato attempted to teach Rocky not to throw a flurry of wildly swinging rights and lefts, Rocky did just that. Nonetheless, after just two minutes of round one, Rocky had sent his opponent to the canvas with a powerful right cross. It was a devastating punch.

A week later, Rocky was entered in the semifinals. He approached the ring, and there he spotted the same kid he had knocked out a week earlier. When Rocky asked him what he was doing back in the ring, the kid explained that Rocky had not knocked him out. He had knocked out the kid's twin brother.

Rocky responded, "Well, kid . . . I'm going to do you a favor. So your brother won't have anything against you, I'm going to knock you out in the first round too."

And true to his prediction, Rocky knocked out the remaining twin in the first round. Rocky now felt he had finally arrived, that he had achieved something that made him proud, satisfying his yearning for respect, not only from the straight world, but also from the wiseguys and the wannabes.

"From that day on, after I took the city title and got my name in the papers . . . I couldn't walk down First Avenue or Second or across 10th Street without everybody stopping me," he said.[3]

Seeing an opportunity to cash in on an up-and-coming young welterweight, the wiseguys and their emissaries came calling. They wanted to sign Rocky to long-term contracts, harness his career to their cash flow, make him one of their earners. Where Terry Young had seen the boxing gloves of a potential champion on Rocky's clenched fists, the wiseguys saw the same gloves with dollar signs pasted on them.

The reactions of Rocky's parents to his newfound celebrity were predictable. His father claimed credit for teaching Rocky to fight from the age of three. He even claimed to be Rocky's manager. Rocky didn't know whether to be amused or angry, or both. His mother was horrified that her beloved son would follow in the footsteps of her drunken, belligerent husband. She begged Rocky not to continue; she urged him to follow on the straight and narrow path of his brother Joey. Again, Rocky didn't know whether to be amused or angry. He did know that he wouldn't wind up like his father, the failed and angry Fighting Nick Bob, and he would not follow the example of his honest, hardworking older brother. While Rocky was a black sheep among his four siblings, he was his own black sheep—and really not a sheep at all, more like a lone and lonely tiger looking to dominate his domain.

Rocky moved on to being a club fighter, getting $15 here, $15 there. He always won and so was always assured of a payday, no matter how small. Where there wasn't money as a payoff, there was a fancy wrist watch; it was quickly pawned, and the money went into Rocky's pocket. Although he was doing well as a fighter, he still thought he could succeed as a wiseguy in some lucrative, illegal racket. The money he earned would serve to pay his way, to finance some grandiose plan that would put him on the same plateau as the top neighborhood wiseguys.

Rocky was introduced to an influential promoter named Eddie Coco, who proceeded to set up a couple of professional bouts for the pugilist. At his first bout, in the Bronx, Rocky heard some tough guys sitting at ringside laughing at him. They wanted to know who the pretty fag was. What joker had put boxing gloves on a guy with such a pretty face? The comments infuriated Rocky; he ferociously ran out of his corner and viciously pummeled his opponent, knocking the guy down. His opponent reluctantly kissed the canvas. After he was declared the winner, Rocky heard the same ringside tough guys asking, "Who's that kid?" He punched like a jackhammer.

Rocky had moved up. His earning capacity had increased. He was now making more than $15 a fight but was still not in the big money. Earning $35 here, $70 there was certainly an increase, but it was nothing compared to what a really good pro could earn. The dreams of being a wiseguy were beginning to fade. Rocky now dreamt of glory in the ring. He could lie half awake and revisit his fights. The dreams were sweet. It was a new and better world. Rocky began to focus solely on boxing as his career. He stopped hanging out with his gang, and he gave Eddie Coco permission to set up one professional bout after another. Rocky felt he was on his way up, and the feeling exhilarated him.

All the while Rocky was boxing, he was on parole. Unbeknownst to him, he had inadvertently violated many of the rules of his parole; he could not have paid attention to those rules, for they existed somewhere outside of his knowledge. For Rocky, boxing was all that mattered now, and he had not seen the booby trap in his parole. He was picked up by the cops and dragged off to a station house. He shouted that he had done nothing wrong, had committed no crime, was clean. It didn't matter. He could have been yelling at trees in a forest. Rocky was charged with statutory rape by his girlfriend's mother, who didn't like her daughter dating a thug. He was locked up, spent a week in jail, and was brought in front of a judge. He thought the judge would go easy on him, for the guy was a celebrity and known to have a big heart. The man in the black robes was the famous "Iron Man," the former great and beloved New York Yankees first baseman Lou Gehrig, slowly dying of ALS. While the rape charge was dropped, Gehrig sentenced Rocky to six months in reform school for breaking the conditions of his parole. Asked if he wished to say anything, Rocky told the judge to go to hell.

Rocky served the full term and, upon his release, finally felt free, free to pursue his career as a boxer, free to walk down the streets of New York without the cops grabbing him for a crime. He felt he could start with a clean slate. He wouldn't have to look over his shoulder and worry about hurting and shaming his mother. He had plans, big plans, and nothing and no one would get in his way; however, two months after his release, he received a draft notice from the U.S. Army. He was to report for his induction into the armed forces.

For basic training, he was sent to Governors Island; from there, he was sent to Fort Dix, New Jersey, with thousands of other young recruits. War was raging in Europe and the Pacific. Yet, it hardly registered in Rocky's consciousness. It was not his concern. All he cared about was himself. To Rocky, the army began to seem worse than jail. It was regimented, stifling, more tightly scheduled than reform school. You were regularly ordered around. Do this. Do that. Yes sir. No sir. The regimented nature of the army made him feel like punching through the rules, breaking out, taking off. Rocky felt it was like being thrown in the hole at Rikers, like wearing handcuffs night and day. Like being a wild animal with hoofs chained to a post. The officers yanked the chain, and the buck privates said, "Yes sir." Why would any man who called himself a man want to be yanked here and there? In a popular ballad, the singer claimed to have life on a string. Rocky felt his life was at the end of that string. Was this the American way? Not for Rocky, a freewheeling hood of the streets, a tough and independent up-and-comer with fists of steel.

He would no more follow the army's schedule than he had followed his teachers' instructions before dropping out of elementary school. He was on his way to becoming a celebrated rebel years before such rebellion was portrayed on the silver screen by Marlon Brando, James Dean, and Montgomery Clift. Rocky spit in the eyes of the army. He rebelled against all orders. He refused to do what he was told to do. "Fuck you" was his response to a corporal, a sergeant, a captain, to anyone who gave him an order. He beat up a corporal and chose to sleep in after reveille and not be in bed until well after taps had sounded. He tried to start up some crap games and initiate a small black-market operation, and often went AWOL, finally being brought before one of the fort's commanding officers, a captain.

Rocky was ordered to stand at attention, being chastised and told he was typical of most New York Jews and Italians, and that the army would knock the New York wiseguy spirit right out of him. As the snarling, angry captain got up from the chair behind his desk, Rocky slugged him, knocking the captain over the desk and onto the floor, where he lay unconscious. From there, almost in a daze, consumed with fear and a need to escape, Rocky managed to sneak out of the camp and make his way back to his parents' apartment on the Lower East Side. It seemed as if Rocky's dreams of becoming a championship fighter would end in another prison sentence.

In New York, Rocky met his old boxing pal, Terry Young, who gave him some civilian clothes. Young took him to Stillman's Gym, a famous boxing establishment on Eighth Avenue in Manhattan; it was where some of the era's most celebrated champions had trained. The facility was managed by Lou Stillman, a gruff-talking ex-cop who chomped on a cigar and wore a snub-nosed .38-caliber pistol in a shoulder holster. He made sure the gym was always filthy, so filthy, in fact, that heavyweight champion Gene Tunney refused to train there. The floors were never swept; indeed, it seemed as if the floors were one giant spittoon. The windows were as black as coal, and the sound of gloves hitting speed and body bags, along with sneakers skipping rope, sounded throughout the place. It was the music, the melody and rhythm of the gym. Boxers, trainers, and managers loved the place, and so did the fans and bookies who paid to watch the fighters train.

Rocky entered Stillman's, not knowing he was entering the school of hard knocks, the place where he would learn to be a world champion, where his eyes would be opened to a new and dazzling future, one where he would not be a criminal on the lam, some punk regularly busted by the cops. Instead, it would open the door to a future, one where Rocky would be celebrated as one of the most exciting fighters of his time, a hero to young and old.

Terry introduced Rocky to his own manager, the kindly and beneficent Irving Cohen, who took one look at Rocky and told him not to become a fighter. He thought Rocky was too good looking to get his face messed up, to wear scar tissue above and below his eyes, to get his nose flattened and his ears pummeled out of shape. And maybe suffer brain damage. Irving pointed out one such sad case who, while sitting ringside, began trembling at the sound of the bell. Is that what he wanted?

"If you knew what it was like, you wouldn't want to be a fighter," he said. "Take my advice. You look like a good kid, a smart fellow. You go find yourself a job that pays $50 a week, and you'll be thankful you listened to me."[4]

Rocky, of course, refused to accept that advice. He asked to have a fight, to get into the ring and show Irving what he could do. He just wanted to earn some money. He was broke. Following Terry's urging to give Rocky a chance, Irving consented. Rocky changed into a pair boxing shorts, had his fists taped, put on a pair of gloves, and entered the ring to fight the former middleweight champion of Argentina. Rocky, eager to show his stuff and collect a few dollars, knocked the Argentine out with a hard right cross to the guy's left temple. He landed on the canvas with a thump.

Before the referee could count to 10, Irving Cohen had changed his opinion; he wanted to manage Rocky and get him one of the best trainers in the business, Whitey Bimstein. Rocky refused. He would no more train than he would take orders from an army officer. He was out of the gym in a flash, letting Irving know he would only be back when professional fights for money had been arranged for him.

Rocky's career as a free man was short-lived. He was eventually picked up by two MPs and was on his way back to prison. After being locked up for a short while, he was told he should return to Fort Dix, where he would undergo a court-martial. He was also told that no guards would accompany him to the fort. He would be on his own. If he proved himself honorable and returned of his own free will to stand trial, his behavior would mitigate his sentence.

Instead of returning to Fort Dix, Rocky returned to Stillman's Gym. He conferred with Irving Cohen, to whom he lied, saying he had been away to get his discharge from the army. Irving didn't know Rocky's surname, and it was needed to obtain a boxing license. Not willing to use his real name in case the cops and the MPs were looking for him, Rocky informed Irving that his surname was Graziano. It was the name of a pal who had been taken off the streets by the cops. Dominick Graziano was no longer around, so why not use his name?

Irving set up a series of fights for Rocky, first with a fighter named Curtis Hightower, who Rocky knocked out in the second round of a fight staged at the Broadway Arena. After that win, Rocky was signed to fight Mike Mastandrea. He, too, went down for the count, and Rocky was now developing a following. It was May 1942, and Rocky finally felt he was sitting atop the world.

However, his world was about to collapse yet again. While in the office of the New York State Athletic Commission on Worth Street in Manhattan for a prefight weigh-in, Rocky was confronted by two cops. It was June 1942, exactly one month after he had exulted in his boxing triumphs and a court-martial sentenced him to one year of hard labor for desertion. He would serve out his time at Fort Leavenworth, a prison for deserters and hardened career criminals.

It was there that Rocky did what all tough kids must do to the local bully: He won the respect of some tough gang members who had initially attempted to intimidate the short Noo Yawk City wiseguy. Rocky was only 5-foot-7, but he challenged the leader of the toughest prison gang, a 6-foot-4 illiterate hillbilly named Harvey Miller. Rocky's unwavering ferocity and pugnacity were enough to cause Harvey to first respect Rocky and then befriend him. He loved to hear Rocky talk of real Noo Yawk City thugs and gangs, and their criminal exploits. When Harvey told Rocky he wanted to find Jews to beat up, Rocky introduced him to his pal, Julie Kaplan. Harvey, who had never met a Jew, refused to believe that Kaplan was a Jew, for he didn't have horns. Rocky explained the Jews looked like everyone else and that Julie was his friend and should be respected. Harvey was amazed but accepted Rocky's pal as another prison colleague.

But it was another man, Sergeant Johnny Hyland, who gave Rocky the opportunity to prove that he was truly a promising middleweight. Rocky had begged the sergeant to let him join the boxing squad, but the sergeant sneered at Rocky's short height and pretty face. Rocky finally said he would fight anyone the sergeant wanted to put in the ring against him. The sergeant, seeing an opportunity to teach Rocky a lesson, put him in against a light heavyweight named Brownie Davis from Chicago. Brownie was a big, solidly muscled boxer who was inches taller than Rocky. Once in the ring, both men squared off, and Brownie began pummeling the shorter, lighter welterweight. Rocky, who was able to absorb an extraordinary amount of punishment, was letting Brownie deliver punch after body punch. While fending off some of the punches and landing a few, Rocky was really just waiting for an opening. He feinted with a left. Brownie went to block it, and Rocky landed his devastating right cross to Brownie's left temple. The light heavyweight sagged to the canvas like a deflated balloon. The sergeant thought it was a lucky punch. Brownie assured him it was nothing of the kind. It was a well-aimed rifle shot.

Rocky went on to beat one opponent after another. The army brought in welterweights and middleweights, not only from the prison, but also from military camps throughout the country. Rocky beat them all. He was now a hero and granted special privileges. The sergeant allowed Rocky to choose Julie as his manager and let Harvey, although awkward and flat-footed, fight as a heavyweight. Rocky was finally enjoying his life in prison. He had his pals and plenty of time to reflect on his life. What had he been doing for 22 years? Was there one thing that was admirable about him? Who was he going to blame for his miserable life? For the time he spent in reformatories, jails, and prison? Not his mother. Not the streets. Not his delinquent pals. Not the army. Yes, he had a grudge against his father, but so do a lot of young men. It doesn't ruin their lives. Rocky was becoming self-conscious. He was able to evaluate the stupid moves he had made throughout the years and view the possibility of a legitimate life as a professional boxer. Once out of Leavenworth, he figured he could go down a different path.

Rocky had three months shaved off his sentence for good behavior. On the train back to New York, he asked himself the same questions he had asked in the gym at Fort Leavenworth.

He said, "So where would I have been today, instead of on a train banging its way to New York City? I would still be a half step ahead of the law, worrying about getting picked up and serving a bit and sweating out parole." Rocky concluded, "Kid, when you walk down them steps, you are going to walk into a new kind of life. You are not the same Rocky Bob Barbella who used to live at 141 First Avenue."[5]

And that new life would revolve around his manger, Irving Cohen, his trainer, Whitey Bimstein, and a woman who would become his wife and best friend for the rest of his life, Norma Unger. As W. C. Heinz said to Rocky, "You married a Jew, and you had a Jewish manager [and a Jewish trainer], and they made you save your money."[6] And, of course, they helped him stick to the goals he set for himself in the gym at Leavenworth.

2

THE TRAINERS AND THE GYM

When Rocky's neighborhood pal, boxer Terry Young, first brought Rocky to Stillman's Gym, fight manager Irving Cohen was skeptical of the buildup Terry had given him. Yeah, okay, Rocky was a tough kid, but could he fight a trained boxer in the ring? Street fighting is not the same thing as boxing. There have been many tough street punks who wound up on their asses because they didn't know how to defend themselves against a skilled pugilist. Irving Cohen, sagacious, low key, and agreeable, finally consented to putting Rocky in the ring with Rocky's pal Terry, who was an up-and-coming lightweight with a lot of promise. Terry weighed 135 pounds, and Rocky weighed 150. Rocky had a powerful right punch and was certainly tough, but he was untrained. Once in the ring, he swung wild, emotionally driven rights and lefts. Terry bobbed, weaved, danced, and feinted. He was a quick-moving, elusive target. He was able to land punches at will.

After a few minutes, it was obvious which man was the professional pugilist. Rocky had a bloody nose and a cut lower lip. He had even been knocked down, or perhaps he slipped. The street brawler could have beaten the boxer on the street; all he needed was a knee to the groin, a gouge to the eye, and a python-like grip around his opponent's throat, and he would have driven his opponent into submission. In the ring, however, the rules of boxing prevailed. That's where a well-trained boxer demonstrates his skills and techniques, and uses them like armor and a sword. It contributes to tactics that build to a devastating strategy. Without those weapons and without knowing how to best deploy them, Rocky would be a whirling dervish of frustrations. Rocky was a smart guy, and his experience in the ring with Young was a well-earned lesson. Rocky knew he would dislike the rigors of a training regimen, but he also knew that if he wanted to be a pro and rise to the top, he would have to learn technique and sharpen his skills. With little formal education and having no trade, boxing was the only legal option available for him. And it offered the ideal outlet for belting out his anger at the world.

It was time for Rocky to meet Terry's trainer, one of the best in the business—former bantamweight boxer Morris "Whitey" Bimstein. As a professional boxer, Whitey had 70 fights, and his countenance was a faded map of those years-ago encounters. His pink, oval face, with puffy tufts of snowy white hair shooting out on the sides of his rounded cranium, gave him a look of gentleness. His coloring and features led many people, upon first meeting him, to think he was of Irish descent, a small, pink leprechaun of a man. But ethnicity mattered little to Whitey. He lived in the world of boxing, where men were judged by their skill, not their ethnicity, race, or religion. A boxer was a boxer, and he was defined by his talent and technical skill—and, of course, his ability to win.

Whitey was brilliant at motivating his fighters. In his book *Corner Men*, Ronald K. Fried has middleweight boxer Vinnie Ferguson saying,

> Whitey was one of the best psychologists in the world. . . . He would light a fire under you. He'd maybe tell you that the other guy insulted you or something. . . . He knew how to get things outta guys. . . . He'd say, "This guy can't carry your gym bag," or "This guy is a baby compared to you."[1]

Fried also reports that if Whitey had a fighter slow to emerge from his corner after the bell sounded, he would jab him in the ass with a pin. He would do whatever it would take to motivate his boxers. As a cutman, he proved equally resourceful: During one of Rocky's momentous fights with the hard-as-nails Tony Zale, known as the "Man of Steel," one of Rocky's eyes was bleeding so badly, he couldn't see out of it. The other was swollen shut. Whitey pressed a quarter against the swollen eye, significantly reducing the swelling so that Rocky was able to see out of that eye. Whitey had also staunched the bleeding of the other eye. Rocky went on to win the fight and the middleweight world championship. (The trilogy of fights with Tony Zale, three of the bloodiest fights in twentieth-century boxing history, is described in a later chapter.)

Whitey had a reputation as a tough guy, a guy without sentiment, someone who only cared about winning. It was not true. He was devoted to the health and well-being of his boxers. He taught them how to protect themselves, how to maintain the highest levels of physical fitness and well-being. Whitey made sure they ate regularly and got sufficient sleep. Indeed, when it came to his boxers, he cared for them like a bear with its cubs. He thought that being a trainer meant you protected your boxers. You didn't let them train in excess; you didn't let them get hurt while sparring. You always had the necessary medicines and tools to patch up your fighters. You always kept up their spirits. Whitey was a combination of psychologist, gym teacher, boxing trainer, father confessor, friend, and motivational speaker. He lived for his fighters, and they knew it. Whatever Whitey said was law, and those laws, tried and true, were delivered with the kindness and understanding of a father instructing his sons.

Whitey had a huge appetite for life, not only the life of boxing, but also life in general. He loved a good drink and rarely got drunk. He loved a good meal and often ate enough for two or three larger men. He seemed like a voracious character straight out of Fielding's *Tom Jones*.

For his ability as a cutman alone, Whitey was known as the Florence Nightingale of cornermen. He had stitched cuts, staunched bleeding lips and noses, and opened eyes that had been swollen shut. He did it all in a matter of seconds between rounds and with the loving care of a benevolent father figure. His fighters loved him, depended on him, felt good knowing he was just a few feet away. There he was in the corner of the ring with cotton swabs in his mouth, tools of his trade in one hand and ointments and lotions in the other. He had never gone to medical school, but he could stitch up a cut faster than any surgeon. He could motivate his boxers faster than any motivational speaker. He not only bandaged and inspired his fighters, but also trained them to be the best they could possibly be. He knew how to point out a fighter's weak points and propose necessary remedies; he knew how to boost a fighter's confidence, to make him feel he was a winner, to turn him into a tiger. Many fighters, Rocky included, might not have won their championship bouts without Whitey.

Indeed, as a trainer, Whitey was regarded by his boxers as second to none. They would do whatever he told them to do, and he never gave bad advice. Mistakes were not in his arsenal of advice. Every word was meticulously chosen to have a positive effect. Whitey was not only a sagacious tactician, but also a far-seeing strategist. He knew what fighters needed to do to win against the weaknesses of their opponents. Whitey had been a cornerman for some of the great legends of the sweet science: Harry Greb, Gene Tunney, James J. Braddock, Tony Galento, Rocky Marciano, and many other ring notables. If ever there had been a championship for boxing trainers, Whitey would have worn the crown.

Of managers and great trainers, A. J. Liebling wrote in *The Sweet Science,*

> Managers, like book publishers, make most of the money, but trainers, like editors, participate more directly in the artists' labor. Bimstein and Brown [trainer Freddie Brown, who had worked with Whitey] are editors of prizefighters. Mediocrity depresses them; they are excited by talent, even latent. What they dream about is genius, but unfortunately that is harder to identify.
>
> Technically, Whitey and Freddie can do a lot for a fighter—excise redundant gesture and impose a severe logic of punching, as demonstrable as old-fashioned mathematics.[2]

Whitey's cleverness was demonstrated by the following incident: One day, his promising lightweight, Terry Young, was scheduled for a bout in Honolulu. But Terry hated traveling by plane. He was willing to take a short flight only if absolutely necessary but nothing that lasted more than half an hour. Whitey told Terry that Honolulu was in New Jersey and the flight would take a mere 15 minutes. Terry agreed to board the plane, and his reaction to being airborne after 15 minutes was never reported; however, he did fight in Honolulu and subsequently returned to New York. No doubt a wiser man.

Regardless of such tricks, Whitey was loved by his boxers, for they knew he had their best interests at heart. Boxers were like his progeny. In fact, he was admired and respected by boxers, as well as their managers, and young trainers who wanted to learn their trade from the expert.

As noted, Whitey never attended medical school; in fact, he never went beyond the eighth grade at PS 62, located at Hester and Essex streets on the Lower East Side of Manhattan. As a student, he had excelled in sports: He played basketball and baseball, and was on the track team. He had never stitched up a cut or placed more than a bandage on a superficial wound. Not long after completing his short-lived formal education, he wandered into a local boxing gym and immediately fell in love with the sport. He took lessons and proved to be a proficient journeyman fighter. He hung out at the gym for hours each day. He skipped rope, shadowboxed, and hit the speed bag and heavy bag. His friends were aspiring boxers, most of whom were poor boys, the children of hardworking immigrants who lived modestly from paycheck to paycheck. Some of the boys who hung out at the gym were aspiring gamblers and runners for bookmakers.

Papa Bimstein was not happy about his son's circle of friends and his life at the gym; he was concerned that young Whitey would acquire the values of those he spent so much time with. Thus, he decided to save his son from a brutal sport and the lowlife figures for whom the gym was a social club and a nonaccredited university. He did not want his son to become a gambler or a bookie—and certainly not a boxer who would have his brain pounded out of shape as if it were butcher's meat. The gang at the gym—and everything it represented—was anathema to Papa Bimstein's ambitions for his son. He decided to move his family to a better neighborhood.

Compared to the dirty, hustling, bustling streets of the Lower East Side of Manhattan, the Bronx seemed like a rural, sylvan setting to Papa Bimstein. It was certainly less crowded and cleaner than the Lower East Side. You could walk down a street and enjoy a quiet evening, without peddlers offering you a deal on something you didn't need or want. Whitey reluctantly accepted the move. He could not effectively object, for he was still a boy unable to support himself. But he was determined to stick with boxing.

Whitey's curiosity brought him to an unlikely venue for boxing; it was St. Jerome's Catholic Church, where the priest, Father Ryan, gave boxing lessons. Ryan didn't care if Whitey was Jewish, for he saw in the young man a natural ability, and he proudly and regularly trained him. Whitey proved to be an apt student, learning a pugilistic catechism of rules and techniques that remained with him for the rest of his life. From the church, Whitey went on to have a series of bouts at the Fairmont Athletic Club. He did well but made little money, especially after paying his cutman and trainer. In any case—like his future stubborn student Rocky Graziano—he hated training. Rather than spend hours in the gym, he preferred to gobble down a few hot dogs before a fight. And, if possible, a charlotte russe or two. Rather than running miles each day, Whitey preferred a leisurely walk.

He had 70 fights, the outcomes of which are long forgotten. Following those fights as a bantamweight, and not being able to earn more than a pittance, even after selling tickets to his own bouts, Whitey joined the U.S. Navy, where he was put to work training sailors in the manly art of self-defense. For Whitey, it was a perfect setup. Rather than fighting, he would train others to fight. He would no longer be susceptible to the injuries suffered by boxers. His head would no longer get pounded. As a trainer, he proved to be a natural teacher, and his students learned the elements of boxing. None would turn pro, but they all became proficient. Whitey had found his true calling, his mission, his life's work. Hence, when he got out of the navy, he figured he could earn a better living training professional boxers than being a boxer himself.

In 1925, he formed a partnership with another legendary trainer, Ray Arcel. The duo trained many great fighters until their partnership was dissolved in 1934, a dissolution brought on by the deprivations of the Depression. Neither one could make much of a living as a trainer. It was hard times. Yet, Whitey couldn't stay away from the sport; it was his life's blood. He lived, breathed, and slept boxing. And many boxers, while not living for Whitey, could not have lived as contenders without him. Fighters wanted to work with Whitey and no one else. Managers wanted to entrust their fighters only to Whitey's pugilistic classroom, which was in the famous Stillman's Gym, the best gym for boxers in New York, if not the country. Those whom he trained were the premier record holders of the twentieth century, men who punched their way to titles and inhabited the status of legends. There was Jack Dempsey, Gene Tunney, Harry Greb, Kid Berg, Benny Leonard, Lou Ambers, James J. Braddock, Billy Conn, Rocky Marciano, Ingemar Johansson, and—of course—Rocky Graziano.

After his partnership with Arcel ended and Whitey was able to get back on his financial feet, he partnered with another legendary trainer, Freddie Brown, and they had great success with their boxers from the 1950s until Whitey's retirement in 1969. His 1959 highlight was Ingemar Johansson, who won the heavyweight title in a highly publicized bout with Floyd Patterson. For 50 years, no other trainer had achieved what Whitey had. His list of champs and contenders was the envy of every trainer.

Yet, he never bragged of his accomplishments, never sought out the press to garner publicity for himself. He was happy to let the spotlight of publicity shine its bright beam of acclaim on those he trained. If reporters approached one of his fighters, Whitey would back away. His work had been done in the gym, in the corner of the ring. His fighters' skills were all the recognition he required. He was happy to have a few shots of schnapps and trade anecdotes with trainers and managers. Some thought his eyes were occasionally bloodshot, but he was never inebriated. His vision never blurred; when it came to his fighters, he was completely clear-sighted. His mission as a trainer was always clear. He was as reliable and steadfast as a loyal watchdog. A day's work done after a training session, Whitey would relax among friends and colleagues at a local bar known as the Neutral Corner, a stone's throw from Stillman's Gym. It was Whitey's regular hangout, where he could imbibe his favorite schnapps and trade stories about famous boxers and bouts. (*A Neutral Corner*, by the way, is the title of one of A. J. Liebling's celebrated books of boxing essays, most of which appeared in the *New Yorker* magazine.)

It was Rocky's good fortune that such a trainer came into his life. Without Whitey's knowledge, skills, and fatherly devotion, Rocky might not have become one of the most exciting boxers of the twentieth century, a man who would dazzle and excite crowds of boxing enthusiasts, whose name alone could sell tens of thousands of tickets to a boxing match, a man whose stardom in the ring was shared by few others. And if he hadn't been a boxer, Rocky very well could have become a lifer at Sing Sing, as did several of his pals.

Irving Cohen, Rocky's brilliant and empathetic manager, had seen potential in the young, rebellious man, a prototype for such fictional screen rebels as the characters portrayed by Marlon Brando, Montgomery Clift, and James Dean. (In fact, James Dean had originally been chosen to play the part of Rocky Graziano in the movie *Somebody Up There Likes Me*. After Dean's death, the part was offered to Marlon Brando, whose ego suffered an uppercut of insult because he was the second choice for the part. Brando turned down the role, and Paul Newman put on the gloves.)

Cohen knew Rocky was raw and unschooled; he needed a trainer, and Whitey would be an ideal trainer for the young man with a chip on his shoulder as big as a brick. And while Rocky was surly in his rejection of training and unwilling to submit himself to the tutelage of another, he knew that boxing was his ticket out of a life of crime. If he didn't train, he might wind up like his pal Terry Young.

Terry, whose real name was Angelo De Sanza, could never be a legitimate guy; he had spent years being a thief, spent years in prison. He was a
holdup man who led a crew of gun-toting robbers. Boxing had not provided him with a way out of his life of crime. He was a talented boxer,
more than proficient, and promoters thought he might one day become a
lightweight or welterweight champ. Throughout the 1940s, he seemed on
the verge of becoming a champion. He had beaten the estimable Beau
Jack, one of the best fighters of that era. Terry won 55 of 69 fights, 17 by
knockout. As good as he was, he could never draw the large crowds of
enthusiastic fans that nearly stampeded into arenas to cheer Rocky.

Terry grew jealous of his friend, the man whom he had introduced to
Irving Cohen and professional boxing; Rocky had become a superstar to
boxing fans, while Terry was more like a B-list actor, never as popular as
his boyhood pal and fellow delinquent, a class-A fighter. Terry resented
the fact that the adulation of Rocky's fans was like that usually reserved
for movie stars or popular singers. Terry would never get the kind of
reception Rocky got when coming down the aisle of an arena and mount-
ing the steps into a boxing ring. While Terry said he made $10,000
annually as a boxer, it was never enough. That money did not satisfy his
need to steal, and since stealing was his métier, he could pursue that when
he wasn't training or boxing. Stealing was a profession he knew well, and
it satisfied his delinquent temperament.

He had been a thief, like Rocky, since his early teenage years. And it
would lead to Terry's conviction for armed robbery and a sentence of two
and a half to five years in Sing Sing prison in 1943, when he was 31 years
old. His end as a thief, a boxer, a wiseguy was predictable and sad. He
was shot to death at a Lower East Side social club, known as the Play Boy
Social Club, where Terry often spent many hours in the company of
fellow criminals. Photos of him in the ring were posted on the walls,
although Terry was never an official member of the club.

One night, while socializing at the club, Terry was shot several times
in the back; he had been drinking in the back of the club and, after being
shot, managed to stagger to the entranceway, where he tried to steady
himself, couldn't do it, and collapsed. He was only 46 years old. By the
time the cops arrived, he had stopped bleeding. His ambitions, his resent-
ments, his promise had bled out of him. He was a corpse, soon to be a
memory. A few local newspapers noted his passing, detailing his record

as a fighter; a couple mentioned his criminal record. It didn't matter anymore.

The transit of Terry Young was an object lesson for Rocky. He was through with crime, through with his old East Side pals. Whitey had opened a door to a new life for Rocky. He would not only save Rocky, but also give him the values that would replace those that had guided his life as a young thug and criminal. Trainer and boxer developed a close relationship, teacher and student, friends. While Irving Cohen mapped out Rocky's future from fight to fight, opponent to opponent, Whitey navigated his fighter through the roadblocks, hidden curves, and dead ends that could have kept Rocky from reaching his destination: the middleweight championship of the world.

For Rocky and Whitey, each was a source of pride for the other. It was Whitey's persuasiveness that got Rocky to train and overcome his deficiencies. And it was Rocky's ambition to be a successful boxer, his drive to one day be the middleweight champion, that inspired Whitey never to give up on his ambitious and talented student. Yet, as much as Rocky wanted to learn from Whitey, he could never completely give up his defiance of regimentation. Training was like going to school, and he hated both. But he wanted the recognition and the money—yes, the money—that would come with being a champion.

Whitey's quote about training could just as easily have been uttered by Rocky. In *Corner Men*, Fried quotes Whitey as saying, "I hated school and I hated training. It didn't make sense to me in those days that a fighter had to waste all that time fooling around with punching bags and getting up at dawn so that he could chase his shadow on the park."

Rocky was Whitey's most stubborn, most recalcitrant student; however, they had shared values. They were both rebels, haters of rules, haters of authority. They were brothers in their shared attitudes. Of course, Whitey no longer had to train as a boxer; he was the trainer and Rocky was the trainee. Speaking of Rocky, Whitey is quoted by Fried as stating,

You gotta give guys who punch with [Rocky] or he don't like it. Give him a boxer in the gym and it's no good.

In the beginning we had trouble getting Rocky in the gym. But once he started to make money, I had no trouble getting Graziano to work. Rock can be very serious about money.[3]

As the years passed and Whitey trained more and more men who would be dominant in the ring, his reputation grew. He was fast becoming a legend, and he did so without ever touting himself. In fact, he had become such a legend he attracted many former boxers who wanted to become trainers too. Whitey's most outstanding young protégé was Al Silvani, who had witnessed his older brother, a professional boxer, being badly beaten in a bout because he had not been properly trained. Silvani, who also briefly boxed, decided he wanted to become a trainer. He would prevent boxers from being unnecessarily injured because they had not been properly trained. For Silvani, training was the essential ingredient for success in the ring. Whitey took him on, and Silvani assisted him in training Rocky. He said Rocky was a rough piece of work, a guy who had a powerful right. "He'd always choke you with his left hand and hit you with the right hand and knock your head in."[4] It was a technique that delivered a series of knockout wins for Rocky.

Apart from Whitey, Silvani was developing his own reputation as a winning trainer. Young boxers, who couldn't get an audience with Whitey, sought out Silvani. Thus, in 1941, when a young Frank Sinatra showed up at Stillman's Gym and requested that Silvani give him boxing lessons, Silvani was not surprised. He agreed to teach the young singer, who was just making a name for himself, the basic elements of boxing. At the time Sinatra met Silvani in Stillman's Gym, he weighed all of 119 pounds. The boxing gloves and boxing shorts made him look like a malnourished kid. While some trainers viewed the skinny singer as an object of derision, Silvani did not. He had seen plenty of lightweight, featherweight, and bantamweight fighters; size did not matter. Anyone who had the right timing, coordination, and flexibility could be taught to box. Silvani liked Sinatra, appreciated his willingness to let another teach him. The two would become lifelong friends, and Sinatra remained an ardent fan of the sport, befriending many boxers, including Rocky, whom he cast in the movie *Tony Rome*. In addition to casting Rocky in that movie, Sinatra, who was known for his kindness and generosity toward those who had stood by him, repaid Silvani by getting him small parts in not only *Tony Rome*, but also *Oceans 11*, *Robin and the Seven Hoods*, and *From Here to Eternity*. Silvani proved such a natural on screen that he appeared as a cornerman in the first three *Rocky* movies.

Aside from getting Silvani parts in movies, Sinatra showed his gratitude and friendship by helping Silvani become a leading trainer for Hollywood stars. Years after helping Whitey train Rocky for his early fights, Silvani was called on to train a young Paul Newman for his role as Rocky in *Somebody Up There Likes Me* and Robert De Niro for his role as Jake LaMotta in *Raging Bull*. LaMotta, by the way, had been a boyhood friend of Rocky's, both having met in reform school.

And where did all that training happen? In an institution variously known as the University of Eighth Avenue, the College of Pugilism, the Graduate School of Hard Knocks: It was Stillman's Gym, located at 919 Eighth Avenue in New York City. To reach the gym, one went up a flight of stairs and entered a large room that smelled of liniment and sweat. Sitting near the entrance like a prison guard, a Caesar of all he espied, was Lou Stillman. Gruff, as hard as nails, vulgar, a true totalitarian, he ruled his domain not only for money, but also for the pleasure of being the boss. He had a big, ugly cigar stuffed into his face that smelled like rotten cabbage and steamed stale tobacco. His hair billowed out from the sides of his head. He wore a shoulder holster that contained a snub-nosed .38. Nearby was his trusty manager, Jack Curley, a dedicated Sancho Panza, devoted to the rules of the gym and its smooth operation and collecting money for the use of the lockers.

Walking through the gym, one couldn't help but notice its filth. The place was never cleaned, never swept, never mopped. The windows were as dark as soot. There were the sibilant sounds of soft-soled shoes skipping rope, the thwack, thwack, thwack of gloves hitting body bags, and the quick pop, pop, pop of gloves gyrating against speed bags. There were guys in shorts shadowboxing and guys in the ring sparring. Loafers, promoters, bookies all sat around, some smoking expensive cigars, others chewing on cheap stogies, sizing up the boxers. There were always guys discussing the changing odds on fights, some of whom rushed to a phone to place their bets. There were always guys looking for inside information, guys looking for a sweet deal. There were managers promoting fights, some against sure losers, others against likely winners. It depended on the betting, the gate, the odds.

If a fixed fight was arranged, no one spoke about it. Only the participants were in the know, in on the fix. Of course, bookies could tell if something was up just by watching the changing odds. If referees and judges were to be paid off for an up-and-coming bout, you didn't talk about it. Not even to the two fighters who would be judged; they often knew nothing about it. But if the proposed loser's manager got wind of the setup, he would go the chairman of the New York State Athletic Commission, and the bout would be called off. Maybe there would be an investigation and licenses would be revoked. The gym was a laboratory for testing the hypotheses of a strategy for winning a bout and cashing in on the big money. Boxing had rules that did not exist in the ring. The gym was a world unto itself, a staging area for making deals.

But the boxers were the real citizens of Stillman's Gym. One could see neophyte boxers learning the elements of their trade. Here and there, pedagogues and pedants of the sport were instructing them to jab, feint, bob and weave, throw a left hook, give a right uppercut, throw a round-house right. It was the geometry of the sport. If you were a good student, you learned all the angles. You learned that the shortest line from your shoulder to your opponent's chin was a straight, hard punch. Euclid would have been proud.

You would also learn how to protect yourself, use your arms as shields, take a punch on the shoulder rather than the chin, pull your head back or duck, hug your opponent's arms so he could not deliver knockout punches. While defending yourself, you should look for that perfect opening, the chance to deliver your own knockout blow to the chin, the temple, the gut of your opponent. Even if you never advanced beyond the gym, never became a pro, you had learned to defend yourself and became a lifelong fan and critic of the sweet science. On Friday nights, you would never be far from a television either in a bar or at home, where you could watch the Friday Night Fights brought to you by Gillette, a man's razor. Following their graduations from Stillman's, many got to wear the gym's emblematic t-shirt with the name Stillman's stenciled on it. It was worn with the same pride as if sporting a shirt with a "H" for Harvard on it.

While Stillman would charge boxers for t-shirts (nothing was ever thought to be free in the gym), he could be generous to poor guys who were down on their luck. For such people, he instructed Jack Curley not to charge them for anything, including snacks at the snack bar. Anyone could experience hard times, and Stillman hid his empathy behind a mask of surly gruffness.

Lou Stillman was a character out of a Damon Runyon story; he could have played himself in *Guys and Dolls*. So where did he come from and how did he get his start? He allegedly started out as a cop; his real name was Louis Ingber. One day, while riding in a trolley car, Lou found himself sitting beside a starry-eyed philanthropist named Marshall Stillman. The two began discussing the plight of poor kids living in slums whose voyage out seemed marred and barred by discrimination and lack of opportunity. Marshall thought that a gym, where kids could learn boxing, would be a refuge from their tenements and a place where they could expend their anger in a socially acceptable sport. He suggested that Lou leave the police force and manage the gym. It didn't take Lou long to agree, and Marshall hired him on the spot. In time, Lou opened his own gym and moved it to a new location. It was all his, and his pride in ownership was his identity.

The gym initially became a Mecca for young Jewish boxers, led by lightweight champion Benny Leonard, who had left another gym after its owner claimed that World War I was started by the Jews. He went on to claim that Jews were responsible for the wrongs of the world: drunkenness, crime, lewdness. Lou welcomed the large contingent of young Jewish boxers, each of whom thanked Lou Stillman for welcoming him. No one ever called Lou Mr. Ingber. At the original gym, he was always called Mr. Stillman by the boxers. So, when he opened his own gym, Lou conveniently changed his last name and went on to become a boxing legend, as did his gym.

Some of the most colorful and memorable champions who trained at Stillman's included Jack Dempsey, Joe Louis, Rocky Marciano, Rocky Graziano, Max Baer, Primo Carnera, Floyd Patterson, and Ingemar Johansson, among many others. For the hundreds of fans who lined up to watch the champs and contenders train, Stillman charged each of them 50 cents. The gym also charged hangers-on, bookies, gamblers, and assorted others. Along with Madison Square Garden, it became a primary focal point in the world of boxing.

It didn't matter that the place was probably the filthiest gym in New York. The floor was one gigantic spittoon; in fact, spitting on the floor was a gym tradition. The air was foul, fetid, and often dusty. Lou Stillman claimed fresh air was bad for fighters. "It'll kill 'em," he said, adding, "The golden age of prizefighting was the age of bad food, bad air, bad sanitation, and no sunlight. I keep the place like this for the fighters' own good. If I clean it up they'll catch a cold from the cleanliness."[5] Lou's comments were taken with more than a few grains of salt. Many thought he just didn't want to waste money keeping the gym clean. A dirty gym seemed to fit his tough-guy image.

No one talked back to Lou Stillman—not fighters, not gangsters, not bookies. If you wanted to be in Stillman's Gym and he verbally abused you, you accepted it either with a grin or a grimace, but you accepted it. After all, Stillman carried a gun, and he had a hair-trigger temper and would let fly with a hurricane of foul-mouthed epithets at anyone who made him angry. Tongue lashings became his pattern; it was how a guy who had never fought in the ring presented himself as someone tougher than the toughest boxer.

The place was his gym, and if you wanted to be there you had to accept Lou Stillman as he was. Boxers and trainers immersed themselves in the culture of the gym and rarely muttered a word of objection. And that also applied to some of New York's most hardened gangsters, who often attended sparring matches at the gym. Even Frankie Carbo (known as Mr. Gray for his monochromatic appearance), a known killer and the gatekeeper for bouts at Madison Square Garden, would not utter a word of defiance to Lou Stillman, the capo di tutti capi of the gym. And nothing and no one seemed to intimidate Lou. And so the gangsters, sportswriters, boxers, managers, and trainers never took exception to an explosion of Stillman's verbal abuse. He ran his gym as he pleased. It was his domain, and no one dared trespass or attempt to take it away from him.

In 1959, ready to finally retire, Stillman sold the gym; it was a sad day in the world of boxing. Many of the gym's habitués sadly showed up for the day the gym was targeted by the wrecker's ball. After the crash of falling bricks, dust rose in the air like a dark and ominous cloud of disappointment. The gym was gone, like a dead man taken off to potter's field and anonymously disposed of. In its place is an apartment building on an avenue in a city that regularly tears down its history and reinvents itself. It is a city with few architectural memories. Today, there is no sign to commemorate the legendary gym; it is known by those who visited it, worked out there, and learned their trade of boxing or training there. It's a fond memory for a dying generation, and when the old-timers vanish into their graves, Stillman's will exist only in the evanescent works of a few writers and as background in some movies. You can catch glimpses of Stillman's Gym while watching Rocky Graziano's story in the movie *Somebody Up There Likes Me*. For some old boxers, the scenes in the movie bring tears to their scarred eyes and smiles to their weathered lips. The gym is now a chapter in the history of the golden age of boxing.

3

THE GIRL FROM OCEAN PARKWAY

Norma Unger was a beautiful, oval-faced, dark-haired Jewish teenager. She was of German descent and lived with her mother and stepfather on Ocean Parkway in Brooklyn. Ocean Parkway was and remains a solidly middle-class Jewish neighborhood. The homes along the parkway are large, stately edifices that bespeak prosperity. In addition to the homes, there are attractive brick apartment buildings containing large, airy rooms, often with terraces. Norma lived in such an apartment with her parents. Yet, like many teenagers, she sought excitement and adventure in another world. Her German-Jewish background was starchy, and conservative: people abided by the rules of society; they worked at respectable jobs and maintained the decorum expected of stable middle-class families. Norma, however, had ideas that extended beyond the circumscribed world in which she was brought up.

She loved to hang out on the Lower East Side, in what was once called an ice cream parlor. There, she met and befriended Yolanda Barbella, Rocky's sister. Although one was Jewish and the other Catholic, one was of German extraction and the other Italian, and one was middle class and the other from a family that just managed to scrape by, the two girls became fast friends. Their separate worlds met in their shared interests. On most weekends, the two met and laughed, talking about boys, their favorite pop songs, the handsomest movie stars, the women they most admired, clothes and jewelry, and their dreams of the future. Their favorite singer was skinny and adorable teenage idol Frank Sinatra, who sang so yearningly of love, love lost, love found, and the loneliness of not being loved. They wanted to take him in their arms. They thought he was perfect.

How did Norma find her way to that ice cream parlor on the Lower East Side where Yolanda passed her weekend nights? Why did the two become friends? Did someone introduce them? A mutual friend? A neighbor? While the details of how Norma and Yolanda met are lost in the faded chronicles of the past, they seemed to have seen in one another reflections of what they wanted to be: Norma wanted adventure and to escape some of the confines of middle-class propriety, while Yolanda saw in Norma not only the middle-class values to which she aspired, but also a possible anchor for her wayward brother, who if he didn't soon settle down could expect to have the short, jaded, and failed life of a petty criminal. Without Norma as an anchor, Yolanda could see her brother as a perpetual convict, or worse: a visitor to the electric chair or shot down one cold, dark night during a failed robbery. Yolanda did not want to be the sister of a convict, and so she regaled Norma with stories about her handsome, restless brother, so daring and headstrong, like a character from the movies. She was determined to be a matchmaker. Time and again, she tried to get them to date one another. Rocky had no interest in dating Norma. He could set up his own dates. He didn't need his sister to interfere in his life. When she couldn't get Rocky to even meet with Norma, Yolanda suggested the possibility of double dating. "What, are you kidding me?" Rocky questioned. He brushed aside the suggestion with a show of annoyance and went out to meet with his gang of thieves.

In fact, Norma felt challenged by Rocky's lack of interest in meeting her. But neither she nor Yolanda was discouraged by his attitude. The right time would come; maybe it would happen spontaneously, or maybe they would have to plan for an accidental meeting. Although they often discussed Rocky, their talk about movies, songs, clothes, and their ambitions for the future continued unabated. The two friends regarded the ice cream parlor on Seventh Street and Second Avenue as their club. They talked for hours and indulged in their favorite ice cream sodas. Afterward, Norma and Yolanda would often walk to the Barbella apartment on 10th Street, before Norma took the BMT subway back to Brooklyn. On the stairway of the apartment building or in its entranceway, they would often pass Rocky as he rushed down to meet his pals. He would mutter a quick "hiya" and be gone. Yet, Yolanda was indefatigable: She kept trying to introduce Rocky to Norma, and his lack of interest bordered on rudeness. While Norma smiled at Yolanda's efforts and pretended she didn't mind, she was annoyed. Yes, Rocky had his own life and would probably continue to ignore her. But Norma also believed that one day, he would pause to notice her and then maybe act like a gentleman. The way it was going, that one day seemed far off. It might never happen, and they could each end up with someone else.

Yolanda, however, would not give up. She could be as relentless as her brother was when fighting an opponent in the ring. There was no end to her persistence. She repeatedly insisted that Rocky meet Norma. He would nod, saying, "Yeah, yeah, don't bother me. I'll find my own girl-friends." He didn't need his sister trying to be his matchmaker. He was a man of the world, a man carving out his own destiny, regardless of what that destiny might entail.

Then one Friday night, after he had knocked out a young fighter named Frankie Falco at the Fort Hamilton Arena, Rocky went home to shower and change into a spiffy, new, bright blue suit with pegged pants, pointy black shoes, a skinny belt, and a white, narrow tie. It was the sharp outfit of a successful hood. He planned to meet his pal Terry Young, also a boxer and young hood. The two of them shared dreams of becoming champions and successful racketeers. On his way down the stairs of the apartment building, Rocky saw his sister talking with another girl in the dimly lit lobby. Oh no, not again. His sister the matchmaker would not give up. Of course, it was Norma, and Rocky figured she would always be around as long as his sister insisted on setting them up. He was determined to avoid both of them.

He pulled the brim of his porkpie hat low on his forehead and tilted his head down, determined to gallop down the stairs and past the girls, avoiding so much as eye contact. Maybe, if he felt like it, he would mutter a muted hello; however, just before he could exit the building, Yolanda grabbed one sleeve of Rocky's jacket and would not let go. Had he yanked his arm away, he would have torn the jacket. Rocky told his sister to let go of his sleeve, but she held on as if she were a cop about to drag him off to the local precinct.

"Rocky, I want you to meet Norma," she said.

Yolanda yanked at his sleeve for emphasis. Rocky turned his face up and pushed back the brim of his hat. He rapidly surveyed the features of Norma's face and the curves of her figure. He wanted to whistle but thought better of it. He later recalled that she had a "nice, trim figure," adding, "She's got nice dark eyes and she's smiling at me like she's a little bit shy."[1] Rocky smiled, nodded at Norma, and said he might see her around some day. She returned the smile and felt that fate was now moving in her direction. Rocky, however, exited the lobby as if the building were on fire. He leapt into his old Ford jalopy and roared off as if he had just pulled off a holdup and the cops were chasing him.

After driving a few miles, not thinking of where he was going and what he was doing, he parked and suddenly realized he was attracted to Norma. She was beautiful. She didn't seem like any of the girls of the neighborhood. She didn't have that phony flashiness for attracting guys. She seemed natural, genuinely beautiful, and he could not forget those lovely dark eyes. He didn't see her again for several days, didn't speak about her with his sister; in fact, he didn't speak with his sister at all for fear of her mentioning Norma to him. He didn't want Yolanda to know he was smitten with her friend. He had behaved boorishly. He knew it and was embarrassed at his own ineptitude, and didn't want to be chastised by his sister for his rude behavior. Yet, he couldn't get Norma out of his mind. He thought she had the most beautiful eyes he had ever seen: deep, dark, and soulful.

One night, he was driving around the Lower East Side in his noisy, rattling old Ford jalopy. The car needed a new muffler and probably could have used a tune-up. Rocky had no idea how old the spark plugs were, as he had never changed them. The wheels of the car splashed through large, dirty puddles as the rain beat on the tin roof and the windshield wipers slowly turned back and forth, almost hypnotically, like metronomes maintaining a dull, steady rhythm to accompany Rocky's meandering daydreams. He had no particular place to go, and he didn't want to go back to his parents' apartment, where he might inadvertently confess to Yolanda that he wanted to see Norma again. The car would soon run out of gas, and with no friends to chip in for a fill-up, Rocky decided to stop for coffee on East Eighth Street.

He parked the car alongside the curb and turned off the engine, and there he spotted her: Walking by herself in the rain was Norma, looking lovely and vulnerable, dressed in a tan, belted trench coat, its collar turned up against the wind. Rocky responded to her as if she were a lost waif in need of protection and shelter. He called out her name, saying, "Norma, hey Norma." Rocky opened the passenger-side door of the car and gestured for her to get in out of the rain. She sat down and removed

THE GIRL FROM OCEAN PARKWAY

the wet kerchief from her head. They sat in the car and talked for a while, steaming up the windows—a small hothouse of blooming love.

After nearly an hour of halting conversation, Rocky offered to drive Norma back to Brooklyn and escort her to the front door of her home. When he started the engine of the car, he remembered that the gas tank was nearly empty and he had less than a dollar in his pockets. He was not going to ask Norma for money; he was too proud for that. After all, he was a boxer, earning decent money. He didn't have to ask a girl for gas money, especially one he was just getting to know. Thus, he suggested that he accompany her back to Brooklyn on the subway. She smiled a shy smile and nodded. They drove to East 10th Street, where Rocky parked the car, and then they walked in the rain to 14th Street to catch the subway to Brooklyn.

A block before they reached the subway entrance the rain had ceased, and a gold crescent of a moon appeared between two billowing, cotton ball-like clouds. It was a warm June night. Rocky held up the palms of his hands to indicate the rain had stopped. They both laughed before descending into the subway station, where Rocky tentatively and nervously took Norma's hand. They sat in one of the cars on the BMT train as it rattled through dusty, dark tunnels, its steel wheels squealing as it maneuvered its way around sharp turns and again as the train came into grim, lonely stations on its route. After about 40 minutes, Norma and Rocky emerged from the subway onto Ocean Parkway; still holding hands, they walked slowly toward Norma's home.

They didn't want the night to end, so rather than going inside Norma's apartment building, they sat on a bench. Wind had brushed the clouds from the sky, revealing thousands of diamond white stars flickering against a black velvet sky. Norma and Rocky talked and laughed until four o'clock in the morning. They later agreed that they had fallen in love on that bench; yet, neither one was willing to admit to such emotions that soon in their relationship.

For the next two nights, Rocky haunted the ice cream parlor like a private security guard, but Norma was not there. He returned to the bench where they had sat for most of the night. He walked back and forth on Ocean Parkway on an odyssey with no end in sight and finally decided to return to Manhattan. He thought that if he kept parading along Ocean Parkway with nothing but longing in his heart, the cops might find his actions suspicious. Who knew what effect his arrest would have on Norma's opinion of him? He didn't want to take any chances. Yet, he was smitten. He was as fixated and obsessed as any teenager enduring the first love of his life.

After one frustrating day on top of another, he decided to go to the large, imposing apartment building in which Norma lived, and there he looked at the names on the directory of tenants. None was named Unger. He couldn't figure it out. She lived there; why wasn't her name in the directory? Disappointed and confused, Rocky returned to the Lower East Side. Something was wrong, but he didn't know what it was. Maybe she really didn't live there. Maybe she didn't want him to know where she lived. Maybe there was something suspicious about her. Maybe she wasn't who she claimed to be. Such disturbing thoughts seemed to be ricocheting around inside Rocky's head. Disappointment and confusion turned into anger, and he suddenly felt like he wanted to flatten someone with his hard-hitting clenched right fist. It was a good thing no one bumped into him on the street, or that person would have become the flattened victim of Rocky's frustration.

He walked and walked, not knowing where he was going. He would often stride into traffic, ignoring traffic lights and beeping horns. His fists were jammed in his pockets, his eyes as alert as eagle eyes, but their only focus was on locating Norma. He passed by the ice cream parlor for a third time and swung his head inside to take a look, knowing she would not be there. But there she was, sitting with her girlfriends, laughing as if she didn't have a care in the world. She and her friends were animatedly chatting away the evening, sipping their sodas and having a good time, when Rocky strode up to their table. In a voice neither friendly nor angry, his tone as flat as a telephone operator's, he greeted Norma and asked if she would like to go for a ride. The girls stopped chatting; they looked at Rocky and then at Norma. Silence engulfed them. Again, they looked at Rocky, then Norma, as if expecting an answer, an explanation of who this guy was. Yolanda was not there to provide an explanation. Norma nodded that she would go with Rocky, quietly saying yes, and her friends nodded, smiled, and said good-bye. As Norma got up to leave, her friends looked unsure, puzzled about what had happened; their raised eyebrows and exchanged doubtful looks made up the silent language that languished until the lovebirds were out of earshot.

Norma and Rocky walked, without holding hands, to his jalopy. He politely opened the passenger-side door for her before walking around the car, getting in, and starting the rackety, loud engine. While the muffler roared, Rocky and Norma remained silent as he drove them around Manhattan and into Brooklyn. As it grew late and the gas in the tank of the car diminished, he decided it was time to drive Norma to her apartment building and escort her to the entrance. He drove the car to the curb, turned off the engine and lights, darted around the car, and opened the passenger-side door for Norma. He took her hand, and they walked to the entrance of the apartment building. He watched her press a button with the name Levine printed under it.

"Oh, so you're a Jewish girl, huh, Norma?" asked Rocky.

"Does that make a difference, Rocky?" she answered.

Replied Rocky, "Nothing makes a difference honey . . . if you'll be my girl."[2]

And so began a romance that would last until Rocky died, a romance free of infidelity and full of gratitude. Rocky couldn't believe he had won over this girl from a world so high above the one that had bred him. Hers was a world of comfort, stability, and security; his had been one of cruelty, privation, poverty, and anger. For Rocky, Norma was a dream made manifest. He believed she could change his life.

Being from different worlds, however, they didn't share one of Rocky's most important and essential interests. In fact, of everyone Rocky knew, Norma was the only one who wasn't interested in boxing. She disliked the idea of two men getting in a ring and punching one another. She never wanted to watch Rocky spar or even train, and she certainly didn't want to watch him fight. She loved him too much to watch him get hurt, bruised, and bloodied. Yet, she would never stand in his way. If boxing was what he wanted to do, needed to do, and if it made him the man he was and helped to define him to himself, it was fine with her. She would never try to get him to quit, never stand in his way. She fell in love with a man who wanted a career as a boxer, and she didn't think it was her place to tell him to box or not box. Hurt or unhurt, win or lose in the ring, Rocky could depend on Norma to welcome him home after a fight.

The only fight Norma witnessed occurred late one night when she and Rocky were walking down Eighth Street in Greenwich Village. It was not a fight with boxing gloves; it was one of those vicious street brawls where someone could get killed. It happened during World War II, and three sailors, slightly drunk, were trailing behind them. The sailors, in loud

taunting voices, wondered what a guy was doing out of uniform. He must
be a 4F civilian, a draft dodger, or a queer, a fag, a fairy. They yelled
offensive epithets as if they were drill sergeants barking out orders at a
nervous young recruit. They wanted to taunt Rocky, drive him into the
night, or maybe beat him up and stomp him. Unable to arouse a reaction,
the sailors started shouting that Norma must be a transvestite. No real
woman would go out with a draft-dodging faggot. They laughed loudly,
yelling insults and following the couple up Fifth Avenue to Ninth Street.

Rocky squeezed Norma's hand and told her not to worry. Once they
turned onto Ninth Street, which was dark and quiet, he told her not to go
far. He swung around and waited for his antagonists. They would soon be
his prey. As the sailors turned the corner expecting to keep up their
harassment, Rocky suddenly slugged the largest member of the group
with a powerful roundhouse right to the temple, crumpling the big sailor
onto the sidewalk like a bag of laundry. The seaman let out a whinny of
pain and lay moaning on his back. Rocky made quick work of a second
sailor, sending him onto the sidewalk with a right, a left, and another
right. The sailor lay beside his shipmate, both helpless. The third sailor, in
his haste to depart, tripped over his fallen comrades, righted himself, and
ran away shouting for help and for the police.

Rocky grasped Norma's hand, and they quickly strode to the subway
at West Fourth Street. While Norma was relieved and nervous, she also
hoped Rocky had not badly hurt the two sailors. After all, Rocky could
have killed them. And as a professional boxer, his fists were considered
lethal weapons by the law. Boxers were not supposed to use them outside
of the ring. And with Rocky's police record, a judge could have sent him
away for a stiff sentence. Norma and Rocky quickly descended the subway steps and found a train just as it was readying to pull out of the
station. Rocky figured they would have nothing to worry about. They had
made a quick, unobserved getaway. In silence, but with Rocky tightly
holding Norma's hand, they rode the subway to Brooklyn; they emerged
and walked in the silence of Ocean Parkway until they arrived at Norma's
apartment building. Rocky wrapped Norma in his arms and planted a kiss
on her lips, a declaration, one never to be rescinded.

After that night, Rocky and Norma were together every day. As young
lovers, they could not get enough of one another. Sitting on a park bench
in the evening, they sang their favorite popular songs and laughed at one
another's jokes, or they went to the movies, went dancing, or simply

drove around in Rocky's old jalopy. They couldn't bear being away from one another. Rocky had found the woman who would be the anchor to halt him from drifting into the sea of criminality; Norma had found adventure with her bad boy, who she would not try to tame or confine. In her eyes, the bad boy had a lot of good in him. And that was enough for Norma.

Rocky preferred to focus his attention on Norma and forget about training. Training for a fight was boring and—he thought—a waste of time. He was a slugger and a brawler, and that was enough for him to take down any opponent. No matter how Whitey Bimstein and Irving Cohen tried to persuade him of the necessity of training, Rocky resisted and followed their regimen with minimum adherence. Whitey and Irving knew that Rocky's preoccupation was with Norma; in fact, that preoccupation was so intense that Rocky could not stand being away from her long enough to train at all. Even without training, he managed to beat his opponents with ferocious attacks, usually ending his fights in the first few rounds with stunning knockouts. So why train? He seemed to want to get the fights over as quickly as possible and be with Norma. If he could be so successful with minimum training, training was unnecessary, he reasoned.

Training was not only an unwanted item for Whitey and Irving to put on Rocky's agenda, but also, at times, it was even difficult to get him to his bouts. Doing so often required Rocky's manager to tell him Norma was seated in the arena. She wasn't, of course, for she hated seeing Rocky fight. Whitey and Irving told Rocky that if he failed to show up for a fight his license could be revoked. Rocky shrugged, insisting that he had never missed a bout. Whitey and Irving threw up their hands. They decided to have a talk with Rocky's friend, Jack Healy, who helped with Rocky's management. One day, while drinking coffee, Healy told Rocky he should marry Norma, otherwise he would drive himself crazy. He was tearing himself apart between his devotion to Norma and his commitment to having a successful career as a professional boxer. Rocky nodded in agreement. It was a good idea. He would ask Norma to marry him. And when he did, she responded with a simple yes. She had been waiting for weeks for him to ask her, and she knew he would.

While Rocky wanted to buy Norma an engagement ring, he had already spent the small amount of money he had made from the few boxing matches Irving had arranged. Without being asked, Norma pawned the

gold Star of David her mother had given her. She used the money to pay
for a marriage license and gave the balance to Rocky. He was upset and
embarrassed at what she had done but also deeply moved by it. He promised to buy back the Star immediately after winning his next bout, and he
was as good as his word.

On August 10, 1943, Rocky and Norma were married at City Hall in
Lower Manhattan. Because the couple failed to bring along any friends to
serve as witnesses, Rocky paid two cops $5 each to witness the marriage
ceremony. Two days later, after winning another fight, Rocky used his
small winnings to retrieve Norma's Star of David. Years later, as Rocky
was coming down the aisle of Madison Square Garden for one of his
bouts, a hand reached out and tapped his shoulder. "Remember me?" a
voice said. It was one of the cops who had served as a witness to the
marriage at City Hall.

Following the marriage ceremony, Rocky and Norma briefly moved in
with his parents. Nick Bob, Rocky's father, refused to talk to the couple.
He thought his son was making what little money he had through thiev-
ery. He thought his son's bruises were the result of street fights. He
wondered aloud what kind of woman would saddle herself with a thief
who had no future, except prison. If Nick Bob had heard that there was an
up-and-coming middleweight boxer named Graziano, he didn't associate
the name with Rocco Barbella. Rocky had refused to tell his parents what
he did to make money, although he often gave his surprised and grateful
mother money for groceries and other necessities.

Instead of telling his father about his career as a boxer, Rocky would
surprise him by letting him witness his once-wayward son winning a bout
in Madison Square Garden. A few nights after moving into the Barbella
apartment, Rocky gave his father two tickets to a fight at the Garden.
Nick did not even mumble a thank you, for he was immediately suspicious, thinking his son had stolen them. He sullenly pocketed the tickets
and left the apartment to go to a local bar. Rocky figured that Nick would
sell one of the tickets and buy himself a few drinks with the money. He
would use the other ticket to attend the fight, excited to be going to the
Garden, where he hadn't been for years. Nick had been so broke for so
long that he hadn't been able to afford tickets to any fights, no matter how
cheap. The bouts he had attended were in gyms and small, smoke-filled
clubs on the Lower East Side where attendees yelled their advice and
curses as they gulped beer.

That night at the Garden, Rocky won a decisive victory over Ted Apostoli. In his dressing room, Rocky was lying on a table getting a rubdown from Whitey Bimstein. His eyes were closed as he relaxed in the glory of another win. He replayed the fight in his mind, unaware of anyone other than Whitey and Irving being in his dressing room. After Whitey finished the rubdown, Rocky opened his eyes and was staring up at the face of his father. Nick had tears in his eyes. He had no idea his son was a professional boxer. And a winning one as well. He couldn't bring himself to say anything, but his pride in his son could only be expressed by the tears of appreciation that poured down his unshaven cheeks. Embarrassed, he smiled and then fled the dressing room, fled from the guilt he felt about himself and the toddler he had long ago abused.

A new chapter had opened in the story of father and son. Rocky grew to empathize with his father's failure and the older man's frustrations, although he could never bring himself to let Nick know how he finally understood the man's anger and unhappiness about his dreary transit through life. He could never express his forgiveness for being mistreated as a child. And Nick never again said a word of criticism about his once-unruly son, the one-time street hoodlum who had been traveling on a dead-end road to prison or the electric chair. There is a photograph of the young, successful boxer and the gray-haired, grizzled old fighter with their arms wrapped around one another's shoulders. They are smiling at the camera, not at one another, but the past had melted away, leaving them united in Rocky's ambition to be a champ.

As Nick came to admire his son, he also came to understand the importance of Norma to Rocky's career. When Nick saw Norma, he smiled and was gracious, for his son had a thoughtful wife who would never interfere with Rocky's career and his inevitable rise to the championship of the middleweight division. Nick appreciated and admired Norma's devotion to Rocky more than Norma knew, for he had given up his own boxing career, in part, to satisfy the demands of his wife. If he had had a wife like Norma, perhaps his life would have taken a different route. It was too late to be angry about that, too late to lament a missed opportunity for pugilistic stardom. Laconic and gruff, he could only show his feelings with a fleeting smile.

Long ago, when he so angry and frustrated at his failure to become a successful boxer, Nick had poured his anger like boiling water onto his wife's psyche, eventually driving her into an asylum for the mentally ill.

Not unexpectedly, his anger hadn't ended at the border of his wife's emotional life; it had rained violence into the distant world inhabited by his young, rebellious, delinquent son. The warfare that had erupted between father and son had almost destroyed each of their lives. Now, everything was different. In Rocky and Norma, Nick finally saw a marriage that worked; it was too late for him to have such a marriage and he was too old to embark on another boxing career, but he could live vicariously through the ring victories of his son.

Norma didn't need to live vicariously through Rocky's fights. He had finally talked her into attending some of his bouts. He wanted her to witness and understand what his profession meant to him, and judge how adept and determined he was in the ring. But after witnessing a few of his contests, she refused to attend any more. She was appalled that men could be so brutal to one another. She was heartsick that Rocky could suffer severe injuries. It was not her world. It was Rocky's. She would never interfere, she just didn't want him to insist that she attend a fight. Imbued with the world of boxing, at first Rocky thought Norma's decision meant she didn't care about his career, didn't care that boxing had turned him from a criminal into a legit guy, an admired athlete. She explained that she couldn't attend his fights because she could not bear to watch him get hurt. The idea of him having his handsome face busted, his nose broken and the bridge of it pushed in, his ears mashed, and his teeth knocked out would be too much for her. Yet, she would always be there after a fight; she was prepared to nurse his wounds, to honor his ambitions, to never let him down.

Before he understood her feelings, he was deeply disappointed that she had turned her back on boxing. One night he had refused to go to a fight because Norma would not go with him. He said the hell with the fight and didn't show up, instead taking Norma to a movie. For that, Rocky was called to a hearing in front of the New York State Athletic Commission. Rocky told the commissioner he was so in love with his wife that given a choice between boxing and being with his wife, he chose to be with his wife. The commissioner could hardly believe the lovesick story Rocky told him, for it was much too sentimental to be accepted. But after thinking about it for a few minutes, the commissioner decided no one could disbelieve such an account coming from a cynical, tough street guy like Rocky Graziano. The Rocky who had not yet met Norma would have laughed at such an excuse. He would have thought the guy a coward. But here was Rocky, standing in front of the commission-er, explaining that he so loved Norma, he couldn't stand to be away from her. Had anyone other than Rocky told such a story, the commissioner wouldn't have believed it. Rocky was apparently telling the truth, so his license to box, which had been revoked, was quickly restored, with the warning that if he ever failed to show up for a fight again, his license would be permanently revoked.

After that, when Rocky fought, Norma would listen on the radio for a few minutes and then turn off the broadcast and go for a long walk, trying not to think about the event. When Rocky had his second fight against Tony Zale in Chicago, which resulted in his winning the title of middle-weight champion, Norma had been listening to the fight on the radio. Up until the time Rocky knocked out Zale, he was taking a terrible beating. One of his eyes was swollen shut, and the other was covered with blood. The announcer described Rocky's condition and the beating he was en-during. Norma could no longer listen to the radio, although her mother, mother-in-law, and Rocky's sister were glued to the station. Knowing the family would not want the radio turned off, Norma dashed into the bath-room, slammed the door, and cried uncontrollably.

When Rocky returned to their hotel after the fight, Norma was still crying. Rocky's face was badly bruised; one eye was clamped shut and the other was so swollen he could only see out of a slit between the lids. Norma and Rocky went into the bedroom, where their daughter Audrey had been put to sleep. Their little girl stood up on the bed and, with a confused look on her face, asked her daddy what had happened to him.

"Now see what I said? Now stay out of the gutter," Rocky replied.[3]

Moreover, W. C. Heinz wrote,

> [Norma] had never, at any time, thought marriage would be like this. . . . [Marriage] would probably be to some ordinary working guy, and they would live in a little apartment. She could never have known that it would be to a fighter and they would have two cars and live in their own house.[4]

Marriage to some normal guy was not what Norma had dreamt of as a young woman; she had always wanted to break the bonds of middle-class strictures. She had found her ideal man in a boxer, although she couldn't bear to watch him fight.

The marriage of Norma Unger and Rocky Graziano was a long, endur-ing, and loving one. When Rocky was with Norma in public, he would often glance at her with a smile on his lips and tenderness in his eyes. Unlike many celebrities, whether boxers or not, Rocky remained faithful to Norma from the time he met her until the day he died. When Rocky was out at some Mafia bar with his old pals who would bring along their goomars, Rocky was always alone. Paul Newman, who portrayed Rocky in *Somebody Up There Likes Me*, asked why he remained faithful to his wife. Newman replied, "Why should I go out for hamburger when I have steak at home?"[5] The Grazianos produced two lovely daughters, Audrey and Roxee, both of whom married and gave birth to children of their own. None became boxers; none needed to fight for their father's love.

4

ROCKY MAKES A NAME FOR HIMSELF

With Norma as an anchor in his life, Rocky was able to devote himself to building his reputation as an up-and-coming boxer. He had been fighting a number of six-round bouts in small arenas. He had fought welterweights, beating most of them. His powerful right-hand punch was a crowd-pleaser, and it forged his reputation as a fighter to watch. He was able to move on to the big time when Irving Cohen booked him to fight in Madison Square Garden. [1]

The results from some of those fights, however, were not what Rocky, Irving, and Whitey had expected. They thought, for example, that Steve Riggio would fall from Rocky's hard right cross. But Riggio managed to stay away from Rocky's wild slugging approach and win two fights, one in 1943, the other in 1944, on points. After witnessing Riggio beat Rocky in two fights, the smart money thought Riggio would go on to be a contender. For reasons never publicly stated, his star was clouded out of view in the galaxy of star boxers. His boxing career faded and dimmed, becoming only a memory to a handful of fans and boxing historians. Riggio turned from boxing to driving a taxi cab. While he did not find glory as a possible champion or even a contender, he was—no doubt—proud of this two sons, Leonard and Steve. Leonard is the executive chairman of the Barnes & Noble bookstore chain, and Steve was the company's CEO.

Another hard-hitting competitor who disabused Rocky of his idea that he could defeat anyone with his powerful right fist was Harold Green. Green was born into a poor family in the Brownsville section of Brooklyn (the birthplace of Murder, Inc.) and began fighting in local clubs and arenas when he was 14 years old. He did so to help support his family. He was awarded a watch each time he won a bout, and many watches came his way. He would pawn each of them for about $10 and give the money to his parents. For years, his boxing prowess provided the means for helping him support his parents and four siblings during the Great Depression. He always made sure no one in his family went hungry and the rent was always paid. In addition, Green's growing reputation as a skillful boxer protected him and his siblings from the onslaughts of local tough guys. He was looked upon as a guy with killer fists who should be avoided. The streets of Brownsville were tread by many gangsters who, for a few dollars, would kill or otherwise brutalize its inhabitants, breaking an arm here or a leg there, slitting a throat, or bashing in a head. It didn't matter, as long as someone paid for the work to be done. Murder, Inc. provided a menu of nefarious deeds, each with a specific price. Yet, even one of Murder, Inc.'s most notorious killers, Abe "Kid Twist" Reles, chose not to tangle with Green.

When he was 22 years old in 1942, Green began his professional career as a boxer. In his first fight, he knocked out Willis Johnson, who was highly regarded as one of the more promising fighters of the 1940s. Green continued boxing, winning fight after fight. He looked like a comer, a guy who would soon challenge for the welterweight title. His career was interrupted by service in the U.S. Army from 1943 to 1944. Immediately after his discharge, he began piling up another series of wins. His record at that time was an eye-popping 24 consecutive wins, 3 losses, and 1 draw. In 1944, *Ring* magazine ranked Green as the number seven welterweight in the world. Yet, he never got a shot at the title.

On November 3, 1944, in Madison Square Garden, Green defeated Rocky in a 10-round bout won on points. The following month, on December 22, Green and Graziano met in the Garden for a rematch. Again, Green outpointed Rocky in another 10-round bout. He even knocked Rocky to the canvas. Rocky went down but was not knocked out. The look on his face was one of disbelief. The fights with Green were frustrating for Rocky, for he was unable, in two highly publicized bouts, to defeat a man he thought would succumb to his power. Finally, on September 28, 1945, Rocky, who had gained enough weight to move up from welterweight to middleweight, and being 10 pounds heavier than Green, got his revenge. He knocked out his opponent in the third round. Rocky felt his future was now secured. He had proven himself against an opponent who many in the sports world thought would be a welterweight or middleweight title contender.

Unfortunately for Green, he didn't have the astute management of an Irving Cohen. He did what he was told by the fight promoters. They never arranged for him to have a title fight. His ring career ended after a loss to Joey Giardello in 1953. He had previously beaten Giardello in 1950. It was time for him to hang up his gloves. Green realized the opportunities he had thought awaited him in the 1940s were no longer available. He retired without a sense of bitterness and went on with his life. He always loved boxing and always would; he was glad he had been an important player in the sport. He died of a heart attack while he slept in his daughter's home in Las Vegas in 2001.

Next on Rocky's and a reluctant Irving's agenda was a fight with Billy Arnold. William "Billy" Arnold was thought to be the best of the middleweights. He had remarkably fast fists, could dance and feint in the ring like Sugar Ray Robinson, and was able to galvanize fans with his colorful ring performances. Furthermore, he was affable and temperate, and he not infrequently elicited the admiration of those who were impressed by his self-discipline, focus on doing well, and desire to reach his goals, no matter how distant or how hard the road ahead. Those who befriended him as a high school student, whether teachers or fellow students, remained lifelong friends.

Arnold, an African American who had been bullied by older, bigger students in his first year in a Philadelphia high school, was encouraged to take up boxing by his gym teacher, Dave Beloff, who had been an outstanding member of the Temple University boxing team. Arnold proved more than proficient. He took to boxing as a bird takes to the air, displaying flair and a natural aptitude that surprised and pleased his coach. He was one of those rare athletes who made it look easy. He had a natural grace that drew the admiration of those who watched him box, developing a large group of fans who loved to watch him perform in the ring. By age 16, he had knocked out his first 28 challengers in front of a cheering section of fans comprised of 20 teachers and fellow students from his high school. Those who had once bullied him tried to befriend him.

Most of Arnold's knockouts had occurred by the second round. Referees often felt they had to stop his fights, for Arnold was pummeling his opponents so badly they feared he would inflict permanent injury. They

would award him a TKO decision. Amid the excitement of his outstanding accomplishments, Arnold regularly attended his high school classes
every day from nine o'clock in the morning until two o'clock in the
afternoon. Upon packing up his books and pencils each afternoon, he
would go to the Olympic Gymnasium to train for hours each day. While
other students cut classes and were truants, Arnold never gave his teachers a reason to complain. His behavior was exemplary. Arnold's attitude
toward and devotion to training was the opposite of Rocky's disdain. One
was a model student, the other a dropout who had roamed the mean
streets of the Lower East Side as if they had been his criminal terrain.

On January 5, 1945, Arnold was to meet the wily professional Fritzie
Zivic, a former welterweight titleholder, for a highly publicized fight in
Madison Square Garden. Arnold was the odds-on favorite to win. At age
31, Zivic was not the fighter he had been. He was nine years older than
Arnold and nine pounds heavier. Because of Arnold's youth, the promoters reduced what would have been a 10-round bout to an eight-rounder.
Arnold fought with the classic skills of a well-trained pugilist. To many in
the audience, he was outpointing Zivic and winning the majority of the
rounds. Thus, when the decision was awarded to Zivic, the fans booed
and hissed, stomped their feet, and loudly yelled, "Fix!" Some of them
threw cigar stubs, crumpled newspapers, and balled up programs at the
judges. The police were called and escorted the judges and referee away
from Arnold's fans. It was an official loss for Arnold but a moral win. He
had won the hearts of the fans for his brilliant display of pugilistic skills.

Billy Arnold was now the man to beat. By 1945, Rocky felt he could
elevate his reputation and become a big moneymaker if he could beat the
crowd-pleasing Arnold, who was a 5-to-1 favorite to defeat the Rock.
This time around, the bookies were ready to clean up on Arnold. Many
thought the smart-money boys had previously cleaned up in the Zivic
fight. They were now ready to put their money on the favorite—or so the
sports world believed. Of course, while the odds favored Arnold, a pre-
scient gambler would have put a large sum on Rocky. If Rocky could
prove the oddsmakers and sportswriters wrong, he could become a title
contender. He would also reward a lot of bettors.

Neither Irving Cohen nor Whitey Bimstein was sure that Rocky could
outpoint Arnold. He would have to win by a knockout. Arnold came out
of his corner with the grace and self-confidence that were the hallmarks
of his style. Rocky, as usual, was wild and aggressive, swinging his fists

and often missing his opponent. As the fight progressed, Arnold was ahead on points, just as Irving and Whitey had feared. Arnold delivered a series of hard punches, all of which Rocky was willing to withstand just so he could slam his right fist into his opponent's chin. And so the fight went: Arnold landing a series of punches, with Rocky waiting for an opening. In the third round, while absorbing blow after blow, Rocky finally found an opening in Arnold's defenses: He stunned his foe with a powerful overhand right that ended the fight.

Arnold was devastated. He had not fully protected himself, and obviously he did not think he would be letting such a punch penetrate his realm of defenses. Rocky was now the center of attention. The referee held his winner's fist high. The crowd roared its pleasure. The dead-end kid from the streets of New York had defeated the stylish, well-trained opponent from Philadelphia. If Rocky could beat Arnold, he could beat all comers, according to the oddsmakers. And to prove them right, Irving lined up a series of matches, drawing the attention of fans, bookies, managers, and sportswriters.

For Arnold, unfortunately, there would be no bright future as a boxer. His will to fight had been temporarily shattered to shards by Rocky. His self-confidence was briefly left behind. He returned to the ring and had 19 more fights. He won 12 and lost 7. Five of those seven were by knockout. The humiliating disappointment that came with his defeat by Rocky Graziano not only took all the steam out of Arnold's drive to the top, but also left the matchmakers feeling that, while the pugilist could go on fighting, he would never be championship material. It was apparent to his fans that Arnold was no longer the brilliant and dazzling fighter he had once been, no longer the hope in whom black Philadelphians invested their dreams of a black welterweight champion, another Henry Armstrong.

At age 22, Arnold, who some said had the genius of common sense, retired from boxing, his confidence as a boxer diminished, but his outlook on life enlarged. Blessed with clear-eyed pragmatism, he invested his money thoughtfully, and to repay his mother for all she had done for him, he bought her a house. He was honored by being one of the first African American men to be featured on the cover of *Life* magazine. He was an honored member of not only his racial community, but also the city of Philadelphia, particularly among its sports fans. During his shooting star of a career as an incandescent pugilist, his left eye had been blackened, cut, and badly injured. The injury worsened, and before it could spread, he had the eye surgically removed. He married Alice Arnold, with whom he had four daughters and two sons. His life was said to have been a happy one. Neither regrets nor bitterness tarnished his pride, and neither anger nor sadness diminished his belief that his life had been well lived.

Arnold was gone, another notch on Rocky's record. Rocky was now focused like a laser beam on his future. But before he could go on to his trilogy of bouts with Tony Zale, fights that are regarded as the bloodiest fights of the twentieth century, he had several opponents he had to dispatch, all of whom were considered top title contenders.

Rocky's first bout was against the tough and sometimes wild Al "Bummy" Davis. Al's middle name was the inspiration of his manager, Johnny Attell, who reasoned Bummy made Al sound like a tough guy, a hard-up guy from the streets who had to fight just to feed himself. Attell, who had been a minor boxer, explained that Bummy would also look better on a marquee than Avrum Davidoff, especially if Bummy ventured beyond the environs of his Jewish neighborhood.

Bummy, like Harold Green, grew up in the Brownsville section of Brooklyn, the tough neighborhood that saw the birth of Murder, Inc., a gang of Jewish and Italian hit men for hire who worked for notorious labor racketeers Albert Anastasia and Lepke Buchalter. Few poor boys could escape the extravagant allures of the gangster life of Murder, Inc., with its implicit promise of easy money, sharp clothes, expensive cars, and self-protective camaraderie. There were also certain types of neighborhood girls who were attracted to the bad boys of the street, and their sexual allure was certainly another magnet for young men and boys. The girls offered excitement and good times. Bummy's two brothers were not immune to those attractions, and so they were pleased to have jobs as debt collectors for the mob. They were strong and could be physically intimidating when confronting deadbeats and other recalcitrant debtors.

Bummy, however, was not like his brothers; he had interests that extended beyond the narrow world of the local hoods. He wanted to be a boxer. The closest he ever came to participating in illegal activities was when he protected his father, who was a minor bootlegger who owned a candy store that doubled as a bootlegger's factory and warehouse. Inside the candy store or outside on the sidewalk, Bummy served as his father's eyes and ears, warning him when cops or federal agents were about to invade the neighborhood. He did so as a loyal son, not an aspiring bootlegger. Bummy preferred to spend his time at a local gym, hitting the speed bag and heavy bag, skipping rope, and sparring, rather than live out his days in a cellar, mixing fermenting liquids. He had begun to box, as had Billy Arnold, when he was a teenager. He demonstrated unusual courage, fortitude, and skill as a teenager, and his prowess and proficiency only increased as the years passed. He so prided himself on his toughness and skill that he was able to stand up to any of Murder, Inc.'s most vicious killers, just as Harold Green did. None of them messed with the young boxer. Nonetheless, in later years, he may have forced their hands and so suffered a grave result.

Fighting under his new sobriquet, Bummy had his first professional fight in 1937. The name Avrum Davidoff was turning into a memory, the identity still held dear by only his mother and father. And it appeared as if Johnny Attell had been correct in giving Bummy his tough-sounding name, for that first fight attracted a full house. Everyone wanted to see the young tough guy, who went on to outpoint Frankie Reese at Ridgewood Grove. From there, he scored 21 consecutive wins. He did not experience any losses until he was matched against Lou Ambers at Madison Square Garden in 1940. Before his loss to Ambers, Bummy defeated Tony Canzoneri, one of the most popular welterweights of the 1930s. Years later, Canzoneri was revealed to be a Mafia soldier. Bummy had knocked out Canzoneri in the third round; it was the only time in his long career that Canzoneri had been flattened in the ring. It proved to be his final fight, and his fans felt he had been humiliated by, of all people, a bum. Canzoneri's fans loudly booed Bummy and called him every vulgar epithet that passed from their brains to their tongues.

On November 15, 1940, Bummy had the most infamous fight of his career, against newly crowned welterweight champion Fritzie Zivic, who had a reputation as one of the dirtiest fighters in his division. In the first round of their bout, Zivic kept jabbing his thumbs into Bummy's eyes. Bummy was furious and appealed to the referee to halt the fight and award him the win based on repeated fouls by Zivic. The referee refused to so much as admonish Zivic, who kept sticking his thumbs in Bummy's eyes. When the referee refused to interfere, Zivic kept on jabbing. In the second round, infuriated, Bummy went after Zivic with his own set of illegal tactics, repeatedly hitting Zivic below the belt, aiming one punch after another at his genital area. Bummy was further incensed that the referee pushed him away from Zivic after doing nothing to stop the eye-gouging.

Bummy refused to stop. He pounded Zivic's groin with punch after punch. Fans had never seen such a rapid and repeated onslaught of illegal punches. When the referee again tried to stop the abuse, Bummy kicked the referee and pushed him away. Judges sitting ringside called for help, and police rushed to the ring. A phalanx of them blocked fans from getting to the ring, while others escorted a furious Bummy to his dressing room. Bummy and Zivic fought again the following year at the Polo Grounds, home of the New York Giants baseball team. It was a far more restrained match, and Zivic won the bout with a technical knockout in the 10th round.

In 1944, Bummy surprised the world of sports by knocking out former lightweight champion Bob Montgomery in the first round of their bout. Montgomery had been a 10-to-1 favorite. Ordinary citizens who had bet on the favorite reportedly lost hundreds of thousands of dollars, while the bookies cleaned up.

Prior to his match with Rocky Graziano, Bummy lost two fights at Madison Square Garden to two superb boxers, Beau Jack and Henry Armstrong, the latter an inspiration for Sugar Ray Robinson. Those two losses portended what was ahead for Bummy in his matchup with Rocky.

On May 25, 1945, he and Rocky met for a match greatly hyped by the media. Rocky knew that if he beat Bummy, he would be unstoppable for a match with Zale. He was determined to have a decisive win. He didn't want to win on points. He didn't want any questions about the decision. He would have to deliver a knockout or at least a TKO. The two fought like demons. More was riding on Rocky's success than Bummy's, for Bummy had already been defeated by two champs. Nevertheless, Bummy didn't want to eliminate himself from ever being a contender, so the two went at one another like snarling pit bulls in a ring. In the fourth round, using his wild, powerful right fist, Rocky found an ideal opening. He delivered a powerful overhand right that dazed Bummy. Bummy was so badly shaken and disoriented that the fight could not go on. Rocky won the fight by a technical knockout. He was congratulated by his corner, Whitey slapping his back and pulling a robe over his shoulders. They knew Rocky was on his way to the title fight he had been dreaming of with Tony Zale.

Life did not go as well for Bummy. Throughout the course of his career, he had made a great deal of money and spent it lavishly—and, some would say, foolishly. He bought racehorses and fancy cars. He spent money on friends and family. When the money supply began to dwindle, Bummy decided to sell a bar and grill, named Dudy's, he owned in Brownsville, Brooklyn. Although no longer the owner, he was the establishment's special guest and would often spend time in the back room, where he drank with friends, regaling them with stories about boxers he had fought and some he knew. His listeners were always attentive, soaking up the latest gossip from the world of sports.

One cold November day in 1945, while enjoying the company of old friends, Bummy turned and looked through the latticework that separated the front of the bar from the back room. Out front were four gunmen, pointing pistols at the bartender and demanding the money in the cash register. As if a teenager still protecting his father's old candy store, he rushed to the front of the bar and punched one of the gunmen, knocking him to the floor, unconscious. Bummy was about to go after another gunman when he was shot in the neck. Another bullet was fired and missed Bummy. He grabbed a napkin from the bar, holding it against the bloody hole in his neck. Cursing, he ran after the fleeing gunmen. He pursued them as if they were prey and he was not the bleeding victim. Bummy was fueled by the adrenaline of his fury, while the gunmen were fueled by fear. A far better athlete than the criminals, the pugilist—although wounded—was gaining on them. Before he could reach them, they turned and fired their pistols, and one of their bullets hit Bummy. He fell to the sidewalk, bleeding profusely and soon dying. The killers ran into the night and were never caught. Many people thought the killers were members of Murder, Inc., who would never have shot Bummy if he hadn't tried to stop them.

Although he had never been called a hero during his brief life, Al "Bummy" Davis was being celebrated as a hero in newspapers throughout New York City. The *New York Times* ran a front-page story about his death. New York's many newspapers extolled Bummy as not only a great boxer, but also a courageous, decent citizen who sacrificed his life to protect the property of a friend. Sportswriters and editorialists agreed that Bummy was an exemplary boxer who died before he could become the champ he was destined to be. He was dead at age 25, leaving behind an impressive professional boxing record of 65 wins (46 by knockout), 10 losses, and 4 draws. He was named one of the 100 greatest punchers of all time by *Ring* magazine, the bible of boxing.

The next opponent for Rocky on his climb to the championship was the formidable Freddie "Red" Cochrane, the reigning welterweight champion. Red was born in New Jersey and began his professional boxing career in 1932. In 1941, he won a decision from Fritzie Zivic in a 15-round bout for the welterweight title. Shortly thereafter, incensed about the Japanese bombing of Pearl Harbor, Red enlisted in the U.S. Navy. To his surprise, he was exempted from naval combat duty because one of his arms was shorter than the other. Such a perceived disability did not have a negative effect on his boxing ability. If he could beat some of the toughest boxers in the ring, why couldn't he be an effective combatant in war? It was a question he asked himself and his officers. Apparently, one had to have two arms of equal length to fire a rifle, machine gun, or bazooka, or toss a hand grenade. The navy's decision seems unsupported by common sense. Thus, while retaining his welterweight title throughout World War II, without having to defend it, Red was instructed to put on boxing demonstrations as a form of entertainment for the troops. In addition, with his uneven arms, he taught men with evenly matched arms how to defend themselves in hand-to-hand combat.

Upon his discharge, Red was primed to reenter the world of professional boxing. He was matched to fight Rocky Graziano in what *Ring* magazine called the fight of the year, although Red's title was not at stake. Red had looked forward to defending his title and earning money again as a champion. He knew about Rocky's wild approach in the ring. Red believed he could outpoint the Rock, but he would need to protect himself against Rocky's wild, yet powerful, right-hand punch. He also knew that Rocky could absorb many punches while waiting for an opening to deliver a knockout blow. Rocky's ability to accept punch after punch and come back with a blistering attack was one of the characteristics of his performances that so enthralled his fans. To outpoint Rocky, while protecting himself against a fierce right, was Red's strategy. In fact, he outpointed the Rock during the first eight rounds.

Red and his corner believed the fight was going their way. Red, after all, was a more skilled boxer than Rocky, who relied on his slugging ability. In the ninth round, Red failed to cover up; he opened a door in his defenses, and Rocky charged through it. Rocky, the slugger, dropped Red onto the canvas with a hard overhand right. It was a blow Red had been unable to block. It looked as if he would be out for the standard count of 10, but the bell sounded and saved him. Red, somewhat dazed, walked on rubber legs back to his corner. He would have to do a better job of protecting himself in the 10th round, avoiding or blocking Rocky's right fist.

The 10th round was not a good one for Red: Rocky was as fired up as a tiger about to pounce on its prey. He quickly charged in for the attack. His right fist was aimed right at the bull's-eye of a target—Red's unprotected chin. Red seemed unable to protect himself; nothing he did warded off the coming of that powerful right punch. He would not be saved by the bell. This time, after being hit, Red stayed down for the full count of 10. Rocky was now being called the new "Million Dollar Baby." It was apparent that Rocky would soon become the highest-grossing fighter in his weight division. He and his corner were jubilant.

In a rematch, two months later, Rocky and Red seemed to reenact their first fight. They stuck to the same script: Red couldn't block or avoid Rocky's fist in the 10th round and so was knocked out, just as he had been in the first encounter. There was no point in engaging for another match. Rocky had proved his superiority over Red.

Those bouts were nearly the end of Red's professional boxing career. His last hurrah came when he defended the welterweight title against Marty Servo in 1946. Servo, a hard-punching, skillful boxer, sent Red to the canvas in the fourth round. Red remained there for the full count. It was the coda to his once-stirring career. Following his retirement, Red operated a tavern in Union, New Jersey, and worked as a liquor salesman. His life as a retired boxer was relatively uneventful; he died at age 77, in Lyons Veterans Administration Hospital in New Jersey. He had suffered from Alzheimer's disease.

Marty Servo would soon be next on Rocky's menu of contenders, but first the Rock would have to take on Sonny Horne. Would Rocky's climb to the top end at the fists of Horne and Servo, or would he go on to meet the mighty "Man of Steel," Tony Zale? That was the question posed by sportswriters to boxing fans eager to see who would be counted out and who would go on to fight Zale for the middleweight championship of the world. The writers were building as much suspense as possible.

George "Sonny" Horne was an outstanding middleweight boxer who, like many of his contemporaries, began boxing when he was a teenager. At age 14, he demonstrated a natural aptitude for the sport and learned easily and quickly. He had been tutored in the fine points of offense and defense by the local police chief in Niles, Ohio, Sonny's hometown. By the time he entered AAU and Golden Gloves bouts, he had proven he was the boy to beat, and no local boys were able to do so. By the time he was 17 years old, he had fought 77 bouts and developed a reputation among amateur boxers that extended from one end of Ohio to the other, from Cincinnati to Toledo, from Cleveland to the borders of West Virginia and Kentucky. His name was known in every boxing gym in the state. He defeated opponent after opponent with his impressive prowess and skill.

In 1941, Sonny's mentor and trainer, Niles police chief Matt McGowan, sent his young protégé to be managed by George Sheppard in New York. That was where the action was; that was where Sonny could make a national name for himself and earn the big bucks that came with major fights. Yet, Sonny was still a naïve Midwesterner. In many ways, he was still a kid. The Big Apple could easily overwhelm and seduce him. Sodom and Gomorrah on the Hudson could swallow young Sonny and spit him out, a desiccated decadent left for dead. Worried the young boxer would succumb to the lurid temptations of big-city nightlife, Sheppard sent Sonny to live and train in the suburb of Valley Stream, New York. It was close to New York but free of the meretricious temptations that could spin a boy's head and turn him in the wrong direction. In Valley Stream, Sonny was taken in hand by an experienced and highly regarded trainer named Al Lang, who operated a local boxing gym.

Sonny proved as devoted a student of pugilism as he had been in Niles. He was progressing to the point that Lang thought his student was ready to leave the ranks of the amateurs. By the time he turned 18, Sonny was boxing professionally. Matchmakers had their eyes on him, knowing that one day he could be a title contender and generate big turnouts and lots of cash. From age 18 to age 20, Sonny boxed in 48 bouts. Of those contests, he lost six, five on points, one by technical knockout. Forty-two wins was an impressive total. In just another two years, he would be featured at Madison Square Garden in a bout with Rocky Graziano.

There he was, at age 24, about to fight one of the biggest draws the Garden had ever hosted. Sonny's bout with Rocky was touted as a $100,000 fight. It was 1946; the war was over; people had money to spend. Tickets for boxing matches at Madison Square Garden were flying out of the box-office cage.

And there was Rocky, just itching to defeat the up-and-coming hope of the Midwest. The Rock was ready and supremely self-confident. He would enter the ring having won his last six bouts, five by knockout. Rocky and his trainer, Whitey Bimstein, had watched a few of Sonny's fights and thought he would be a formidable opponent, so a strict training regimen was put in place, and Rocky willingly subscribed to it. For two weeks, Rocky trained vigorously at Greenwood Lake in New Jersey. Every day he ran several miles, sparred, skipped rope, pounded the heavy bag, and tattooed the speed bag. He was primed to be a winner.

He returned to New York City, where he resumed training at Stillman's Gym on Eighth Avenue, where Sonny was also training. That the two fighters were able to observe one another's training routines was odd, but it gave each of them insights into how best to launch successful attacks. Whitey worked intensely to make sure Rocky would not depend solely on his powerful right hand. He got the Rock to develop a left jab and uppercut, which Rocky demonstrated in his sparring matches with Sidney Miller. When the opening bell sounded in Madison Square Garden, the two fighters came at one another with their best shots. It was a hard-fought match that went the full 10 rounds; Rocky seemed more disciplined than in his previous fights. It was not surprising that he outpointed Sonny.

An exhilarated Rocky was proud that the judges and referee unanimously awarded him the win. It wasn't as good as a knockout, but it was better than a split decision, which sportswriters could have disputed. The fight was considered such a crowd-pleaser that the two combatants would go on to have two more matches, in 1948 and 1949. To the delight of the managers, each fight filled all the seats, and although Sonny lost both contests, he was still an attractive asset fans would pay to see. Regardless of who he fought, Sonny was admired for his skill and tenacity.

He continued fighting with vigor, skill, and style until 1951, when his high level of energy seemed to have inexplicably leaked out of him like air leaking from a tire. His reflexes would drowse and then seem to be shocked awake, his energy returning only in spurts. It became increasingly apparent to everyone watching that his career would soon become dormant. He should stop fighting, his friends advised. Although he knew that something was wrong, he refused to listen. He tried every known panacea for his lethargy, but nothing worked, not caffeine, not alcohol, not even priming himself for a fight. Fans sadly witnessed a once-superb, fleet-of-foot athlete plod through his bouts. They wished him well. They didn't want to see him humiliated in the ring. The best thing was to retire, to go out as he had come in, leaving his admirers with memories they could cherish. Instead, they watched as Sonny engaged in a series of fights in which he seemed little better than a tired, washed-up palooka. Disappointed, his fans said Sonny had become just another pug whose time was up. It was too bad he didn't know it.

Unable to find a remedy and escape the downward spiral of his career, a worried Sonny finally took himself to a doctor, then to a hospital for a complete diagnosis. Doctors informed the startled boxer he had ALS, Lou Gehrig's disease. Although as upset and anxious as anyone would be when given such a diagnosis, Sonny did not retreat to a waiting list for the eventual arrival of a hearse. He decided to keep on boxing; it was what he knew best, and he would do it until his time ran out. He would fight as best he could and not be complicit with his diagnosis. He had never given up, even after multiple losses in the ring. He was always ready to sign up for another bout. It was his life, and he might as well die doing what he loved rather than be the pitiable vision of a man waiting for death. His persistence was admirably sad and sadly admirable.

Even with small reserves of energy, he demonstrated impressive will-power to go on and not give up. He knew one day the disease would floor him for a final count of 10 and he would never get up. Meanwhile, he would rely on his persistence and determination to keep going. Although important and necessary prompts for any boxer, neither persistence nor determination could take the place of his slowed reflexes and inability to go 10 rounds, toe to toe, fist to fist, with vigorous, young, healthy fighters.

Sonny lost his last 13 fights, the final one to Lalu Sabotin in Warren, Ohio, on August 29, 1951. It was a heroic loss, for Sonny was so weak he should never have been permitted to enter the ring. He died one month later, having lived his last two years in the home of his friend Russ Baxter in Youngstown, Ohio. He left behind a wife and two children. He was 35 years old and remembered not only as a great boxer, but also for the courage he displayed throughout the debilitating agonies of his final years. Fighting through ALS, Sonny had brought tears to the eyes of many who remembered the early promising years of a strong, athletic teenager, the hometown boy from Niles, a son of Ohio, who many thought would go on to be a conqueror.

After the Horne fight only one combatant stood between Rocky and his challenge for the middleweight championship. It was Marty Servo, a tough, first-class welterweight who had never been knocked out in any of his previous fights, including two with Sugar Ray Robinson, both of which Servo lost on points. In the last of those two fights, many fans and sportswriters believed Servo should have been awarded the decision. If he could outpoint Sugar Ray, many sportswriters said, he should be able to outpoint the Rock. He just had to stay away from that powerful right fist.

Servo was born in Schenectady, New York. In high school, he was a track star, as well as a successful featherweight boxer. He was popular with his fellow students, eliciting their admiration for his outstanding athletic abilities. Coaches, teachers, and many students thought Marty would go on to become a successful professional boxer. As an amateur, he had an impressive career of 91 wins and four losses; his record included his Golden Gloves and Diamond Belt Featherweight championships. Promoters had their eyes on young Servo; they thought that with the right management, he could go right to the top.

Servo was regularly encouraged to become a pro by one of his relatives and a successful boxer named Lou Ambers. Ambers also imparted to Servo many of the finer points about the necessary tactics for succeeding as a pro; however, there was only so much Ambers could do, as he had his own career to pursue. When Servo finally made the commitment to leave the ranks of amateur boxers and enter those of the pros, Ambers introduced the youngster to famed boxing manager Al Weill. Weill was not only sagacious in choosing opponents for Servo, but also he had a sense of what the public would find attractive in a fighter. He imagined his fighters' names in lights on Broadway. He thought that by shortening and Americanizing the names of his fighters, he could attract large numbers of fans to their matches. If a fighter was perceived as too ethnic, he would only attract members of his own race or religion, or—if the son of immigrants—he would only attract those who identified with the fighter's parents' land of origin. The same thing was going on in the movie business, where stars had their names airbrushed and vowels cropped to eliminate even a hint of ethnicity. While in Weill's care, former high school athlete Mario Severino became Marty Servo. Luigi Giuseppe d'Ambrosio had already been transformed into Lou Ambers, and, most famous of all, Rocco Marchegiano became Rocky Marciano, a powerful slugger who retired as an undefeated world heavyweight champion, 49 bouts, 49 wins.

By the time Marciano fought his first fight, Graziano had been attracting large crowds for five years. A somewhat shortened Italian name had become acceptable, and Marciano was easy to pronounce; furthermore, Weill figured it would be easier for headline writers to fit Marciano onto a page than Marchegiano. And why not another Rocky? After all, Rocky Graziano had become the most popular boxer in the United States. Another Italian Rocky would simply carry on the tradition. And there were exactly 16 letters in each of their names. Perfect—it all worked.

Servo, with his new Americanized name and his management astutely setting up crowd-pleasing fights, was heading toward a championship bout. From 1938 to 1942, he had 44 bouts, winning all but two, and those two were draws. Then Weill made his first mistake: He matched Servo with Sugar Ray Robinson. Servo lost the bout on the unanimous decision of the judges and referee. Yet, Weill and Servo thought a rematch would have a different result. Again, Servo lost, but this time it was a highly disputed split decision. Both fans and sportswriters were divided; many thought Servo had been robbed of the win. Fans complained the fight wasn't even close; some sportswriters agreed. Servo's career would have been better off had he not fought Robinson. And now he would have to temporarily leave the ring and be scored a loser in the record books.

Shortly after that encounter with Robinson, Servo joined the U.S. Coast Guard, serving from 1942 to 1945, as a boxing instructor, under the command of former heavyweight champ Jack Dempsey. Upon his discharge from the military, he reentered the world of boxing and began training for his fight against Freddie "Red" Cochrane for the welterweight championship of the world. Servo intended to make up for his losses to Robinson and either win by unanimous decision or knockout. He badly needed a win if his career was to advance. The fight was a fiercely fought bout, each fighter throwing punches that bloodied the other. In the fourth round, Servo hit Red with a powerful left hook that sent Red collapsing onto the canvas. Red attempted get up, but his legs wouldn't support him. He was counted out six seconds before the round would have ended. Although it was a joyful win for Servo (for he was now the world welterweight champion), the win generated a mirage of confidence in Weill, and perhaps Servo too.

Servo and Weill agreed on a decision they would come to regret. It was a worse decision than matching Servo against Robinson. If there had been a rematch for the welterweight title, the results of that second bad decision might have been avoided or postponed. To get Servo a shot at the title, Weill had to guarantee Red a $50,000 fee for the fight. Servo couldn't afford to pay Red and Red's manager. A rematch could have wiped out that debt. But a rematch wasn't in the cards; there wasn't enough money for such a fight. Instead, Weill and Servo agreed there should be a big money-making fight with Rocky Graziano, who outweighed Servo by eight pounds. If Servo won, he would have more than enough money to pay off Red.

Rocky was so eager to challenge Zale for the middleweight championship that he wanted to make quick work of Servo and move on to the big money and national fame a championship would guarantee him. Rocky could not have been more aggressive; he battered Servo in the first round. In the second round, Rocky delivered a series of powerful lefts and rights. Poor Servo suffered a technical knockout in that round and never really recovered. Rocky had so badly broken his nose that doctors, while repairing the injury, warned Servo that he should never fight again. If he did and his nose was broken again, he would have to breathe through his mouth for the rest of his life. Still eager to prove himself, Servo foolishly fought two more fights, losing the first, winning the second. His nose may not have been broken again, but to many he seemed a broken man. His defeat at the hands of the Rock broke something more important than Servo's nose; perhaps it was his self-confidence, perhaps it was his desire to continue in a sport where his options would be limited. His postboxing career was filled with unsatisfying jobs: bartender, auto salesman, steel mill foreman.

In 1950, while experiencing difficulty breathing and sharp pains in his chest, Servo sought medical attention; doctors diagnosed him with lung cancer. Like most boxers, he had no medical insurance, and his subsequent medical treatments robbed him of whatever savings he had accrued. Being a favored son of Schenectady, however, Servo became the focus of a fund-raising drive organized and managed by the *Schenectady Union-Star* newspaper, which raised $13,000 to help defray the costs of his medical treatments. He died at age 49. His indigent end demonstrated a sad truth about many boxers who hadn't made a lot of money during their careers and failed to have remunerative postboxing careers: Too often they died in poverty, being taken care of in their final years by their families, surviving on welfare and the generosity of former fans and a few colleagues.

Boxers have no union to represent them, no pension plans to cushion their later years; many suffer serious health problems brought on by years of having their brains hammered, while many boxing managers enjoy comfortable retirements. Managers of titleholders and contenders reap significant sums of money, taking 30 percent from each of their fighters; if a manager had a full stable of good fighters, he could retire as a multimillionaire, his brain untouched by blows in the ring.

In his later years, Rocky Graziano often reflected on the fates of boxers less fortunate than himself; he would often give money to those he knew and/or defeated, and regularly patronize their businesses. But after his stunning defeat of Marty Servo, Rocky had no time for reflection: He was focused like a shark on the body of Tony Zale. He wanted to kill Zale. Their bouts would be so bloody some sportswriters were amazed neither fighter died.

5

MEETING THE MAN OF STEEL

Rocky's entourage was a band of men united in their common goal: Each was looking forward to Rocky winning the middleweight championship of the world. There was the fighter himself, plus the manager, the trainer, the cutman, friends from the Lower East Side, and those who thought they might be considered friends. They were in a large hotel suite in the West 80s in Manhattan. At Rocky's house, there was his anxious wife Norma and his in-laws, parents, siblings, and grandmother. Prior to the fight's commencement, Norma was beset with anxiety about Rocky's safety. Her relatives tried to keep her calm, distract her from worrying too much, and assure her that Rocky would be fine. Their efforts had little effect on Norma's nerves, which were being fed by electric currents of apprehension.

On the streets, there were thousands of Rocky's fans, who had lined up to buy tickets in anticipation of the greatest middleweight fight of the year, perhaps the century. Those people would not have paid the same tribute to a movie star. Rocky was theirs, a man unique in his heroism and promise. His destiny was theirs. And if they had been parishioners in church they would have prayed fervently for the Rock's anointment as champ of the world.

The hype for the fight was as intense and unrelenting as the PR men could generate, and some of the best—the most creative and daring of the breed—were working overtime for the managers and promoters. They were on the phone with up-to-date information for sports pages and up-to-the-minute information for the wire services. Much of what they touted was pure fabrication, and all of it was in an effort to create the largest possible audience. Much of their information had to do with the rapidly changing odds for the fight. Some of it was about who would fight the winner and if there would be a rematch. By keeping the news pipelines full and flowing, the publicists earned every dollar they were paid. The fight wouldn't need a chorus of cheerleaders, for the publicists had such a repertoire of cheery stories to peddle that the papers and wire services couldn't print it all. Nevertheless, the flow continued right up until the bell sounded for round one.

Irving Cohen told Rocky the mission of the press, whether they knew it or not, was to park a body on each seat in Yankee Stadium and sell the fans programs, cigarettes, cigars, beer, soda, and hot dogs. For Rocky, it was the promise of a huge payday. The gross from the fight would result in fattened bank accounts for not only the fighters, their managers and trainers, and the promoters, but also scores of vendors.

The fight would be the most popular since Max Schmeling and Joe Louis had slugged it out in two famous contests for their patriotic fans in the United States and Germany. Rather than the United States versus Germany, however, the Graziano–Zale fight would be the streetfighter, the Italian delinquent, the ex-convict who fought like a junkyard dog (Graziano) against the upright, all-American, clean-living good guy from the country's industrial heartland (Zale). It would be the gritty streets of the Lower East Side, with its peddlers and gangs of tough young ethnics, versus the steel mills of Gary, Indiana, where the muscles, bones, and sinews of diligent factory workers turned out steel for autos and appliances. They were the ones who kept the U.S. economy humming. It was America's industrial heartland versus America's immigrant slums. It was the rebel against the conformist, the young former thief against the steady and reliable military veteran, the rule breaker against the rule supporter.

The fighters had their supporters, and they were from two distinct worlds. Allegiance depended on not only where you lived and what you did for a living, but also who you could identify with, who could you imagine yourself being. When a punch was thrown, could you imagine yourself throwing it? Or could you imagine the pain of being hit? Did you flinch from imagined pain, or did you feel vicariously aggressive? Regardless of which fighter was the object of their loyalty, the fans bet like frantic stock traders on the floor of the New York Stock Exchange. The market price of one boxer rose as the price of the other fell, and then the action would reverse itself, becoming topsy-turvy. No one dwelled on the fact that one group would go home full of joy and satisfaction, while the other would be left feeling empty and disappointed.

Although Rocky and Tony were determined to win, Rocky wanted more: He wanted to earn the largest amount of money he had ever banked. It was almost as important as beating Zale for the title. To be the middleweight champion of the world would wipe away the shame he had felt for his past mistakes, and the money would show those who had known him when he was nothing but a poverty-stricken street urchin and petty thief that he could now afford to buy anything he wanted. To be crowned champion of the world and be a rich man were the two goals that fueled Rocky's anger and determination going into the fight. To earn such a large sum of money in one night without being a racketeer, a profession to which he had once aspired, seemed nothing short of amazing. It was lawful. No one could take it away from him.

But Rocky couldn't get ahead of himself. He had to pace himself, cool down; he was eager to get into the ring, eager to earn that big payoff, but he had to be calm and thoughtful, and on top of his game. He could not let eagerness overwhelm him and cause him to rush headlong into defeat. He had to be calm, aware, and strategic, using all the tactics in his arsenal, and then go for the knockout. The knockout and the big payday.

The fight and the title were so close, he could imagine the contest and play it over and over again in his head, like a movie on the screen of his mind. It was a continuously playing loop, both in his dreams and when he was awake. He knew his future might depend on one lucky punch. If his right cross could find the perfect opening, he would be the champ. Such knowledge can cause one to postpone an event, or it can make one an anxious, restless caged animal. It can cause even the calmest, most stoical of boxers to lose sleep. Waiting for that initial round, when your fists are up and you move toward your opponent, can seem like a tortuous eternity. The minutes slowly drip by as if from a leaky faucet, one slow minute followed by another. The second hand rounds the minutes in slow motion, finally pushing the minute hand to the next digit. And then suddenly the bell sounds for round one, and the fight is on. Fear and anxiety vanish. There's no turning back.

It's no wonder fighters get jumpy before a bout, easily lose their tempers, and lash out at friends, trainers, and managers for making seemingly innocent remarks. Although many fighters have confessed to experiencing fear before a bout, none of them would ever show or admit it in public before a fight. To do so would not only call their manhood into question, but also lead their opponents to believe they were weak and cowardly. Those confessions, when uttered, usually come in reminiscences long after fighters have retired from the ring.

If Rocky was fearful, no one knew it. He could have been a prisoner of that emotion, as he was of varying others. He could be as restless as a Mexican jumping bean or as calm as a Zen meditation master. Before his fight with Tony Zale, he had been one and then the other. There he was in the bedroom of his hotel suite trying to sleep late. His trainer, Whitey Bimstein, wanted him to rest, to contain his energy and strength for when he would need to rely on every bit of it later that night. Rocky had gone from being as still as a glass of water to as storm-tossed as an ocean during a hurricane. He couldn't sleep. He would sit on a chair just to get up as quickly as if he had suddenly been shocked by high-voltage electricity. Rocky was fortunate to have Whitey by his side, for Whitey was always the concerned, indulgent older brother type: mature, practical, calm. More than anyone he knew how to soothe his restless young boxer. He knew Rocky needed to keep moving; it was the only way he could transform his restlessness to calmness. There was a tightly tied knot of tension in Rocky's gut, and he needed to loosen it and then untie it. Movement was the solution—keep moving like a tiger in a cage. Later the cage door would be flung open, and Rocky would come roaring out, ready to do battle, to kill, if necessary.

But for now, Rocky was focused on the minutes leading up to the fight. And Whitey was focused only on Rocky. Neither Rocky nor Whitey mentioned the fight. All the talk, all the advice, and all the training had been going on for weeks. There was nothing new to say, nothing new to learn. It was just a matter of waiting and waiting and waiting. To the men in the suite, Rocky was distant, uncommunicative. The caged tiger paced from one corner to another. He looked as if he was ruminating on plans. Rocky's entourage, including Whitey, Jack Healy, Eddie Coco, and Al Pennino, knew not to intrude into Rocky's self-enclosed silence. They would occasionally glance at him and then return to their own conversations. They spoke about baseball, sports in general, cars, clothes, food, the weather, and a couple of guys they knew doing time in Sing Sing—anything but boxing. Their chatter was soft and pleasant, almost like background noise. It was meant to soothe, not disturb.

Earlier, after getting out of bed, Rocky had been dressed in only a pair of boxer shorts. Having padded around the suite on bare feet for several minutes, he decided to get dressed. He put on a pair of neatly ironed dark blue slacks and a gray cotton polo shirt. The guys unobtrusively observed Rocky; again, their glances were quick and casual, almost surreptitious. Peripheral images of Rocky moved in and out of their focus. Rocky's face seemed to relax as he walked around, restlessness seeping out of his pores. While the restlessness dissipated, reserves of energy remained. He would need every bit of his energy and determination when he got into the ring with Zale.

For a man who could spend hours running, shadowboxing, and hitting the speed and heavy bags, his prefight confinement was a punishment. There was no place in the hotel suite to punch a speed bag or jump rope. He could do push-ups and sit-ups, but they did not provide the same release as rapidly flying fists. If he didn't find an outlet, he might punch a wall, knock over a lamp, or smash a glass on the floor. He always felt he was better off pounding the sidewalks than sitting around and letting his mind focus on something that might cause him to be angry. From the time he was a kid on the streets, stealing coal and firewood, bread and rolls, milk and cream, he was always moving, always outrunning the grip of the law, always avoiding being tripped by a good citizen. Stand still and you would feel the cold, hard grip of a cop's mitt on your shoulder, or a billy club, night stick, or rubber blackjack across your back or the back of your head, he thought. Keep moving, and move fast, and you wouldn't be decked, you wouldn't be sent sprawling onto the sidewalk and hauled off to the local precinct. The same was true in the boxing ring: Keep moving and you won't be sent sprawling onto the canvas.

Avoiding a cop's grip and evading an opponent's punch required quick reflexes and rapid movements. Restlessness had saved Rocky. It was as natural to him as his hard right-hand punch. He could no more sit still than a dervish could not whirl. Even after Rocky had given up a life of crime, he was always up early and out on the streets. He couldn't stand being confined, not in a cold-water tenement, not in a gymnasium. If the temperature on the streets was below freezing, it never had mattered to the young Rocco Barbella. It was always better to be out and moving; if his hands were cold, he would jam his fists into his jacket pockets or breathe hot air onto his palms and fingers and rub them together. If his feet were cold, he would stamp them on the sidewalk. If his entire body was cold, he would stand on a subway grate for a few minutes.

On the Lower East Side, Rocky couldn't see the far horizon—what his future would be; he only saw the old brick tenements with rusting fire escapes and grimy windows. It was his world, street after street, avenue after avenue, a grid of crisscrossing streets. As dirty as the world outside was, it was still infinitely larger and more enticing than the world inside a tenement. It may have only offered the opportunity for minor crime sprees, but it was better than hanging around with his parents, a father who drank too much and a mother who cried when not silently depressed. Escaping the dark, dreary world of tenements and poverty was his modus operandi.

Having escaped from the Lower East Side, from school rooms, from the army, he made his way to Brooklyn. His path was full of signposts, each a testament to his winning career as a boxer. There, on Ocean Parkway, Rocky bought a spacious, elegant house, a testament to his drive and success. He would never fit the image of a typical suburban squire, but he was a man of property, a father, a husband, a man with lots of money in the bank. He would never have to steal again. He was able to buy his wife and daughter everything they needed. And not just them: He bought himself a powder blue Cadillac convertible and had his name, just Rocky, no last name, stenciled on the front doors. He parked it in his own garage. There, on his own property, he could work off his nervous energy by swimming in his own heated swimming pool. It was a luxury the young Rocco Barbella had never seen in a dream. During the summer, poor boys and girls would open a fire hydrant and splash, jump, and skip through its shooting jets of water. They would sunbathe on the rooftops of their tenements, known as tar beaches. That was all in the past; the Rock was now a man riding a rocket aimed at the ultimate success for a middle-weight contender. He could imagine the championship belt wrapped around his waist.

Rocky, hair slicked straight back from his forehead and his face smoothly shaven, paced about in his hotel suite. The tiger was ready to spring but had no opponent to spring at, no one to absorb his violent, pent-up energy. The hotel suite was comfortable, but it was too confining. He wished he was back at his house on Ocean Parkway, but his manager and trainer did not want their fighter at home with his wife and kids before a fight as important as the one with Tony Zale. At home, Rocky would empathize with Norma's anxiety about the fight. Such empathy could result in not throwing himself completely into the fight. It could stifle his killer instinct. The worst thing he could do would be to reassure his wife that he wouldn't be hurt and then not fully engage in the fight. Irving and Whitey did not want Rocky to be hampered by any anxieties and concerns regarding his wife and daughter.

Going into a fight, a boxer needed to be supremely self-confident, to burn with the ambition of defeating his opponent—and, if necessary, during the heat of combat, to even want to kill his opponent. He had to suppress his sense of fear, and although it might exist, he could not let it supplant his need to win. Fear could be driven out of oneself by the violence and anger necessary for winning. It was the job of the manager and the trainer to make sure their fighter was as powerfully motivated to win as possible. They would say anything, true or not, to make a fighter want to take the head off of an opponent. And then when it was all over, many fighters wanted to congratulate an opponent and honor him for having the courage to wage an impressive battle. They were enemies in the ring and brothers in courage after a bout was over.

Yes, the hotel suite was stifling. A change of scenery was necessary, so later that day, the group of men drove to Eddie Coco's house in the Bronx, where Rocky had a light dinner and surprised his friends and hosts by being able to nap before heading for Yankee Stadium. People at the house remarked how cool, calm, and collected the Rock was. Imagine being able to nap before entering the ring to fight for the middleweight championship of the world. When neighbors asked where Rocky was, they were told he was napping. Most men would be a bundle of jittery nerves at such a time, they agreed. It seemed that his usual restlessness had been replaced by a self-induced Zen-like calm. It seemed as if Rocky had emptied his mind, made it a blank.

When he awoke, he said nothing about Tony Zale, although the fighter's reputation as a hard-hitter with a jaw of steel was a preoccupation, and not just for Rocky, but also Whitey and Irving. They had originally attempted to dissuade their fighter from engaging with the "Man of Steel." Better to put it off, rack up some more wins. It might be too soon. It could be the wrong career move, if the fight ended badly for Rocky; however, after decisively defeating Billy Arnold and Marty Servo, two of the most promising contenders, Rocky insisted he was ready. "Get me Zale! Get me Zale!" he had insisted. And so it was done.

The bout in Yankee Stadium looked as if it would be the biggest event in the careers of the two boxers. For each of them, the final trajectories of their careers would be mapped by the outcome; unbeknownst to them and their mangers and trainers, the two men were about to enter the history books of pugilism as two of the most brilliant middleweights the sport has ever witnessed; their bouts would be regarded as the bloodiest, most intensely fought middleweight fights of the twentieth century. The boxing world had never seen anything like it and still hasn't.

Nearly 40,000 fans paid $342,497 to witness two of the toughest gladiators to ever meet in a boxing ring. For Rocky, it would be his biggest payday thus far. He knew he would carve out a large chunk of that money for himself; and if he won, he would be the world middleweight champion, with the ability to command even larger sums—and not just from boxing matches, but also from commercial endorsements. The money would flood into his bank accounts. The combination of money, fame, glory, and redemption were his powerful motivations. There was more riding on his performance that night than most men would face in a lifetime, than most men could withstand without fear coldly coursing through their bodies, rattling their nerves, drying their throats, and causing their bodies to ooze perspiration. Self-contained, determined, and strong-willed, Rocky seemed cool and calm, with not a bead of perspiration on him. He didn't yell at anyone, didn't lose his temper, didn't curse and throw things at the wall. He was focused solely on defeating Tony Zale. If he felt fear at the prospect of going up against a winner of four middleweight championship bouts, he didn't let anyone know about it. He wouldn't even admit to himself.

His method had always been to absorb as many punches as necessary while waiting to find an opening and slam an opponent with a hard right. Zale, he knew, might require many such punches to be knocked out, but Rocky had an arsenal of those punches in reserve, and he was prepared to fire as many as necessary to bring down the Man of Steel.

And what of Tony Zale? He had worked in the steel mills of Gary, Indiana, hence the nickname Man of Steel. But there was more to the sobriquet than just the steel mills of Gary: Other fighters said Zale was as hard as steel—not just his body, but also his punches. His chin was made of steel, a few sportswriters noted hyperbolically. As with Rocky, Zale could absorb a tremendous amount of punishment and come back to defeat an opponent. He was known as a crafty tactical and strategic fighter, but he also resorted to a repertoire of dirty tricks that were often overlooked by referees. For example, in his fight with George Abrams for the middleweight title in 1941, in Madison Square Garden, Zale drove one of his gloved thumbs into Abrams's left eye in the first round. In the beginning of the fourth round, Zale headbutted Abrams, causing a severe cut above Abrams's right eye. There was a curtain of blood covering Abrams's face, and he could barely see. Yet, he courageously fought on. In the ninth round, Zale delivered a series of hard, rapid punches to Abrams's midsection, which were difficult to block. Zale was known for his powerful gut punches that drove the air out of fighters, leaving them helpless, although rarely unconscious.

By the end of the fight, Abrams looked like a wounded war casualty. While the judges, as expected, awarded the win to Zale, the Associated Press wrote that Abrams won eight rounds, with Zale winning seven. Once again, the opinion of the judges was called into question, and many fans believed they had been paid off by bookies and mobsters. Others said Zale had proved to be the more aggressive fighter and so deserved the decision of the judges. Many of Abrams's fans, however, were primed to witness Zale receive a humiliating beating by the gloved fists of the former street fighter from the tough streets of the Lower East Side.

For Zale, the present was what mattered, not some disputed judgment from the past. It had always been that way, ever since he began his professional boxing career in 1934, at age 20. His birth name was Anthony Florian Zaleski. Tony Zale sounded less ethnic, more American; it was short and crisp, easy to remember, and a comfortable fit for headline writers. (It was a tradition of managers and promoters to shorten the names of their fighters, especially those with multisyllabic, ethnic monikers.) By the time Zale was to fight Rocky in 1946, he had fought in 75 bouts. Of those he had lost 16, two by knockout, one by a TKO.

Prior to his fight with Rocky, Zale had won and retained the middleweight title four times. It was an accomplishment that added luster to Zale's reputation and polished his Man of Steel image. For his fans, the steel could not have shone more brightly or been any harder. His bout with Rocky would be his fourth attempt to retain the title. He was now 32 years old and had been in the navy for four years, and some said he was not as tough, not as strong, and not as fast as he had been. Others said the military had made him even stronger than he had been in 1942. The boxing world was eager to see who was right.

Physically, the fighters were almost mirror images of one another. They were nearly the same height: Rocky was 5-foot-7, while Zale was 5-foot-7½. Zale's reach was 69 inches. Rocky's was 68½ inches. On the afternoon of the fight, Zale weighed 160 pounds, and Rocky weighed 154. Zale was six years older than Rocky. Some said the six-year difference would benefit Rocky; others were not so sure.

Prior to his fight with Zale, Rocky had had 54 bouts. He succumbed to six losses, none by knockout, and experienced five draws.

Fans, sportswriters, and bookies thought the fighters were evenly matched, although many from Indiana gave the edge to Zale. They said steel is stronger than rock, that steel could drill through rock, cutting it into shards. There was a local cartoon of Zale's fists of steel shattering and splintering Rocky's jaw. In New York, however, fans and trainers thought Rocky had the edge. After all, they insisted, Zale had not defended his title since 1941. Four years without a professional fight meant Zale might have lost the speed and endurance he used to display. In addition, he was six years older than Rocky, who at 27 had the exuberant fitness and energy of youth. A 33-year-old's muscles are not as big, hard, and flexible as they had been at age 27. Moreover, the more youthful Rocky had an impressive winning streak against some of the best contenders in boxing. He was primed and proven, ready to challenge Zale and take away his title. The bookies outwardly stated that the two fighters were evenly matched, although the odds fluctuated following different news reports and gossip from ring insiders.

On September 27, 1946, the two men entered the ring to the applause, shouts, and cheers of 40,000 fans, many of whom acted as if the ensuing battle would be between conflicting ideologies. The fans had chosen their sides, and the only things missing were flags and uniforms. As the fight would go on and both fighters were bruised and bloody, there would be shouts of, "Kill him, finish him, drop the bum, smash him." Some liquored and/or overly exuberant fans mimed uppercuts, right crosses, and left crosses. Their vicarious presence would serve as an amusing sideshow, for none of them could withstand so much as an indignant slap across the face. Being a fan was safe and exhausting.

Zale, square-jawed and stoical as a cinematic cowboy hero about to face down an opponent on the streets of Tombstone or Dodge City, stared—slit-eyed—straight ahead. His mien was imperturbable; he exuded cold self-confidence. In front of fans and reporters, he stood proud and erect, a man who knew what was ahead of him and what was expected of him. He was prepared to meet the challenger and confident in the result. As the time of battle approached, a small, confident smile seemed to play on his face. Or perhaps it was the way the light caught his features. At such times, a fighter wants to impress his opponent and demonstrate that he is the superior pugilist, that his skills, strength, and determination will win him the decision or propel him to a win by knockout.

Zale certainly looked the part of a heroic winner: His features appeared to be geometric and proportional; previous fights had not misaligned his eyes or diminished the vertical line of his nose. He was a conventionally handsome man: middle American and solid.

Rocky carried himself with the bounding energy and restlessness of a man eager to get on with the fight. While Zale's face was a mask that did not reveal his emotions, Rocky's was that of a silent film star. You could look at him and get a sense of what he was feeling. He was all emotion.

His eagerness to begin the bout was apparent. He was like a racehorse that had to be held back at the starting gate. He was where he had wanted to be for years. This fight would be the defining event of his life as a boxer. It would be his biggest fight, and win or lose, he would walk away with $100,000. Yet, just as much as he wanted the money, he wanted to win and win big. He didn't want the fight to be like the disputed Zale–Abrams bout. This one had to be decisive. With a win, he would never have to slide into the mud of defeat, never have to end up at the bottom like his father. He would rather be dead.

Different in appearance from Zale's conventional good looks, Rocky looked ethnically handsome, a product of the Mediterranean: slightly swarthy with jet black hair. He looked as if he could have sprung from Naples, Sicily, or Florence. He wore his black hair slicked back with a modest pompadour crowning his forehead. If you could imagine him 10 years younger, you could see him playing a juvenile delinquent in a movie. He was better looking than any of the cinematic dead-end kids but just as recalcitrant, ever the rebel, the defiant one, ready to flatten anyone who stood in his way. And that was the attitude he brought to his bout with Zale. Zale was an obstacle that had to be pushed aside, knocked over, or stomped—or even killed.

Rocky the rebel was on fire with rage and an ambition to take off Zale's head. Later on in the fight, tasting his own hot blood, it would be like fuel poured on the fire of his rage. He was determined to slam his opponent into absolute submission and grab the golden title, wearing the thick, heavy championship belt for all the world to see.

The word on the streets of the Lower East Side was that Rocky was the betting favorite: His recent performances against tough opponents had convinced friends, fans, and other local fighters that the Rock was on a roll. He was destined to win, they believed. Zale, in terms of athletic ability, was approaching the status of being middle-aged. And that four-year layoff in the military meant he might have lost his killer instinct. Rocky believed it too. He told his pals to bet on him. They would clean up.

And then they were in the ring. The referee, Ruby Goldstein, called them into the center. He instructed the fighters on the rules and told them to touch gloves and give the fans a good, clean bout. He dispatched them to their respective corners. The bell sounded for round one. The two men were primed for instant, intense combat. They seemed like two gladiators at the Roman Coliseum, rushing at one another with their weapons raised. Zale hit Rocky with a left hook, and Rocky went down with a bewildered look on his face, his mouth and eyes wide open in surprise. He seemed to blink in disbelief, pressing his lips together in a sign of determination. This wasn't supposed to happen, and certainly not in the opening round. With hot flames of fury burning inside, Rocky sprung to his feet and went after Zale as if he wanted to kill him. In fact, after the fight, that's exactly what Rocky said. Rocky faked with a left, and Zale ducked out of range, leaving an opening for Rocky to drive a hard right to Zale's chin. He may have seen that one coming but had no time to get out of the way. It was Zale's turn to hit the canvas, and he did so with a loud thump that caused fans to leap to their feet and erupt with cheers, ooos and aaahhs, and shouts of, "Finish him, Rocky." Zale stayed down, seemingly dazed. When the referee had reached the count of three, the bell sounded, ending the round. Zale, still dazed, but lucky, shook his head like a wet dog coming in from the rain and made his way back to his corner. He had been as surprised as Rocky had been in the first round.

In the third round, Rocky went after Zale again, this time to finish him, to knock him out well before the bell sounded. He pounded him with lefts and rights. Zale's face was a mask of blood. The handsome Mid-westerner looked as shattered as if he had been in a terrible car crash. Rocky grabbed Zale's head with his left glove and pounded it with his right. A plume of blood flew in an arc from Zale's face with each punch. Rocky's gloves were wet with his opponent's spattered blood.

In the fourth round, Zale emerged as if by some magic transformation. He seemed like a new man, appearing refreshed, energized, and determined. Something had infused his will, and he went after Rocky with a series of powerful body blows. There was the Zale of old, delivering hard, rapid, pile-driving body blows that could hammer the air out of an opponent, making him feel as if his heart and lungs were deflated and dying.

By the fifth round, Zale was indeed on the offense, shooting punch after punch against Rocky's bruised and reddened midsection. Zale drove Rocky back against the ropes. Rocky had nowhere to go, and Zale kept up the assault. Again, inflamed by anger and a burning desire to win the fight, Rocky launched a furious counterattack, driving Zale back with a series of powerful punches. Lefts and rights, lefts and rights, and more lefts and rights, each shot against Zale's head. Rocky's right fist landed with explosive power against Zale's mouth, and blood spurted from his ravaged, torn lips. Before Rocky could finish Zale, the bell sounded, ending the round—another lucky break for Zale. Frustrated, Rocky shook his head as if he couldn't believe Zale was still standing. The bell seemed like a caustic curse, an ironic laugh of fate. Just when Rocky could have dropped Zale, the damned bell saved the guy—not just once, but twice. Rocky's right fist had been cocked to deliver a stunning final blow, the coup de grâce to end the fight. Now it hung by his side as he returned to his corner of the ring. There was a groan of disappointment from the crowd, but they were also eager to see what would happen in the next round. It was one of the most exciting fights they had ever seen.

At the outset of the sixth round, Rocky was determined to send Zale to the canvas for a full count of 10 and do it well before the bell could sound. Rocky reopened old cuts on Zale's bruised face, as well as some new ones. He pounded away with rapid-fire rights and lefts. Zale's head was wobbling as if a toy on springs, his face contorted from each blow Rocky delivered. Instead of continuing to go after Zale's head, Rocky changed tactics and aimed a hard right at his foe's midsection. It was a costly mistake. Zale saw his opening. It was his last opportunity to put Rocky away, to save himself, to save his title. He drove a hard right into Rock's solar plexus. Zale's fist looked as if it penetrated inches into Rocky's midsection. Rocky gulped and gasped. Air, as if from a burst balloon, escaped from his mouth. He couldn't catch his breath. Breathing was momentarily impossible. He felt as if he would soon lose consciousness.

Zale followed up with a left hook against Rocky's chin. Trying to suck in air, Rocky went over like a dead tree. He sat on his ass, looking as if he had been thrown off a rapidly spinning world by centrifugal force. Goldstein, the referee, counted him out. Yet, just as Goldstein said 10, Rocky sprung up and attempted to rush at Zale. It was too late. The fight was over. Rocky had lost. He felt as if his dreams had been shattered by a sledgehammer. Whitey Bimstein and Ruby Goldstein yoked him back to his corner. Zale was the bloodied winner; Rocky was the comparatively unmarked loser. "Hell, he looked like the loser, me the winner," was Rocky's comment to reporter John Devaney.[1]

When Rocky got home that night, Norma couldn't stop crying. Having listened to the fight on the radio, she feared he had been badly hurt, that bones in his handsome face had been broken, teeth dislodged. But when she saw that he had not been damaged, that his face was as handsome as ever, she cried some more, this time relieved that he was in one piece, safe, and in her arms.

Rocky's friend, boxer, holdup man, thief, and thug Terry Young, who was serving time in Sing Sing prison, heard the fight on a prison radio and was so upset by the outcome he smashed two of the prison's windows. The guards threw him into solitary confinement, known as the "hole," after accusing him of attempting to start an insurrection.[2]

The next day was not so bad; although sore, tired, and disappointed, Rocky knew he would have another shot at Zale, and he would not open himself up for another devastating body blow. He would stay true to his original instincts and go for Zale's head. The sense of optimism that had caused him to tell Irving and Whitey to get him Zale returned. He didn't have to say it again. The fight would take place, and having come so close to knocking out Zale in their first bout, Rocky knew he would succeed in the second go-round.

Rocky decided to refresh himself by visiting his old neighborhood. Although he had moved away, the Lower East Side still had a grip on his imagination. It was his neighborhood, it was where he had defined himself, and it was still filled with his people. They were the people who had come out of their apartments and stores to congratulate him as a conquering hero every time he won a bout. He was a true son of the Lower East Side. There were stores, bars, restaurants, bakeries, barbershops, grocery stores, shoe repair shops, and the pool hall, each one a touchstone from his youth. Visiting the place would wipe away some of the sense of loss he was feeling, further strengthen his self-confidence, and put the bounce back in his swagger. There, on his street, in his neighborhood, Rocky strode down 10th Street as if he owned it.

Although not a conquering hero this time, he knew he was still a hero to his people. He had overcome poverty and his criminal past. He was a success, someone to be admired. He certainly displayed heroic endurance and fortitude in the ring. He expected to be admired for that too. He didn't realize, at that moment, he was only a hero in his own mind. He whistled, he waved to kids, he called out hellos to store owners and familiar faces on the street. When he saw guys who he had hung around with, he was surprised to see them cross to the other side of the street and avert their eyes. He called out to them, but they ignored him. He muttered to himself and shrugged his shoulders. He headed to an old hangout, a poolroom, where he expected to be greeted like a warrior returning from battle, wounded and now healed, scarred but not bowed. He entered the place, and there was not one greeting. No one came forth and slapped him on his back. No one playfully punched his shoulder. Old friends, some guys he had pulled heists with, acted as if he were invisible.

He couldn't figure it out. Sure, he had lost the fight, but everyone loses fights. And some of the sportswriters said he had really won the contest. Just look at Zale. He was beaten black and blue and bloody; he could hardly make it out of the ring. He was two inches and 10 seconds away from being taken out on a stretcher. If it hadn't been for a fast count, if Rocky had gotten up one second sooner, he figured he would be champion. The guys should know that. He was robbed by a miscalculation. The fight was his. The title should have been his. He would get the title the next time. So why the silent treatment?

An old pal finally filled him in: Rocky had told everyone he would win; it was a sure thing. He told everyone to bet on him. He felt it in his bones, in his heart, in his determination. The guys in the poolroom, his old buddies in crime, they had bet everything they had that Rocky would win. They thought the fight was fixed for Rocky. That was how they saw the world. The fix was always in. If Rocky said he would win, he would win. It was fixed. No doubt about it. He not only let them down, they figured, but also sold them out. He must have been paid off big time to take a dive. Why else would Rocky sit there on the canvas just watching the referee counting him out before making a big show of pretending he still wanted to fight?

He was a fake, a fraud, a heel. He was in it for himself. He had forsaken his old pals for a quick and easy payoff. They figured they couldn't trust their old pal. He was a sellout, a fink; he should have told them to put their money on Zale. They didn't know Rocky would sooner be humiliated than take a dive. They didn't understand how proud Rocky was. Sure, he had once been a thief and served time in protectories, reform schools, jails, and prisons, but he had never finked on a friend, never ratted anyone out. If he said he was going to win, he genuinely thought he was going to win. He was proud and self-confident, perhaps too self-confident, but never a sellout. Rocky's entire career had been aimed at winning. If you take a dive for the easy money, you may never get a chance for a title fight. It could wipe out your chances. In fact, when approached by shady characters at Stillman's Gym or other venues, offering him $10,000 to take a dive, he would laugh and tell them to take a hike. Yes, he wanted money, but he wanted to earn it by winning, by being the champ. There was a lot more money to be made as a champ than as a guy who took dives and never got to be a titleholder.

Rocky knew what he had; he knew the power of his right fist; he knew how much punishment he could withstand; he knew his ambition and desire to be the champ. He had come so close; all of New York City knew who Rocky Graziano was. They loved him. Just read the *Daily News*, the *Daily Mirror*, and even the *Journal-American*. The fans filled every seat in the Garden when he fought there. They had filled 40,000 seats in Yankee Stadium. They would hardly do that for a guy who wasn't all heart, who didn't fight to win, who gave his all every time he stepped into the ring. For them, Rocky had the heart of a lion. He believed he would win the next fight with Zale and show the doubters and disbelievers in his old neighborhood that he was a real champ. He would train as he never had before. He would make the cynics love him again.

In the book *The Top of His Game*, W. C. Heinz wrote,

> When Graziano fought, you could breathe the tension. When he fought in the Garden, you could feel it over on Broadway, and the night he fought Zale for the first time you could sense it two hours before the fight between the cars jammed along the Grand Concourse, half a mile from Yankee Stadium. When he trained at Stillman's, he packed that

place to the walls. They would be stacked on the stairway to the balcony, and they would be packed on the balcony, too.[3]

Rocky needed to clear his head, put everything in perspective, look to the future and put the loss to Zale behind him. Nothing would be gained by punishing himself about the fight, by thinking about the friends who had turned on him. He would make up for it in a rematch. He had just earned $100,000, the largest single sum of money he had earned thus far. He would enjoy it and the time he had between fights. He took Norma, little Audrey, and his in-laws on vacation to Florida. There, they would relax in the sun and frolic in the waves, and Rocky would count down the days until his rematch. Rocky spent days at the beach with Norma and Audrey. He was joined by Jake LaMotta, his fellow reform school chum and middleweight boxing colleague, and LaMotta's wife, sitting poolside at their hotel. In Miami, there were other guys from the world of boxing, and Rocky was glad to hang out with them.

Before his planned return, Rocky received a call from Irving Cohen: He wanted Rocky to come to New York to prepare for a tune-up fight with Reuben "Cowboy" Shank. It was a fight to help get Rocky in shape for a rematch with Zale. Against Shank, Rocky could try out new tactics. The fight would keep him primed, on his toes. While working out at Stillman's Gym, Rocky pulled some muscles in his back. To relax those muscles, he got a rubdown; it didn't help. The pain only got worse. The pain spread to his side, and he couldn't twist his torso from side to side. When he threw a punch at the heavy bag, the pain shot like electricity through his entire torso. Irving decided Rocky would not fight the Cowboy. It made no sense. Better to let the muscles heal through massage and hot baths than take a chance and suffer an injury that would put the Zale fight out of reach. The fight with Zale was postponed. Unbeknownst to Irving and Rocky, something more than a bad back would cause a postponement of the Graziano–Zale rematch. For the first time since his prison days, Rocky would be in legal jeopardy.

6

HUNG OUT TO DRY

It happened so suddenly, so quickly, and so unexpectedly; Rocky may have felt as if someone had tied him to stakes on the ground and attempted to castrate him.

On a sunny January morning, he left his home on Ocean Parkway, heading out for a drive in the country. His wife, Norma, and daughter, Audrey, were vacationing in Miami. He had the big house all to himself. Occasionally, some of his pals would drop by for a card game, snacking on beer and pretzels and swapping tales about the boxing fraternity. But most of the time, Rocky was alone. On that day, he had been without the company of his friends. And being a social animal, Rocky didn't enjoy being solitary. In addition, he missed his family and would call them every evening. Little Audrey loved hearing from her father, loved the sound of his voice, his Lower East Side Noo Yawk accent. Her father's deep voice was as reassuring as his strong arm around her shoulder.

But just sitting around, reading the papers, listening to the radio, watching television, gabbing on the phone with friends, and hearing gossip about some members of his old gang did not provide the warm embrace of family or the good-humored camaraderie of his pals. The pleasure of getting in his car, turning on the engine, and listening to its lion-like purr for several minutes gave him the enjoyable sensation that he could conquer his restlessness. Pulling out of his driveway or away from the curb in front of his house meant he was on the move, on the go, leaving his loneliness behind. And movement would be essential to Rocky for as long as he lived. The joy of driving, while listening to Frank

Sinatra and other singers on the radio, erased the gray clouds of tedium and boredom that made Rocky restless; he was like one of Jack Kerouac's characters in *On the Road* who had a sense of being a freewheeling guy.

Getting into the left lane on a parkway or turnpike, Rocky liked to gun his Caddy, for its big eight-cylinder engine produced an enormous amount of horsepower. With a firm tap of the gas pedal, he could put the car in overdrive and make it surge ahead, passing other cars. Driving that big beauty of a machine made Rocky feel as if he owned the roads on which he drove. One can imagine him singing along with his favorite pop songs, for he knew most of the lyrics. His style of driving consisted of shooting through red lights as if they were no more than Christmas ornaments. He was a man without troubles.

Then, as one song ended, Rocky heard the ugly, pulse-quickening, rudely blaring siren of a black unmarked police car. He had learned not to antagonize cops during his prison days; it only made them angry and treat you roughly. He slowed the big Caddy and glanced into its rearview mirror, where he could see the flashing red police light on the car's dashboard. A hand from inside the car grabbed the flashing light and stuck it onto the roof of the car. The light was spinning like a top. Rocky pulled his car alongside the curb and stopped. He felt slightly embarrassed and hoped no one he knew would see him. He lowered the car's window and tilted his face out toward the unmarked police car. As a detective approached the car, Rocky turned down the volume on the radio. Maybe his celebrity would be enough to keep a speeding ticket at bay. His celebrity and the offer of a cigar always had done the trick in the past. He certainly wasn't going to offer the cop a cash bribe, the way some guys did, folded alongside the license and registration. That might only make matters worse.

As Rocky started thinking of excuses for why he broke the speed limit and zoomed by red lights, the cop asked him if he was indeed Rocky Graziano. Rocky nodded his head yes several times, saying, "Yeah, sure I am." But neither his speeding nor his blasé attitude toward red lights were why he had been pulled over. Rocky diplomatically grinned and extended his right hand to shake the cop's hand. It was done politely but perfunctorily. The cop apologized for stopping Rocky and said he and his partner were fight fans, had seen a number of Rocky's fights, and thought he was one of the best of the middleweights. They, like many other cops, were regular readers of the city's daily newspapers, all of which had substantial sports pages where some of the era's best sportswriters practiced their craft. Regardless of which paper they read, they all knew about Rocky Graziano, for each of his fights was reported on in their pages. Some even ran front-page headlines about the fistic powers of the raucous former dead-end kid. The cop knew all about Rocky: his reform-school past, his time in prison, and his position as a formidable boxer. He was the kid who had no future but fought his way into the limelight with a powerful right fist that sent many opponents crashing to the canvas.

Rocky knew the cops no longer had it in for him. They liked him; so why were they stopping him, Rocky wanted to know? They told him it wasn't for traffic violations. This was something different, something a lot more important. The district attorney wanted to speak with him; it was an important matter, and they wanted him to come with them. He had been clean since his last scrapes with the law years prior. He had served his time, some of it in solitary confinement. He had no outstanding fines. He wasn't on parole. He was not a witness to a crime. Sure, he was no fan of cops, never had been, but he respected them and usually got along with them. He saw no point in antagonizing them.

Rocky was a new man. He was no longer the wild kid of the streets, fighting, stealing, and running from the law. He had turned over a new leaf (or turned the leaf), as he affirmed to his mother and grandmother when he started his boxing career. He had become a role model for poor kids, especially those in the old neighborhood; he was an example of how to avoid crime and become a celebrity athlete. Italian Americans honored Rocky, admired his courage in the ring, took vicarious pleasure in his bon vivant's sense of humor. Other than Frank Sinatra, Rocky Graziano may have been the most popular Italian American celebrity in the United States. His face appeared in newspapers and on the covers of magazines. He had been hired to promote such manly products as Gillette razors and Barbasol shaving cream. He was presented to the public as what was then known as a man's man (today, such an expression would have an entirely different meaning). So why the hell was he being called to the D.A.'s office? Why send detectives? Why not just call him on the phone and politely ask him to come in for a discussion? But a discussion about what?

The cops were vague, even obscure, in their responses. One of them finally said he didn't know the reason for Rocky being called in. They were just told to find Rocky Graziano and escort him to the D.A.'s office.

Then, shrugging his shoulders almost apologetically, the cop said they would follow Rocky back to his home on Ocean Parkway, where he could park his car, and they would then drive him to the D.A.'s office. To Rocky, the cop sounded as coldly official as an officer in the army; his tone of voice made Rocky feel uncomfortable. Rocky clenched and unclenched his right fist. Something was up, but he knew not what.

He didn't know how hard he was about to be hit. And he wouldn't be able to hit back. He was about to be smacked with an avalanche of humiliation; it would cover him in obloquy from coast to coast. It would be a nightmare from which he could not awake. Toss and turn, yell and moan, curse and pound the walls, there was nothing that would alleviate the pain he was about to suffer. There it would be for his fans, friends, and family to hear about and read. His humiliation and ignominy would be blared on radio stations and emblazoned on the front pages of newspapers.

A big, bold headline on the front page of the *New York Times* shouted, "Graziano Loses His License; Censured for Silence on 'Fix.'" The story was reported by James P. Dawson, whose lead paragraph spelled out the sleazy course of events that led to the revocation of Rocky's license to fight:

> Ruling that Rocky Graziano, East Side middleweight and the outstanding challenger for the championship in his class, was "guilty of an act detrimental to the interests of boxing" when he failed to report a $100,000 offer to fix two bouts, the State Athletic Commission yesterday revoked Graziano's license as a fighter effective immediately. [1]

For 18 hours, from Saturday night to Sunday morning, assistant district attorneys and detectives grilled Rocky. He had never before sat through such a long and intense grilling. In his earlier days as a criminal, he was asked a few perfunctory questions and smacked around, sometimes with a billy club or a blackjack, before being tossed, pushed, or shoved into a cell. Now, he felt he was being treated as if he had already been found guilty.

The D.A. implied he was willing to offer Rocky a plea bargain but only if he would come clean. When Rocky said he wanted to confer with his lawyer, the D.A. discouraged him from doing so, telling him it wasn't necessary, for Rocky was in no legal jeopardy. He was told it wouldn't help the mess he was in. They told him a lawyer didn't know the answers to their questions and thus could be of no help to Rocky. Their warnings were ambiguous, obtuse, and meant to confuse. They tried to rattle Rocky, scare him, let him know they held the fate of his career in the palms of their hands. One detective held up a page showing Rocky's boxing record. He held it front of Rocky's face for several minutes before tearing it in half, then in quarters, then in eighths, and letting the pieces float like dissolving snowflakes into a wastepaper basket. The message, the menace, the implied threats were clear. But their scare tactics failed. Rocky sneered at their attempts to coerce him. The old, recalcitrant Rocky evidenced a spine of steel: He would not bend for them.

Seeing that their tactics were only making Rocky angry and adamant that he would not cooperate, the D.A. and the detectives changed direction: Where accusations and threats had failed, they now employed flattery; they told him how much they admired his skill, his endurance, his heart as a fighter. He was such a phenomenon that he was sure to beat any opponent. He would do to the middleweight division what Joe Louis had done to the heavyweight division. They told Rocky he was a wonderful and inspiring role model for kids and young men. Did he want to spoil his reputation in their eyes? The D.A. and the detectives said they only had Rocky's best interests at heart; they were actually trying to protect him. The last thing they wanted to do was injure his career, hurt his reputation. They were his biggest fans. They had hoped to help his career by freeing him from any taint of having done something wrong.

Rocky bit his lip so as not to grin defiantly at their bullshit. To Rocky, the unctuous flattery being spouted was like the foul odor of a rotting corpse. When he pinched his nostrils together, no one said anything. Rock was smart to avoid snarling with anger or smirking sardonically. Better to be stone-faced. He saw his opponents as bullies, no different than the cops who had pushed him around when he was a teenager. In those days of his delinquent life, he had suffered real beatings at the hands of cops who knew how to do it without leaving any marks. He had been pummeled by fists to the back of his head; a rubber hose had been used on the backs of his legs; and a set of brass knuckles had been driven into his gut, forcing him to gasp for air. In those days, he would either lie motionless on a cement cell floor or spit at the cop beating him and let him know he wasn't hurt. He didn't give in to them then, and he wouldn't give in now. He didn't believe their threats or assurances. In the ring, he was capable of absorbing more punishment than any other fighter, and he would take whatever these guys were prepared to dish out. After all, Rocky was known for being able to take a beating and then come out of a crouch swinging like an angry wild man, sending an opponent to the darkened land of forgetfulness. He was not about to cave in front of a firing squad of accusations.

Rocky was proving too tough for the D.A. and the cops. They just couldn't get him to crack. They tried to chip away at his refusal to admit he had done anything wrong. The Rock was too hard for their puny chiseling tools. He refused to admit he had been offered a bribe. He hypothesized that if someone had offered him $100,000 to throw a fight, he wouldn't take it. The prosecutors quickly pounced, turning the hypothesis into a premise and then a confession that someone had, in fact, offered Rocky that sum of money to throw the fight with Cowboy Shank. Rocky told them they were crazy. Cowboy Shank? He was a pushover, hardly worth a fight. If he had taken a bribe and lost to the Cowboy, everyone would have known it was a fix. And Rocky wouldn't take a dive for anyone.

The D.A. informed Rocky that failure to report a bribe offer was cause for a boxer to lose his fighting license. Did Rocky want to sacrifice his career? Rocky reiterated that to lose to a nobody, to a bum, like the Cowboy, would be as ridiculous as the heavyweight champion taking a dive in a fight with Mickey Mouse. No one would believe it. It was absurd. It was the stuff of comedy, of daydreaming cartoons. Forget about it. He insisted there was no bribe; there had been nothing to report. The biggest bookies would never even try to set up such a fix, and boxing fans would see it coming from a mile away.

But even if Rocky had been offered $100,000 and turned it down, he would never have run to the D.A. with such news. It went against his code of honor. In Rocky's world, no one snitched, no one ratted, unless, of course, you were a punk.

Next, the prosecutors accused Rocky of faking a back injury, pretending he had injured himself so he would not have to disappoint his pals and the gamblers who planned on betting against him. It relieved him of being a participant in a no-win situation. The prosecutor said he understood that Rocky had no choice but to feign a back injury. His life would surely be in danger if he won such a bout and the gamblers were cleaned out. He would have wound up sprawled and bleeding, and breathing his last breaths in a dirty, dark alley. And if he had taken the money and then intentionally lost to the Cowboy, fight fans would lose all respect for him, to say nothing of the self-respect Rocky would forfeit. If he had done such a thing, his reputation as a boxer would be forever tarnished and perhaps shattered. Would he ever get another important fight if he had lost to the Cowboy? They said it was unlikely. So, either way, he had no choice. He had to fake an injury to extricate himself from being victimized by two conjoined disasters. They understood, and Rocky had no choice but to come clean. Nonsense, ejaculated Rocky. He had a genuine back injury. He pounded the desk in front of him. He leapt to his feet, overturning his chair. He called the D.A. a liar. He didn't have to stand for this shit. He had come on his own free will.

The prosecutors had devised a credible and clever scenario, but without Rocky's confirmation, there was no evidence to back it up. Having failed again and again to get Rocky to cooperate, the prosecutorial team tried to get Rocky to admit he had taken bribes in the past. Why he would confess to such an accusation, especially when he would not admit to being offered the alleged bribe for which he now stood accused, made no sense. Rocky denied the accusation. Sure, there were always guys hanging around boxers, whispering in their ears that they could earn big money for taking a dive. But most boxers just laughed it off. Maybe a few guys whose careers were going nowhere or some old palookas with no futures would succumb to the temptation of easy money, but a boxer, a contender, a rising ring star on his way to becoming a champion would never take the bribe. Certainly, no titleholder would jeopardize himself by taking a bribe to surrender the championship. He might never regain it. Why would he sacrifice it all for a bribe when there was a chance of earning millions? For Rocky, there would be plenty of money once he won the championship, and it would be clean money, nothing in an unmarked envelope slid under a table.

At one point, after hours and hours of needling Rocky with threatening questions interspersed with words of praise and admiration, Rocky stated, "Fighting done everything for me. I got a good life today on account of fighting. You cops know my old record. You know you ain't got nothing on me today, because I live a good, clean life. So don't go knocking the fight business."[2]

Although Rocky had been discouraged from calling his lawyer and was not represented by legal counsel, he had requested that his manager, Irving Cohen, be present, for Irving would confirm his claims. He was not only a character witness, but also an eyewitness. After all, Irving had been present at Stillman's Gym, in Rocky's dressing room, in Rocky's ring corner, in his hotel room. He had seen Rocky go bare ass in and out of the shower. Thus, Irving would surely know if Rocky had been offered a bribe or faked his back injury. Irving was like Rocky's shadow, always present, always aware of what was going on. Rocky was Irving's most important investment, and he wouldn't let himself or Rocky risk that investment to accommodate some mob guys who wanted to cash in on a fixed fight. Irving was as faithful and protective as a seeing-eye dog.

Unshaven and carelessly dressed, Irving arrived at the D.A.'s office in the middle of the night; he looked bedraggled, tired, and withdrawn, but he was eager to defend his friend, his client, his fighter—to protect their investment in the future. While Irving confirmed everything Rocky had told the prosecutors, his words didn't change the course of the questioning or move the situation toward a conclusion. The prosecutors regarded Irving's words as nothing but echoes of what Rocky had claimed. To them, Irving was nothing more than a good uncle covering up for his delinquent nephew.

At three o'clock in the morning, the prosecutors decided that the entry of a new actor into their little drama might change the final act. They called upon Colonel Eddie Eagan, head of the New York State Athletic Commission, to make a dramatic entrance. The prosecutors thought Eagan might inspire Rocky to give up the name of the man who had allegedly offered the bribe. Eagan not only had the power to revoke Rocky's license to fight, but also he had acted as Rocky's friend and confidante before this dark night of grilling had gotten underway.

Eagan, who had been an Olympic boxer, had often called Rocky into his office to give the young fighter lessons on the sweet science of pugilism. During such sessions, which Irving had urged Rocky to attend for the sake of good relations, Rocky would spend most of the time ducking and backing away from poorly aimed left hooks and slow-moving uppercuts. Rocky thought such sessions were ridiculous charades during which he would have to humor the self-important Eagan. Irving, however, was always worried Rocky would emerge from the encounters bruised and perhaps too injured to meet a genuine opponent in the ring. Had he witnessed those lessons in absurdity, he would have laughed rather than worried.

When the lessons concluded and Eagan was exhausted from throwing his out-of-shape punches, he would fling a tired, avuncular arm over Rocky's shoulder, tell him what a great athlete he was, and remind him not to tell anyone about his private lessons, for such information could lead to questions about favoritism. And it shouldn't be known that the Colonel had taught Rocky tricks unbeknownst to the world of boxing. Such tricks could give Rocky an unfair advantage when fighting an opponent. Rocky would nod obediently and have a solemn, appreciative look in his eyes as he bit his lower lip so as not to laugh or smirk. It was ridiculous, but it was important to have Eagan as a friend, to humor the self-important blowhard, who couldn't help veering toward unintentional buffoonery. You never knew when such friendship would come in handy. Rocky looked forward to the Colonel's participation in the the current drama.

The Colonel, however, was planning on playing a role that Rocky had not previously witnessed; he was no longer the meddling uncle and self-important coach. Eagan started off his part of the inquisition by letting Rocky know how much he admired and liked him, how he was just present to help Rocky reach the right decision and get on with his career. Self-importance was about to veer into self-righteousness. The vile odor of a rotting corpse returned. The Colonel said he knew Rocky wanted to make the right decision, and the Colonel would help him get to that point. Rocky wanted to spit. Instead, he simply refused to cooperate.

Eagan took a deep breath and seemed to puff up his chest, like a rooster about to strut. He held his head angrily erect, his expression a cross between disappointment and disbelief. He reminded Rocky of a reform-school warden, lecturing a rebellious delinquent. He solemnly told Rocky that his license could be revoked for not reporting a bribe. He would hate to do it. After all, Rocky was one of his favorite boxers. He had devoted a lot of time to advancing Rocky's career. But if he had to revoke the license then so be it, and Rocky would never fight in New York again. Rocky insisted that attempted bribes happened all the time and that if a fighter reported each one, he would spend more time in the commissioner's office than in a boxing ring. Most such offerings, Rocky declared, were made by screwballs, people who just wanted to get close to a fighter. No one paid much attention to those jock-sniffing wallflowers. The Colonel looked distressed, as if he had just caught his star pupil cheating on an exam. He turned away from Rocky and patted his right index finger on his lips.

Seeing that he was getting nowhere, that his presence hadn't brought about the desired result, the Colonel conferred with the assistant D.A.s in a corner of the room. It looked like a huddle of losing football coaches. Across the room, Rocky and Irving could hear the buzzing of whispers, like bees around a hive. The buzzing stopped after a few minutes, and Eagan emerged from the strategic huddle, scowling and shaking his head from side to side as if failing to convince a recalcitrant juvenile delinquent to go straight. He walked over to Rocky and placed a firm hand on his shoulder, which Rocky attempted to shake off. The Colonel, with sadness in his voice and a look of disappointment on his face, told Rocky he was free to leave. His words hung on Rocky like a noose.

The following week, newspapers throughout the country reported that Rocky Graziano's license to box in New York had been revoked. Colonel Eagan made the formal announcement: "Boxer's license No. 514, issued by the New York State Athletic Commission to Tommy Graziano, ring name Rocky Graziano, is hereby revoked."[3]

W. C. Heinz wrote, "The afternoon that Eagan announced that Rocky Graziano was banned, ostensibly for life, from boxing in New York State, I covered that. In that crowded hearing room, I watched the fighter, who had seemed to have finally found his way in this world, drop his head into his hands, his elbows on the table as he sat there across from Eagan, and I rushed back to the paper and wrote the piece that ran under the eight-column headline that bannered page one."[4]

It didn't matter that Rocky had testified in front of a grand jury that refused to indict him. It didn't matter that those jurors believed in Rocky's innocence. It didn't matter that there was no evidence—not even circumstantial evidence—of Rocky's guilt. None of it mattered. He had been condemned by Eagan and the media. Rocky felt as if he were the victim of vigilante justice.

To make matters worse, to inflict additional wounds, a former inmate of Rocky's from Leavenworth sold a story for $300 about Rocky slugging a corporal, knocking out a captain, and going AWOL. And for emphasis, it was noted that Rocky had done this, behaved like a common thug, a criminal, a draft dodger, during wartime, when other brave, patriotic men were dying to defend democracy. The verdict was that Rocky may be tough in the ring, but when it came to his country, he was no patriot. Maybe he was even a coward. Words of righteous indignation poured from the teletype machines of major newspapers and magazines, microphones of radio announcers, and soi-disant patriots, each ricocheting around a cavernous echo chamber, growing louder and more ferocious with each repetition. For Irving Cohen, it sounded like a bloodthirsty lynch mob, each person carrying a torch that lit up their faces of fury in the darkness of their anger.

For Rocky, his own fury was nearly apoplectic. Wrote Heinz,

> And then it all came out, all the expletives, all of the vulgarities. The close air in that car was filled with the obscene oaths and unprintable invectives. He was throwing them wildly, the way he threw punches in the ring, where he had found a way to fight back against all the hurts he had invited and that society had inflicted upon him. Now, cornered and wounded again, he was seeing society as his enemy again, personified by Eagan.[5]

While setting up Rocky as a man without character, a stooge, and a liar, there were some things that neither the D.A. nor the commissioner of the New York State Athletic Commission understood: The rules of honor on the Lower East Side had not originated in the state capital or with the city council. The rules were not promulgated by legislators wearing high, stiff collars and speaking in sanctimonious and self-righteous effusions. Rocky had imbibed the rules of the street well before he reached puberty. You remained true to your code and conscience, and did not rat on friend or foe. If you had a problem, you or you and your gang dealt with it. You never called in the cops. When sporting men, emissaries of gamblers, approached the Rock to pay him to take a dive, he laughed and showed them the door. If they kept coming around, he told them to pound sand. How could Rocky Graziano, the hero of the Lower East Side, an idol to teenage boys, take a dive and expect his friends and neighbors to remain in his corner? Look what happened when he unexpectedly lost to Tony Zale. People crossed the street to avoid him because they thought he took a dive. Friends from his boyhood wouldn't talk to him.

Rocky certainly would not take a dive for a pushover like Cowboy Shank, a man Rocky referred to as a bum. It was laughable. It was insulting. It was ridiculous. Sure, the gamblers would clean up if Rocky were to lose such a fight, for the Cowboy was more than a 30-to-1 underdog. Had Rocky taken a dive it would have been headfirst into a pool of incredibility. The laughter, the disappointment, the anger, and the criticism would have buried him in a tank of obloquy and humiliation. Had Rocky taken a dive, it would have been to boxing what the crash and immolation of the *Hindenburg* was to the rigid airship industry. Why not just take a razor to his wrists and watch the blood of life pour out?

Rocky was neither a rat nor a fool, neither a stooge nor a dummy. He had his eyes set on the prize, and that prize was the championship of the world. The transit of his career had gone from nightmares to dreams of glory. He would rocket into the stratosphere, where only champions dwelled. Below him would be a heap of knocked-out opponents, men like Billy Arnold and Marty Servo, whose boxing careers lay like abandoned car wrecks in Rocky's rearview mirror. Rocky was going right to the top. He would become the superstar of boxing. The KO king. The man who no one could hold back, not the D.A., not Colonel Eagan, no one. He believed his destiny was to be the middleweight champion of the world.

He was the former Thomas Rocco Barbella, juvenile delinquent, petty criminal, ex-convict, draft dodger, transmuted into Rocky Graziano, the best, most colorful middleweight the world had ever seen. He had broken the bonds that had once destined him for a life of crime, a life in prison, and perhaps even an ending in the electric chair. Some of his old cohorts had followed that path right to its desperate, miserable end. Rocky now played and fought by the rules of the straight world. He also had his own rules of honor and strictly adhered to those rules.

What did pompous, pusillanimous politicians, who called bribes "honest graft," know about the world of boxers? Had any of them put on boxing gloves, gotten into a ring, and fought against a fierce opponent? A man so desperate he wanted to rip your heart out? Did they know the courage it took to get into a ring and ask yourself if you might endure permanent brain damage? Had any of them stood up to gamblers displaying snubbed-nose .38s and thugs who menacingly flashed switchblades? Men who would break your bones if you didn't pay off a debt? Had any of them taken a beating from cops in the back of a precinct? Had any of them been thrown into solitary confinement and stomped on by soulless, sadistic prison guards? No. The politicians played the game of favors: You rub my back, and I'll rub yours. You scratch my back, I'll scratch yours. It was laughable. Rocky believed he had done nothing wrong. He had turned down the easy money, the hundred-dollar bills in number 10 envelopes, the bribes that could have ended his career, and he steadfastly went on pursuing his goals. Sure, he didn't rat on the gamblers. What good would that have done? It would have served to make Rocky look like a fink. It was not his way. His way was like the inspiring Frank Sinatra song of many years later: "I Did It My Way."

Rocky was like a man pushing against the powerful wind from a hurricane. It might attempt to stifle him, to force him backward, but Rocky could not, would not stop moving forward. He would do it his way.

7

THE BAD-BOY CHAMP

"**I** cannot box in my own town, New York City. I cannot box in the same city where I fought bootleg amateurs and nobody stopped me, where I fought while I was on parole and nobody stopped me, and where I fought while I was AWOL from the U.S. Army," wrote Rocky Graziano in his autobiography *Somebody Up There Likes Me*.[1]

Rocky was devastated. He felt as if he had taken an unfair brutal beating. No defense would have been adequate. He had been utterly helpless. He looked more defeated than he ever had in any encounter in the ring or while in jail or prison. They had attempted to emasculate him. A fighter without balls is no fighter. He felt that the tools of his trade, his very arms and fists, had been put in storage or pawned to satisfy some pretentious and pseudo-pious tribute to public virtue, a thoroughly dishonest tribute to self-righteousness and a smugly self-satisfied hypocrisy. What would he have to do to redeem himself? How was he to make a living, to support his family, to stay on the path of decency? He had worked so tenaciously to fight his way to the top of the mountain, and he was almost there. And now they wanted to push him off a cliff.

If you rob a man of his means to make a living, you turn him into either a bum or a criminal. Rocky was neither. He would never return to his old hoodlum days, and he was too restless to be put on a shelf and left to rust. He was a climber, a man of burning ambition, and, most importantly, he was consumed with becoming a championship boxer: It defined him, made his life worthy of respect. He could look at himself in a mirror and be proud of what he saw. But, without the right to box, Rocky looked into his future and could see only a dark abyss. He had a dream about being thousands of feet up in the air and diving into a bottomless swimming pool or off the precipice of a cliff. The dive was cold and endless: a drop into the darkness of infinity. He was more alone than he had been when fighting an opponent in the ring. At least in the ring he had a good chance of beating his opponents. Now, he felt, the fix was in, and he was the loser.

That Rocky had risen to such heights and savored the respect and admiration of hundreds of thousands of people, and then had it all snatched away because he had refused to snitch on a lowlife who had attempted to commit a crime but didn't carry it out, seemed—at worst—a minor infraction. Maybe, just maybe, at the very most, he deserved a slap on the wrist, a warning, a call for a public admission that he had made a mistake and regretted it. But to take away a man's livelihood for not accepting a bribe, for staying on the path of legality, struck Rocky as a decision issued by a world turned upside-down. His ensuing anger was like magma erupting from a volcano, burning hot and unstoppable.

And then there was that phony friend, Colonel Eddie Eagan. Damn him. Rocky would have liked to give him a nose-breaking, jaw-shattering thrashing. Eagan had always pretended to be Rocky's good pal, his "how-you-doin' buddy," followed by a couple of pats on the back and a big smile. He had said to Rocky, over and over again, that Rocky was his favorite. Of all the boxers Eagan knew, Rocky was his particular favorite, his absolute favorite, and no one else even came close. His hypocrisy, his oily pretense to friendship, his back-slapping good cheer, his unctuous greetings—it was all an act, all for naught. He wouldn't lift a finger to help. He was a typical political appointee, an opportunist with an eye out for the main chance, who knew only one loyalty: to himself.

"It was Mr. Eagan who hurt me most of all," Rocky wrote. "I had thought the Colonel was my friend. He had told me I was his favorite fighter. He had told me I woke up single-handed the middleweight division. I never thought that he would use me to play politics with."[2]

There were 12 daily newspapers in New York during the late 1940s, and their sportswriters supported Rocky. He was the best thing that had happened to boxing in years. Crowds flocked to watch him, cheer him on, and celebrate his victories. Bill Corum, Red Smith, and W. C. Heinz were three of the most prominent and prolific sports reporters who wrote article after article in support of Rocky. Taking away his license to box was outrageous. It was mean-spirited. It was wholly without cause. Would a high school principal expel a student for not reporting that another student had asked him to help him cheat on a test? Would an accountant be indicted and have his license to practice his profession revoked because a client had asked him how to cheat on his income taxes and the accountant then refused to help and also did not report the aspiring cheat to the IRS? Would a doctor have his license to practice medicine revoked because he had refused to sign a phony medical report that claimed that his patient had an injury for which the patient sought compensation from an insurance company and the doctor didn't report the attempted fraud? The comparisons went on and on, and each drove home the point that Rocky was being singled out, being made an example of for something that was commonplace.

The forces judging Rocky acted as if the fighter had been a common hoodlum, a punk, a wiseguy. Taking bribes or not reporting attempted bribes would be typical of such a lowlife character, they said. What should the public expect from a guy who spent time in prison, whose closest friends were criminals? But Rocky was not intimidated by such accusations; he stayed true to his own code of honor. He was not a snitch, a fink, a rat. He simply refused to take a bribe to lose a fight and then forgot about it. Why report a crime that did not take place? It was absurd to report such a nonevent. Attempts at bribery happened all the time. The very nature of boxing invited such endeavors. It was easy compared to other sports: In baseball or football, one had to bribe an entire team, or at least the key players. The same was true in basketball and hockey. But in boxing, one only had to bribe one boxer to take a dive.

Offers of money swirled around the heads of boxers like mosquitoes on a hot, humid summer night. After a while, one just swatted them away or told them to take a hike. Most boxers, unless they were on the way down, didn't take the money: It was not only too risky, but also could prove to be an irreversible detour away from a possible championship bout. Yet, there were always bookies and promoters who were out to manipulate the odds. It was part of ring culture.

Fans couldn't believe that the New York State Athletic Commission would revoke Rocky's license because of a crime in which he didn't participate. Rocky received thousands of letters of support; he received messages from cops, firefighters, construction workers, members of the fraternity of boxers, corporate executives, ex-convicts, and even a handful of convicts and mobsters. Colonel Eagan may have thought he was being the good guy, portraying himself as someone who rode into a lawless town and would throw the bad guys in prison, the guy in the white hat who wouldn't let personal feelings get in the way of doing the right thing. Instead, he became one of the most disliked men in New York at the time, but that didn't stop him from basking in the light of his own self-righteousness. He thought that if he came out onto a public stage and stood under a self-shining spotlight he would be cheered by an audience of politicos and editorialists. He would have been surprised had he appeared in front of a crowd of boxing fans at Madison Square Garden, for there he would have been vilified and forced to take cover from torpedoes of tomatoes and the farting roar of Bronx raspberries.

In Rocky's world, however, the spotlight that had once shined on his career had been turned off. Eagan, in fact, had taken pride in switching it off. He let darkness engulf Rocky, and the darkness that engulfed him was bitter, cold, and humiliating. While Rocky slunk through his days, not knowing if there was a tunnel or bridge out of his daily grimness, Irving Cohen, ever loyal to Rocky, was looking for a means of escape and renewal. While sitting despondent, morose, quiet, and almost catatonic in his living room, Rocky received a phone call that brought renewed light into his world. It was Irving, letting Rocky know he had signed Rocky for a rematch with Tony Zale for July 16, 1947, in Chicago, at Chicago Stadium. Rocky leapt out of his chair with a whoop of exultation. He was jubilant. He shed his despair and desolation as if throwing off a ragged outfit of dirty, malodorous rags. His old energy returned, as he had been given a sudden shot of adrenalin.

To get in shape for his rematch with Tony Zale, Rocky had a pair of tune-up fights, both of which he won easily. One of the fights was with Eddie Finazzo in Memphis, Tennessee. Finazzo was so much a fan of Rocky's that he had asked for Rocky's autograph before the fight. Rocky was nearly dumbstruck. That had never happened to him. No opponent had ever been a fan. How could you punch such a guy into oblivion, a guy who had just requested your autograph? In fact, Rocky was so touched he decided not to draw out the fight. Why spend round after round beating up a sweet kid, especially one who was serving as your punching bag? Rocky, with the nimbleness of a skilled executioner, knocked out Finazzo in the first round, saving him from a savage beating. There wouldn't be a mark on the kid, not a bruise, not a cut. In fact, Finazzo wore his defeat by the fists of the great Rocky Graziano as a badge of courage, a source of countless stories. He could dine out on it for years. He would always be grateful to Rocky, always be one of his fans. For Finazzo, defeat had been a kind of triumph.

After that fight, Rocky quickly disposed of Jerry Fiorello. It was an easy bout for Rocky, who claimed he hardly worked up a sweat.

Rocky now felt primed and ready to face Tony Zale. He would prove to the world (and himself) that he could be the world champion, that he— in fact—deserved to wear the crown of middleweight champion, for he would do everything in his power to win it; he would use every trick, every weapon in his pugilist's arsenal, and once he had achieved that victory, the petty, pusillanimous powers that controlled his license would have to restore it in the city that was his, the city that had bred him and taught him to be the toughest kid on the block and led him into Stillman's Gym, where he became the brazen slugger who typified the gritty lower-class struggle to make something of himself. He would not be a failure; he would not follow in his father's failed attempts to be someone.

Once the crown of a champion was placed on his head, those who had taken away his license would have to restore it. How could they not? The fans would demand it. The editorial pages of the newspapers would demand it. Sportswriters would clamor for it. They could not possibly continue to deny a license to box to the world champion. After all, they were politicians, and politicians always held up a wet index finger in the wind and ultimately went with the flow of public opinion. Rocky's defiant reaction was to hold up his middle finger. The winds of change would soon be blowing his way. If the politicos resisted, they would be pissing into the wind. Rocky was going to teach them that they had been wrong, that they had been petty and foolish. Vengeance would be his. Eagan would have to swallow his pride and pretend it was not rotten beef.

In fact, Irving told Rocky Eagan would—no doubt—be the target of snide laughter and satirical jibes if he failed to restore the license of the man who had just ascended to the middleweight throne. Eagan and his compatriots would have no choice. Irving, igniting a fire of anger and motivation in Rocky, agreed with him that his entire career would be determined by the outcome of his fight with Zale. He must win it. If he didn't win, he might as well kiss his career a short, sad good-bye. Bury it. There was no alternative.

As driven as Rocky was to win the bout, he still felt he was pulling a heavy load of mistakes and bad memories behind him. Society would not let him forget. Powerful moralists never stopped to remind the public of the bad Rocky, the kid who had spent time in jails and prisons, who belted an army officer, who went AWOL. He was just no good and shouldn't be allowed to represent the world of boxing as a champion. From such an onslaught, Rocky sometimes felt whipped, like a dray horse who was expected to spend the rest of his days pulling his guilt like cement blocks behind him, trudging through the mud of accusations. It would always be there. He would never be free of the past. The accusations could be briefly washed away, but then they would be there for him to trudge through again and again. He could look back in anger and see that he had been called a coward for avoiding military service during the war; he had been accused of faking a back injury to avoid a fight; and he had been beating Tony Zale round after round in their first encounter and lost the fight.

Amazing. No one could believe it. When you looked at their faces, Rocky looked like the winner and Zale the loser. His old pals thought Rocky had taken a dive. Even the New York State Athletic Commission wondered if he had. The bookies thought they had been screwed out of a certain win. Around every street corner Rocky turned, he thought others were whispering their condemnations of him, disparaging him, and questioning his courage, loyalty, and ethics. Failing to be a stand-up guy was a curse in Rocky's neighborhood. It was the equivalent of being a traitor. He felt haunted, defamed, slandered. He imagined the boos and catcalls he would elicit when he fought Zale in Chicago, for he was no upstanding, churchgoing altar boy with Midwestern values. He was the Wop, the Guinea, the guy with olive-oil hair, the Noo Yawk greaseball from the Lower East Side. He was the thug, the former gangster wannabe. Rocky had come out of the darkness, while Zale emerged clean, angular, and strong out of the sunlight.

Zale was the Midwestern golden boy: honest, upright, modest, virtuous. Rocky was a rogue from the garbage-strewn streets and tenements of New York. One only had to gaze upon Zale to see a clean-cut all-American. Rocky knew and understood the different images they projected. He figured the Midwesterners would be cheering for one of their own. Rocky's only fans would be those in his corner. He would have to close his ears to the boos and catcalls, and focus on shooting down Tony

Zale and sending him crashing onto the canvas like a fighter pilot in an aerial dual. He knew it would be the hardest ring fight of his career. He had enlisted for it, trained for it, and the fight was now his to win or lose, but win he must.

When Rocky landed in Chicago, a cacophony of loud, contradictory thoughts wildly bounced around in his cranium; he felt startled and confused. His skin itched. He felt as restless as a hunted alley cat. He wanted to escape to his home turf. And so like an animal sensing imminent danger, he sought a means of escape: He went back to his own turf, to New York, back to the streets he knew so well. He hailed a taxi and told the driver, as if in an old detective movie, to get him back to the airport—fast. Once on a plane, an old twin-engine DC-3 prop plane, its engines sputtering smoke and roaring in the dank darkness, Rocky settled into his seat and told the stewardess he'd like a Scotch on the rocks. In his cocoon of safety, Rocky was flown from anxiety to safety, from Chicago to New York. He disembarked and sniffed the familiar air. He was back in his city. He could see the Empire State Building and felt a sense of relief.

Once a taxi had deposited him in his old neighborhood, he wandered the late-night streets. Each site, each building, each storefront was like a piece of a puzzle. He had to assemble it all in his head, get a picture of who he was, where he had come from, where he intended to go. It was a night of quick self-analysis: a series of images that told him who and what he was and who he wanted to be. He told no one of his presence. He didn't phone his wife or his mother. He just kept walking. He walked down to the East River, where there were no lights and the river looked as black as tar. He heard the mournful fog horn of a freighter or a tugboat. In the distance, he could see the boat's blinking red light, but he couldn't make out its ghostly shape. He looked up at the stars and felt small and insignificant. That's not what he wanted; he had fought all those fights to escape the imagined curses that came with the barrage of accusations, to beat the pain out of his life, prove himself worthy, and not be his father—and certainly not be small and insignificant. He would show them all. He would get back on a plane and fight Zale. Not just fight him—slaughter him. It would be a massacre. He had no choice. Kill or be killed. He had to prove to himself and the world that he was not a coward, a liar, a fink. He would prove he was a stand-up guy, both literally and figuratively. He would show the world a kind of courage they had never seen before. He would live up to his name: He would be as hard and indestructible as a rock.

About the match, Rocky wrote, "This was no boxing match. It was a war, and if there wasn't a referee, one of the two of us would have wound up dead."[3]

He would not run away. He would fight through a trial by blood, bruises, and serious injuries. He might suffer a broken nose or jaw, or worse, but he would prevail. He would not lie down. He had trained harder for his rematch with Zale than for any previous fight. The training would not go to waste. It had been intense and deliberate. Because Zale had gone after Rocky's midsection in their first fight, Rocky had to undergo stomach-strengthening exercises: Day after day, a hundred times a day, Whitey Bimstein threw a 100-pound medicine ball at his fighter's stomach. Rocky ran five miles a day, sometimes twice a day. He lifted weights. He hit the speed bag and the heavy bag. He jumped and skipped rope. He shadowboxed. He fought faux Tony Zale sparring partners. He was a tightly wound spring, ready to spring catlike at his opponent. He came out of those training sessions in the best shape of his life. Whitey thought Rocky was rock hard. Rocky let it be known he was ready to kill Zale or die trying.

The day of the match arrived, and the sports pages turned up the heat and cooked up as much palpable excitement as possible. It was like a witches' brew, and its aroma was in the air and people could breathe in the excitement. Newsstand dealers shouted out the coverage, the odds, the favorites, and the stats, and customers were told, "Read all about it!" Even the mayor said he wouldn't miss the fight for a million dollars, which caused a number of cynics to ask how much the mayor would accept to miss the fight. A lot less than one million dollars, they said. Some even said the mayor had Al Capone's onetime second in command, Jake "Greasy Thumb" Guzik, on his payroll.

More than 20,000 fans, including Frank Sinatra and J. Edgar Hoover, arrived at Chicago Stadium, as if it were the reincarnation of the Roman Coliseum, where they could savor the fiercest gladiatorial combat of the decade. In fact, the fight was billed as the most exciting middleweight rematch in boxing history. When the fighters emerged from their dressing rooms and headed to the ring, the fans lustily cheered, loudly whistled, hooted, and shouted the name of their favorite boxer. Some opposing fans got into shoving matches and had to be threatened with expulsion by the police before they refocused their misplaced aggression on the main event.

The bell for round one clanged, and the fighters rushed from their corners, not waiting to feel one another out. They immediately started slugging one another. Rights and lefts were flying, faces were quickly bruised and reddened. In the first round, Zale landed a powerful right to Rocky's left eye. The lid closed like a coffin, and blood from a cut above that eye veiled half of Rocky's face. Rocky was now a one-eyed fighter. The bell sounded, ending the round, and Rocky made it back to his corner. Whitey rapidly repaired the cut and stanched the bleeding. It didn't matter, for in the second round, Zale went after Rocky's eye again. Punch after well-aimed punch opened the cut, and blood flowed more profusely than it had in the earlier round.

After Whitey closed the cut for a second time, Zale pounded away at his foe's midsection, hoping to drive the air out of his lungs, as he had done in their first fight. But Rocky's washboard abs and well-muscled pectorals were an effective shield against the onslaught. That wasn't enough, however. Rocky's offense wasn't working. Fighting with one eye closed, his perception was askew; he was fighting from an angle, so Zale dodged punch after punch by rapidly bobbing his head. Nothing was landing. Rocky's fists chased a ghostlike Zale, but not one of his punches landed on his elusive target.

Seeing that Rocky was in trouble, Zale changed tactics and went for a quick knockout. He connected with Rocky's chin, sending him sprawling onto the canvas. Rocky sat there for a moment, a look of disbelief and anger on his face. Then, consumed by rage, not wanting to lose and feeling the heat of blood on his face, Rocky leapt off the canvas and charged at Zale. He was swinging like a madman. But, again, none of his punches landed. Zale, by more deft means, was throwing well-aimed punches, finding vulnerable targets time and again. And so it went for rounds two and three. Rocky, his face a mask of blood, was finally saved by the bell, and he staggered back to his corner.

He was exhausted, and fans thought the fight was just about over. Whitey again worked on closing the cut above the left eye. The right eye was also in bad shape; the skin around it was purple and swollen to the size of an egg. The referee, Johnny Behr, came to Rocky's corner and said he wanted to stop the massacre. He didn't think Rocky should go on taking such a beating. His face looked like raw, bloody hamburger.

Whitey urged the referee to let Rocky have one more round to try and save himself. If he was going to lose, let him lose in the ring, not sitting on a stool.

In the fourth round, Rocky found new strength and energy to pursue Zale as if he intended to kill him. He delivered shot after shot to Zale's head. Rocky had to stand sideways since he could not see out of one eye. But his punches were finally connecting, and Zale's arms were tired. Zale was now the one who was missing shots; he threw a wild, desperate punch, throwing himself off balance. The force of the missed blow caused Zale to crash onto the canvas, landing on his face. The round ended, and the fans were primed for something dramatic to happen.

The fifth round looked as if it could be the final, decisive round. Before the round could begin, Rocky had to be able to see out of his right eye, which was swollen shut. He couldn't win the fight while seeing out of only one eye. What to do? W. C. Heinz wrote, "Frank Percoco [one of Rocky's cornermen] took a quarter—two bits—and pressing it between his fingers, he broke the skin of the swelling under the right eye. When the blood came out, the swelling came down enough for the fighter to see."[4]

The fifth round was not the decisive one fans had expected; it produced more of the same action: Rocky going after Zale, Zale counterpunching. Maybe the sixth round would be the one. In that round, Zale seemed exhausted. His arms were not as tense and did not shoot the same kinds of rapid punches that had been in his arsenal during the earlier rounds. Rocky grabbed Zale's neck with his left glove and punched his head with his right fist. Zale fell against the ropes, and Rocky kept punching his head. That bloody, bruised head looked like an inanimate, disengaged speed bag that was turning a brighter shade of red with each punch. Rocky's fists were being driven by pure fury; it was as if a switch had been flipped inside of him and an electrical current of anger could not be turned off. Punch after punch rained down on the seemingly helpless Zale.

The referee grabbed Rocky and pulled him away from the sinking hulk of Zale's body. Not realizing he had won the bout, Rocky attempted to charge at Zale. His fury would not die. The referee kept telling Rocky he had won. The words didn't seem to register. Rocky was so electrified with anger he acted as if he wanted to kill his opponent. The referee held Rocky in place, and it took a few minutes for the Rock to realize the fight was finally over. He had won but at the cost of considerable damage to his face. He was such a bloody mess that anyone who had not been watching the fight would have thought he was the victim, the poor, bloodied loser. He looked as if he should have been taken to the nearest hospital. The referee kept telling Rocky he had won. It was those words repeated over and over that finally doused the flames of Rocky's anger. When Behr announced to the crowd that Rocky was the new world champion, Rocky grabbed the microphone and shouted, "Ma, Ma, your bad boy done it, he's world champion."[5]

The fight had been a mirror image of the first one. At the end of that contest, Zale looked like the beaten, bloody loser, and Rocky was relatively unmarked. At the end of the rematch, Zale, although bruised and bloody, was not the garish mess that was Rocky: Rocky's eyes were so badly damaged that the cut below one required stitches, and the other had to be bandaged. When he got back to his hotel room, Norma kissed his bruised and battered face, and cried about the damage.

When they had met and married, Rocky was handsome, his face relatively unmarked by his profession. In the years since then, however, boxing had taken its toll, as it does for all fighters. It didn't matter to Norma. She loved her Rocky, and the two hugged one another. Rocky was with her; he was away from the ring, and she felt safe in his embrace. Rocky went into their bedroom, for he had promised little Audrey a goodnight kiss. At the sound of Rocky's voice, Audrey awakened, took one startled look at her daddy, and asked what had happened to him. She stared at the eye with the closed, bruised lid. He told her that is what happens when you play in the gutter and that she should remember never to play there. The gutter was no place for sweet little girls.

According to Rocky's autobiography, after Norma and Audrey had fallen asleep, Rocky—sweating from the oppressive heat in the hotel and bone tired from his fight—went to open a window. He needed to suck in a large amount of fresh air; his lungs hungered for it. The window seemed jammed shut; it wouldn't open. Rocky hammered at the window frame with the fleshy parts of the palms of both hands. He had to gulp in some fresh air. The window wouldn't open, so he pushed at its frame with all his strength. The window was like an opponent, and Rocky thrust himself into defeating its resistance. He cursed the window and used the power of his biceps and shoulder muscles to give one forceful thrust. The window shot open, and Rocky suddenly lost his balance. He started to tumble forward, headed for a 12-story nosedive toward the street below. As he was about to plunge into the night, Frankie Coco entered the room, saw his buddy about to take the worst dive of his life, and made his own flying leap. Before Rocky could tumble out of the window, Frankie grabbed his legs, as if tackling him. He caught him just in time. With hearts racing and adrenaline shooting through their veins and arteries, the two men fell back onto the floor. Breathing rapidly, they were too stunned to speak. After a few minutes, Frankie picked himself up, went into the living room, and got drunk. Rocky, exhausted from his fight with Tony Zale and stunned by his near embrace of death, fell into a deep sleep and did not awaken for 20 hours.

The following day, a refreshed Rocky, a proud Norma, and an excited Audrey boarded a Chicago train for Grand Central Terminal. On 42nd Street, just outside of the terminal, there was a procession of Cadillac convertibles, each occupied by a notable local politician, many of whom were of Italian descent. Rocky was invited into the lead limo. He climbed aboard, planting his feet on the rear seat and his ass on the car's trunk, the way many campaigning politicians do. It was a perfect perch from which to wave to his fans. He was joined on his throne by Norma. The cars tooted their horns as they proceeded downtown, and Rocky and Norma waved to passersby. The procession was accompanied by a police motor-cycle escort, sirens blaring, lights flashing. It was just short of being a ticker-tape parade, the kind of event reserved for winning generals, World Series champs, and, at a later date, astronauts.

The procession finally came to a crawl in Rocky's old neighborhood, the Lower East Side. Once on 10th Street, Rocky was greeted by a surging sea of cheering fans. Their rising, rushing tide pushed up against the car. They had been his neighbors. They were the populace of his small ethnic village, the village that could not contain him. He was now the conqueror returning home from battle, scarred and bruised but obviously a winner, the champ. He raised his arms, hand clutching hand, and pumped the air over his beaming countenance. His face hurt, and one eye was still shuttered, the other bruised blue and purple, but the pleasure he got from the crowd far outweighed the pain from his championship bout.

A new crowd of cheering boys now poured like a wave toward the limo; they just wanted to touch him, to feel the muscles in his arms, to touch the fists that had brought him the middleweight crown. In addition to the boys, there appeared men both young and old—shopkeepers, clerks, pool sharks, peddlers—all shouting their approval, applauding their hero. He had brought pride to them, their neighborhood, their tribe. He was one of them: a poor Italian kid who had done better than good. He was spectacular. He was a star. No one would dare call him a no-good guinea thug again, certainly not to his face. He was an Italian champion every Italian male could look up to, admire, and say, "He's one of us."

And because he was a family man, devoted to his wife, his daughter, and mother, the women of the community held him in high regard. He was an example for their husbands. It didn't matter that Norma was Jewish or that little Audrey might be raised as a Jew. Technically, they were not members of their tribe. But Rocky loved his wife and daughter, and they loved him. They were a great family: happy, healthy, and obviously delighted to be in one another's company. That homecoming was an event all three of them would remember and cherish.

Now that he was a champ, Rocky thought the world was his oyster, its pearl his alone. He thought his problems with the New York State Athletic Commission would be put aside. You could hardly deny a champion the license to box, to defend his title. But that's exactly what happened. The Illinois Boxing Commission banned him from boxing, and the National Boxing Association declared that a boxer who had gone AWOL and served time in prison for striking an officer and was given a dishonorable discharge should not be permitted to fight. In addition, the commissioners claimed that Rocky "ran out" of a fight with Ted Apostoli. Altogether, Rocky would be a bad example for boys throughout the country. Men with military sensibilities who are not reluctant to dispose of young boys as cannon fodder could not tolerate anyone who had escaped their net and run out of basic training. For them, avoiding military service seemed one notch below treason. (Years later, the same breed tried to prevent Muhammad Ali from pursuing a successful boxing career because he had refused to be drafted into the army.)

Rocky could not believe such a decision had been reached, one that was intended to prevent him from fighting anywhere in the nation. He felt that those making the decision were nothing but self-righteous sons of bitches. He had paid his dues. He had served time at Leavenworth for his crimes against the military. How long would he be pursued?

Although Rocky felt defenseless, there was one man who always stood by him. And while he was not a boxer, he fought with his brain to protect Rocky. He was Rocky's devoted manager, Irving Cohen. He managed, and not for the first time, to pull a rabbit out of the boxing bureau-crats' hat. He got the National Boxing Association to agree to let Rocky fight Sonny Horne for charity in the Uline Arena in Washington, DC. Rocky would get a single dollar for the fight; the rest of the gate would go to charity. It would be the ideal public relations performance to let the world know Rocky was a good guy, and it would provide the association with the cover it needed to reinstate Rock's right to earn a living as a boxer. After such a bout, the national ban against Rocky would be lifted.

Before the referee could make his initial ring announcements, Sonny Horne had almost diffidently approached Rocky. With trepidation in his voice, Sonny asked if Rocky would please not knock him out. Rocky liked Sonny, thought he was a good guy, not some mean-spirited, thumb-in-the-eye, knee-to-the-groin fighter, and so he agreed. He had smiled at Sonny, nodded his head in agreement, and patted Sonny on the shoulder. During the bout, Rocky threw no wild punches. He did not lunge at Sonny or grab Sonny's head with his left glove and batter him with the right. Instead, Rocky boxed like a classical pugilist, jabbing with his left fist and aiming right crosses that would do no damage. Of course, he made sure he would win on points, but he never indulged in a savage attack, never attempted to inflict serious injury. After Rocky had won the bout, he bounded over to Sonny and gave him a hug and kiss. Sonny was relieved and grateful. On the train back to New York, trainer Whitey Bimstein told Rocky his fight with Sonny was his cleanest win. Rocky felt he was back on the professional road. He might not be able to box in New York and Illinois, but the ban on fighting in the rest of the country had dissolved like a bad dream.

No more roadblocks, no more dead ends, just a slight detour to New Jersey: Rocky signed for a third fight with Tony Zale, which would take place at Ruppert Stadium in Newark. For fans, this would be pure gladia-torial combat; it would be blood and gore. It was promoted as a grudge match between two of the toughest middleweights in the history of pugi-lism. Bets of $1, $2, $3, $5, and $10 were placed with bookies throughout the land. For the wealthy sports, bookies would commonly receive bets in the hundreds and thousands of dollars. Ticket scalpers made out like bandits, and Rocky was promised the sum of $120,000. Sports editors reported the large sum as if it were a king's ransom. For middle-class fight fans, such a great sum of money in the spring of 1948 was impres-sive; an annual salary of $7,500 was considered more than sufficient for a family of four in those days. Promoters predicted that because the fight would draw so many fans from New York and New Jersey, Ruppert Stadium would leave many spectators stranded outside or standing in the aisles. Better buy your tickets now, they said. And the scalpers acted as if they were selling food to starving men.

Tony Zale couldn't wait to take back the crown from Rocky. Once again, he hoped to wear the belt awarded to the champion, a belt of such gilt and shiny, ostentatious brass it would be a target for thieves and sports memorabilia collectors. It was a belt with a large gold-colored oval at its center, topped by a golden eagle. Below each of the eagle's wings was a miniature American flag. Two small, golden ovals, each containing a bas-relief image of a pair of boxing gloves, stood like sentries at the ends of the belt and were joined together by a red, white, and blue ribbon and a pair of intertwined gold-colored chains. It would be many years later, in 2015, long after Zale had donated his belts to the Boxing Hall of Fame, that they were stolen, never to be recovered. Rocky's belt would become a point of contention in a family dispute reported in tabloid newspapers. But all of that was far off in the future.

In 1948, hundreds of thousands of boxing fans eagerly waited to see who would emerge from the collision course charted by Rocky Graziano and Tony Zale. The two men were like a pair of speeding drag racers shooting down the same highway but coming from opposite directions, each one aimed head-on at the other.

8

THE END OF THE TRILOGY

Something left Rocky after his second fight with Tony Zale. He had reached a goal, redeemed himself, and proven to the world that he was a true champ. The hunger had been satisfied. The fire that had driven him had not cooled, but it burned with a lower flame. He now lived a life of comfort and experienced a kind of contentment he had never previously known. Rocky took enormous pride in being a suburban homeowner. The home occupied by the Graziano family on Ocean Parkway in Brooklyn was something Rocky could not have dreamt of when he was scrounging the streets of the Lower East Side. Stealing fruit and vegetables from peddlers seemed like ancient history. He had been a combination of the Artful Dodger and Billy the Kid, and then he had transformed himself into a happy member of the mid-century middle class in the United States.

He was a suburban squire, seen in the local supermarket, hardware store, barbershop, and liquor store; he could be seen playing with his young daughter, walking his pony-size Great Dane, and driving his powder-blue Caddy along Ocean Parkway. Rather than a scowl on his face and a hard look in his eyes, he had an inviting and ready smile for neighbors and fans. Local merchants didn't have to worry that Rocky would run off with their merchandise. He was a man of substance. He finally had enough money in the bank to feel secure. In his pocket was a thick roll of bills; he would wrap his powerful right fist around the roll, and it felt like a life raft. He could gaze at his stately house and know he would never face foreclosure. His shiny Caddy convertible told the world he had made it; he had achieved success. And best of all he had a beautiful family.

The need to kill an opponent in the ring was gone. A priest who might have known the young delinquent and then met the middleweight champion of the world would see a man who was a symbol of redemption. The reformed Rocky would have been an unbelievable stranger to the delinquent boy. The boy may be father to the man, but this man outgrew the boy he was.

Along with his attitude about himself, Rocky's daily routine had changed too: He no longer had to limit himself to the high-protein diet prescribed by Irving Cohen and Whitey Bimstein. He could go out with his pals to nightclubs and drink until his bonhomie and laughter lit up his face. Joshing, breaking balls, telling jokes, and bullshitting were part of his good-time repertoire. On other nights, he would go out to dinner with Norma and eat a four-course meal: pasta, calamari, clams on the half shell, veal, sausage, chicken, and broccoli rabe. They would start out with a cocktail and toast one another (Rocky the romantic remained in love with Norma until his dying day), and have a bottle of wine with dinner.

The suburban homeowner would sleep late and not have to awaken to the prospect of 10 miles of road work. He was a man of leisure, easygoing, affable, and pleased with himself and his family. He would relax in a Barcalounger and light up a cigar or cigarette and enjoy a cold beer. Everything he had earned, everything he had accomplished was better. In fact, it was more than a dream come true; in the bleak, cold, oppressive days of his hard-bitten youth, he could never permit himself to indulge in dreams of the kind of success he now enjoyed. At best, he could have hoped to become a big-shot rackets guy, wearing a $200 custom-made suit and avoiding a long prison sentence, which some members of his old gang were enduring.

Rocky had taken a different voyage, following the directions on a map drawn by Irving Cohen, which brought him to a destination unknown to old friends, relatives, and guys from the pool hall and the old neighborhood. The tough, young punk from Alphabet City was but a distant memory for Rocky; he was a boy he had left in the past. There were other boys like Rocky, but few of them were able to travel the same road Rocky had. There are perhaps only a handful of boys who could have survived such a journey, never mind ascend to the top of the heap.

The one thing that still bothered Rocky was that his New York boxing license had not been restored. If he could only get his license renewed, he would feel like king of the world. With all of his success and comforts, Rocky still felt like he could only wear his crown in lands not his own.

Yes, he was still a boxer, a titleholder, albeit one getting a little rusty, a little too heavy in the midsection. He would still go to Stillman's Gym, but only to watch the young and upcoming boxers. He would kibitz with the trainers and managers, smoke cigarettes, and regale his coterie with tales of the ring. He was happy but restless. He knew he needed to get into a boxing ring, not so much for the money—he had plenty—but like most boys who grew up in dire poverty, Rocky always had a desire to earn more. Yet, unlike many of those who became wealthy, Rocky was never tightfisted with money. He spent it freely, loaned it to friends, and simply gave to those in need. As one of his pals commented, Rocky didn't have fish hooks in his pockets.

His trade was boxing, and he needed to box to ensure that his success was not fleeting, that it was no mirage. It was a hard climb up the brutal ladder of boxing, from club fighter to champion. And Rocky wanted to remain champion of the world. He could not stay atop his perch without eventually having to defend his title. He knew he would have to get back in the ring. He also knew he would have to give Zale another shot at regaining the title. Such a bout, win or lose, would be a financial windfall for Rocky.

Yet, the state of New York wouldn't let Rocky engage in another match. He, the middleweight champion of the world, a beloved character, a boxer who could pack any arena or stadium in the country, was not permitted to box in his hometown. He was not a layabout, a do-nothing. He wanted the action, wanted to experience the surge of adrenaline that fueled his fights. He wanted to trade punches and know he was the best there was and maybe the best ever. Boxing defined him. He would have danced a naked jig on Broadway with a flower pot on his head and a long-stemmed rose clenched between his teeth if it would have resulted in the return of his license. But the license was beyond his reach.

Sure, the New York State Athletic Commission told him he could box in New Jersey, but it wasn't the city he loved. Cross the river and fight there, but don't expect to get a sanctioned match in New York—not at Madison Square Garden, not at the Polo Grounds, not at Yankee Stadium. He felt the commission looked at him like he was some young guinea punk, a tough wop, a greaseball. They were too timid to spit on him, but they could withhold a license to fight in New York, and it was perfectly legal. Go ahead, box across the river in Jersey, but it wasn't the Big Apple, it wasn't the jingle jangle of Broadway, it wasn't passersby yelling out his name. It will never be the Big Apple. It's not even a little apple, not even an apple core. It's just the plain old sticks, a speck of a place compared to the city of bright lights and big dreams.

There he was, the middleweight champion of the world, permitted to box in other states but not New York. He loved the city; it was his, it had nurtured him, fed him. Sure it had treated him like dirt at times, but it was his home. From his turf in Brooklyn and the Lower East Side to the fancy apartments on the Upper East Side and the sporting guys of Times Square, it was his home. He loved it, and New Yorkers seemed to love Rocky in return. He was their bad boy gone good. He was a true Noo Yawk character. Take him to Miami, Chicago, San Francisco, and he couldn't wait to get back to the Big Apple. It was his apple—big, shiny, and delicious to its core.

Years earlier, Irving Cohen had changed the transit of Rocky's life. It was time for the ingenious navigator to draw a new map and guide Rocky to the promised land of another title fight. Rocky had been enjoying his leisure, but it was tiring. It robbed him of energy. Life was pleasurable, but it lacked the driving purpose of having to put one's body in the line of fire, of having to take severe punishment to deliver that great knockout blow that had made Rocky's reputation.

Irving Cohen would reinvigorate Rocky as if shooting vitamin B-12 into his tired, lethargic veins. Rocky was not hard to convince; he wanted to get off the couch. He wanted to hear the bell announcing round one. If he could get another fight, he and Irving knew the crowds, the money, and the attention would be greater than anything they had previously experienced.

Irving, his mind awash in possible scenarios, sped into action. He quickly got Rocky to agree to a rubber match with Tony Zale. The fight world (fans, promoters, advertisers, bookies) would go nuts at the prospect of another rematch between two of the hardest-hitting boxers in the middleweight division. The dollars would set a new record for everyone involved. Fans would pay top dollar, for they couldn't wait to see the two gladiators draw blood. The two fighters were a throwback to the killer days of the Roman Coliseum, where gladiators thrilled cheering, bloodthirsty crowds. Rocky had even said that during his second bout with Zale, he had wanted to kill him. He liked Zale, but he wanted to kill him. It had been many years since fans had seen two fighters go after one another with such fierce intent, such ferocious zeal. Without a referee between them, surely one would have been killed.

It didn't take Irving long to set it up. He was a great dealmaker. Once the elements were in place, the deal went as smoothly and easily as rolling a ball down a hill. Rocky signed for what sportswriters called the greatest gory glory trilogy in the annals of middleweight pugilism.

Rocky hadn't been this excited since his bout with Zale in Chicago. Lethargy leapt from his body like a cat into the night and vanished. Irving had taken a broom to the cobwebs that had been weaving a web of pessimism and disappointment around Rocky's life. Again, the air seemed fresh, clean, and fragrant. Sunlight illumined the day. It was set: Irving negotiated the finances, made the subsidiary arrangements, and set the parameters. Rocky quickly scrawled his signature on a contract to fight Tony Zale in New Jersey. Yes, he had wished to fight Zale on his home turf, but this was better than nothing, better than letting one's skills rust before one's time is up. So, Jersey would have to be it. It was an easy ride, not like traveling to the Midwest, the West, or the South. He would get home and be in Norma's arms while the moon was still smiling on them.

The fight was an opportunity to spring out of the hammock of a forced retirement, to see his pugilistic identity in the mirrored eyes of fans. For Tony Zale, the fight was the opportunity to regain what he had lost, what he was convinced he should have won. He was now the hungry lion. After that second fight, Rocky looked like he should have been carried out on a stretcher to the nearest hospital, while Zale was relatively un-marked. Zale understood and appreciated Rocky's powerful right fist; he appreciated Rocky's ability to absorb punch after punch as he was wait-ing for an opening to land his famous knockout right. Zale appreciated Rocky's stamina and determination. The guy could just keep going, keep coming at you for as long as he could stand. Zale wanted to knock Rocky off his feet and leave him in the embrace of the canvas. Their fight would not be decided by the judges and referee, but by the power of a brutal assault.

Zale also knew he was the more skillful and strategic boxer, the man who did not dismiss training, strategy, and tactics. He would rely on his brain and instincts, his power and skill. He would work to outbox Rocky and outpunch him. He knew what to expect from Rocky, weighing it in his strategy for winning. He believed it would be a grueling, brutal battle but that he would prevail. Fans had their own opinions, as did the sportswriters. Regardless, it would be the fight of the year.

The two men, eager, nervous, and suppressing fear, as all boxers do before a bout, met on June 10, 1948, in Ruppert Stadium. More than 21,000 fans paid in excess of $300,000 to witness what some predicted would be the bloodiest battle in the trilogy of encounters between the two middleweights. Without the presence of a referee, death in the ring was a possibility with these two guys. It was said again and again. It was unclear whether the crowd wanted to witness a murder or was hopeful it wouldn't happen.

As champion, Rocky would receive the lion's share of the payout; for less than 30 minutes of actual fighting, of defending his title, he would earn $120,000, while Zale would get half that amount. If Zale were to lose the fight, he would witness his earning power sink like a boat rapidly taking on water. His financial incentive to regain the crown he had worn so proudly was intense. The first bell of the fight would sound in his ears like a starter's pistol going off. He would be out of his corner, fists firing on all cylinders, aiming to punch the air out of Rocky's lungs and send Rocky's head into the velvety darkness of unconsciousness.

For Rocky, the once-angry street fighter, brawler, and scrapper with a chip bigger than a brick on his shoulder, the prospect of the fight did not ignite the expected killer instinct that had previously inspired his ring performances. He was a happy man, maybe too happy, who took enormous pleasure in being a father and husband. He was financially well off; he could afford anything he wanted. He had undergone an amazing transformation from the poor, snarling alley-cat kid, a scavenger and scrapper who had prowled the streets stealing coal during the winter and food year-round, and belting anyone who got in his way. Other fighters would have hung up their gloves and invested their money. Not Rocky. He had become a New York personality, almost an institution. He was not about to pass into history and exist only in the record books of boxing. He loved the public attention, as old men, young men, women, and children could all identify the inimitable Rocky Graziano. "Hi ya, Rock," complete strangers would call to him. People stopped him on the street, patted him on the back, bought him drinks, and waved from taxis and buses. Newsstand vendors invariably asked, "Howya doin' Rocky?"

He was always willing to sign an autograph. He signed with a pen, as well as a smile and a nod of the head, implying the privilege was all his. No one in New York or New Jersey wanted to see the Rock lose his title. Everyone who loved him wanted to see him succeed. Seeing him lose would be like the Statue of Liberty losing its lantern, the Empire State Building its spire, the Yankees their stadium, or the Dodgers Ebbets Field. (And when that did happen, fans wept as if at a funeral.)

Irving Cohen and Whitey Bimstein understood Rocky's appeal, and they knew Paul Cavalier, the referee for the fight, would give the champ every benefit of the doubt to hold on to his title, for even in New Jersey, Rocky was more of a hometown hero than Tony Zale could ever be. The crowd had come to see the champ whip his opponent one more time. And the referee could not hide his own feelings. Yes, he was a fair man, a good man, a solid referee, but his courtesy was expected to be tilted toward Rocky, the crowd's favorite.

Rocky had been living it up since becoming world champion. He had earned the goods of the good life and partaken of it all as if his mortality was just around a corner, as if he might step off a curb and be trampled by a heaving city bus. His practice was to live for today and enjoy it to its maximum potential. That was the life of a champ, but not a contender, and Rocky had not suspected how hard he would have to contend against Zale. Never a fan of rigorous training, Rocky was absent from many scheduled training sessions. The old truant, the soldier who had gone AWOL, still lived in Rocky's rebellious soul. He did not look forward to those vigorous workouts prescribed by Whitey. The 100 throws of Whitey's medicine ball had diminished to a few hard gut shots; the daily 10-mile runs had been shortchanged. Yes, Rocky had trained, but not like he had for that second bout with Zale.

Said Graziano, "After I became champion . . ., I went the way of all fighters—drinking, smoking, having a good time until all hours of the night, you know. I was the king of the world. I don't think there ever wuz a more popular champion than me except Joe Louis."[1]

Yet, he was in surprisingly good shape; his weight was within ounces of Zale's: Rocky weighed 158½ pounds, while Zale weighed 158¾. Even though Rocky's living had been soft, his body was still hard, lean, and muscular. His stamina was still that of a racehorse. Of course, his strength had been diminishing ever so slowly as he aged, as well as his flexibility and speed, but he was not aware of the slow diminishment of his power.

When the fans saw Rocky, they did not see a man who had been eating sumptuously for months, an out-of-shape palooka. He still looked strong and able to take on and take out the toughest of challengers. When he removed his robe, stretched, and flexed his muscles, the crowd whistled and applauded the presence of their hero. He was still their young tiger.

The first bell sounded, and the fighters came out of their corners, like bulls out of their chutes at a bull fight. Each was determined to reenact a past victory. Rocky, however, proved to be an easy target for Zale, who drove him against the ropes with a series of rapid-fire punches. A swift left hook caught Rocky on the side of the head, and he fell to the canvas; he was flat on his back but rose momentarily into a sitting position; he shook his head and leapt to his feet before the referee could begin his count. If you hit him, he would come back at you with fire in his eyes, his jaw clenched tight and his fast-flying fists in your face. Rocky jabbed and threw right crosses. He attempted to go after Zale and drive him against the ropes, where Zale would have few opportunities to throw his powerful body blows.

Rocky threw a dynamite right cross at Zale's head, but it missed the target. His punch had been telegraphed too soon and came too late. Zale saw his opportunities open like an unfolding welcome mat, driving rights and lefts at Rocky's head and midsection. Rocky aimed a hard right uppercut at Zale's chin, but Zale jerked his head back and the blow missed. Once again, the punch was telegraphed too soon and arrived like a man just missing a bus, the doors closing against his hard-charging breathing.

Rocky was driven against the ropes again, absorbing punch after punch. He seemed to be almost absent from the fight. He looked like a man who was watching himself being defeated. The bell sounded like an alarm clock, shaking Rocky awake, and he looked slightly stunned, dazed; he returned to his corner to absorb a minute of restoration and renewal.

The bell sounded for round two, and Rocky emerged from his corner, having discharged the spirit of doom. He was the old Rocky, going after Zale with a will to kill. He landed powerful hard rights and lefts against Zale's head and jaw; for a moment Zale looked surprised, but then he turned up the flame on his own aggression. He counterpunched like a jackhammer. The two men pounded one another, blow for blow, each demonstrating a drive and determination to defend against a possible loss. For a brief while, Rocky seemed to draw on his inner resources to rally as if he were about to win. He gave the battle all he had. He forced Zale into a defensive crouch, but Zale wouldn't accept it. He bravely battled back. To the crowd's amazement, Rocky seemed to outbox Zale in that round, and his fans cheered him on, waiting for him to take Zale out in round three. The Rock, they believed, was on his way to another victory.

In the third round, Zale was the aggressor, driving Rocky against the ropes, where Zale pounded Rocky, who momentarily lost his footing and nearly fell like a drunk into the arms of the ropes. He seemed to wobble as if his lungs were gasping and his brain needed more oxygen. He was not the sure-footed, sure-fisted fighter he appeared to be when he emerged from his corner at the beginning of round three. Zale caught him with a flurry of punches—rights and lefts, rights and lefts, followed by a right to the head and a left hook to the chin. That last punch sent the champion tumbling to the canvas. The crowd was stunned into a whispered murmur of surprise and disappointment.

Their Rock lay prone, one hand clutching a ring rope as if it were a life preserver. He managed to pull himself forward, inch by inch. He stumbled and raised himself into an upright position, a dazed expression on his face. At the count of eight, he was deemed ready to submit to the final indignity of a loss. He nearly fell against the ropes again, his rubbery legs barely able to support his own weight. Zale couldn't wait to get his man, to finish him off and reclaim the title. Zale bounced on his feet, a look of imminent victory in his narrowed, gleaming eyes. Rocky had just shaken the cobwebs from his brain, and Zale was on him with a flurry of punches. A hard left hook sent Rocky sprawling onto the canvas, where he lay as supine as a dead man about to receive last rites. After the referee counted him out, Rocky's mouthpiece was gently removed by Whitey. He knelt alongside Rocky's body like a priest saying good-bye to a beloved parishioner.

For Tony Zale, victory was sweet. He had regained his crown, and his earning power had soared. He was the first middleweight fighter to regain his title in a rubber match since Stanley Ketchel had done so in 1908, against Billy Papke. Zale was pugilism's new hero, its wonder boy come back from the dead.

The loss, although treated in the press as if it were the end of the career of Rocky Graziano, was not an accurate obituary. It was surely a low point, but fate placed other points of destination on the map of Rocky's career. Sure, he felt broken, humiliated, and ashamed of his performance. But the damage was not permanent. After his wounds and ego healed, and he felt completely recovered, he told Irving he wanted another rematch with Zale. It was the old Rocky, the guy who would never give up, never give in, never accept defeat. But Zale and his manager said no dice. Enough was enough. Zale had fought bravely and won back his title, and he was not about to put it in jeopardy. For Rocky, it would take years for him to reflect on his life and understand that out of his defeat, new and gratifying opportunities presented themselves to him. Rocky Graziano, former world middleweight champion, would be reborn as a new kind of Rocky, a more well-known and celebrated character than either Rocky Graziano the middleweight champ or Rocky Graziano the beloved New York character had ever been.

But the Graziano–Zale fights would always be a singular trilogy, one examined and reexamined by boxing fans the world over. In their senior years, Rocky and Zale were interviewed on ESPN and other sports channels, and the two old fighters took pleasure in one another's company, joking, trading anecdotes, and complimenting one another on their skills and toughness, while also laughingly admitting their weaknesses. Their sense of humor and irony about the past made them engaging, beloved figures. It was obvious to viewers that the two men liked one another and knew their names would always be linked in the annals of great ring encounters. Like most professional boxers, they respected one another for having the courage to get into the ring, risk severe punishment, some of it permanent, and take a chance on fame and fortune. Some made it to the top, some didn't: Rocky and Zale, however, were two extraordinary standouts.

After his loss to Zale, Rocky still would not hang up his gloves. He still boxed, but his post-Zale fights were preliminary bouts to a new career. Rocky still wanted to make money boxing, and Irving had promised him he could still expect top dollar for his ring performances. Rocky would go on to have more than 20 additional fights, all but three of which he won and none of which were as bloody as his bouts with Zale. He fought Tony Janiro (ranked as one of the top 10 middleweight contenders of his era) three times; the first time, the judges agreed the fight was a draw. For the second encounter, the judges agreed unanimously that Rocky had won. Their third encounter required no decision by the judges, for Rocky won by a knockout.

Many fans thought Janiro could be another Rocky Graziano: He was good looking; hated training; was a powerful puncher; and enjoyed the company of flashy, louche friends and nights out drinking, having fun. He finished his career with an impressive 83 wins, 11 losses, and 2 draws. After Janiro retired from boxing, he became a bartender at the Neutral Corner, a popular tavern located near Stillman's Gym frequented by members of the boxing fraternity and made famous by *New Yorker* boxing writer A. J. Liebling. Rocky often visited Stillman's Gym to take a look at the new talent, and he would then mosey over to the Neutral Corner. He loved to engage Janiro in stories about other boxers, and before leaving, Rocky would always leave a big tip for his former opponent. If Rocky was accompanied by friends, he would always suggest that they too leave generous tips for Janiro.

Rocky also fought and beat Sonny Horne again. But there was one man who represented the pinnacle of boxing talent, and it was that man who Rocky wanted a shot at—the man who would test his skills like no other. He was Sugar Ray Robinson, who, pound for pound, is considered the finest boxer to ever enter a ring. His fight with Robinson and one later with Chuck Davey would bring Rocky's ring career to its end. The obituarists had been premature. For Rocky, each of those post-Zale fights added to his burgeoning bank account, but each contest would also be a milestone and a signpost to a future free of training, bruises, cuts, knockouts, and wins and losses.

9

FIGHTING THE SWEETEST OF THE SWEET SCIENTISTS

On May 7, 1949, the *New York Times* ran a headline informing boxing fans that Rocky's boxing license had been restored by the New York State Athletic Commission. John Rendel wrote, "Rocky Graziano, the New York boxer who formerly held the world middleweight champion-ship, was reinstated by the New York State Athletic Commission . . . ending a suspension in this state that had been in effect since February 7, 1947.[1] Next to the article appeared a photo of Rocky grasping the out-stretched hand of Commissioner Eagan, who seems to avoid Rocky's gratefully intense gaze. For more than two years, Rocky had felt aban-doned, disowned, rejected, and ridiculed by self-righteous bureaucrats who had attempted to deny him the right to earn a living by the only means he knew.

California followed the example of New York, lifting its suspension of Rocky's license. When that occurred, Abe Greene, commissioner of the National Boxing Association, also rescinded his organization's suspen-sion of Rocky's license. The final suspension to be rescinded was the one imposed by the Illinois Athletic Commission, which had revoked Rocky's license after its members had learned Rocky had gone AWOL from the army and been dishonorably discharged. The commission's erst-while rule that no boxer could be granted a license to fight if he had been dishonorably discharged from any branch of the military was declared unconstitutional by the commission itself. The commissioners now dis-agreed with their previous decision and decided that Rocky should not have been deprived of his right to earn a living as a boxer. Boxing was his profession, a legal means of earning a livelihood, and to deprive him of it was to deprive him of a basic human right. Why they couldn't have come to that conclusion earlier remains a mystery.

Rocky now felt he had been dealt a royal flush. And he was ready to bet his chips on a new campaign to take back the middleweight title. Sweet vindication. Rocky was back on top of the world.

While facing Commissioner Eagan, Rocky, like an apologetic and remorseful truant, a reformed delinquent with a steady, sincere, level look, had to promise the New York State Athletic Commission he would "keep boxing on the high level it now enjoys."[2] Eagan paternalistically warned Rocky not to let him down; Rocky gratefully affirmed he would not. Following that political exchange, Eagan said Rocky could finally apply for a new license. Rocky, relieved and happy, immediately did so.

The boys at Stillman's Gym were pleased by Rocky's return to New York boxing, although many had smirked and guffawed at the words of Parson Eagan. There was a certain amount of backslapping and laughter, and a few hoots of, "Praise the lord" and "Raise the ante." Rocky was still the biggest draw in boxing, the most popular pugilist since Max Baer had filled the gossip columns of Broadway scribes in the 1930s.

One day shortly thereafter, Irving Cohen eagerly phoned Rocky to let him know he could get a new shot at the title if he would be willing to enter the ring against Sugar Ray Robinson, a dazzling ring performer who most boxing aficionados consider one of the finest, if not the finest, boxer of the twentieth century, an inspiration for Muhammad Ali and other champions. Rocky was initially reluctant to accept such an invitation, for Sugar Ray was such an extraordinary boxer that many who fought against him did so just for the money and to say they had been matched with the greatest middleweight of the era. Rocky's reluctance was certainly understandable. But Irving was not willing to take no for an answer. He challenged Rocky to meet his own expectations. He could not go on saying he wanted to fight Sugar Ray and then decline to do so. In addition, there would be a fat payday for Rocky, a lure he was always eager to accept. Rocky finally succumbed to Irving's entreaties and the challenge of combat. He ordered Irving to bring it on, to sign the deal

In a book about the 100 greatest boxers, Burt Sugar, the "Mad Hatter" of pugilism (for he never removed his hat), rated Robinson as the number-one boxer of all time. Sugar Ray Leonard, Muhammad Ali, Roberto

Duran, and Joe Louis rated Robinson as the greatest boxer pound for pound. The term *pound for pound* means Robinson was absolutely the best boxer, the apex of the pyramid, regardless of weight classifications. Compared to any fighter from featherweight to heavyweight, Sugar Ray was the best fans, promoters, and sportswriters had ever seen. He was the most skillful, the most daring, the fighter armed with the cleverest strategies for winning. He was as graceful as a cat; his punches came in lightening quick combinations, and his footwork was that of a dancer, which he had done professionally. More fighters attempted to imitate the style of Sugar Ray than any other boxer in the twentieth century, and it was only Muhammad Ali who came close to succeeding as another Sugar Ray, although Ali was certainly sui generis on his own terms.

If Rocky was the most charismatic white boxer of his generation, Robinson was the most charismatic black boxer of his. And if one erases the category of race, Robinson was probably the most charismatic fighter of the 1940s and 1950s. His appeal spread across color lines. White fans loved him as much as black fans. He was to boxing what Marlon Brando was to acting, what Gershwin was to music, what Lenny Bruce was to comedy: a complete original, an archetype. Even Woody Allen, a person one would not readily suspect of being a boxing fan, thought of Robinson as a true artist, a genius at his craft. Writer Jack Newfield said Robinson was the greatest fighter to tie on a pair of boxing gloves.

His record was extraordinary: Fighting as an amateur, Robinson scored 85 victories, 69 by knockout, and no losses. The majority of those knockouts occurred in the first round. When Robinson turned 19 in 1940, he registered as a professional. And his record as a pro was no less impressive than the one he racked up as an amateur: He had 128 wins, 84 by knockout, and only 2 losses. In eight years, from 1943 to 1951, he was a compelling wizard of punches, having beaten 91 consecutive opponents. It was a winning streak that dazzled both fans and sportswriters. It remains a record unequaled by any other boxer.

For his fans, Robinson was like the Pied Piper of boxing. They turned out in huge numbers whenever and wherever he fought. His fistic ability seemed almost magical, for his sleight of hand combination of punches not only dazzled onlookers, but also left his opponents bewildered victims of shock and awe. There was no one like Robinson, who could dance around his many flat-footed and often-plodding opponents, and deliver devastating and unanticipated rapid-fire combinations of punches that seemed to play tricks on one's visual senses. "Wow!" and "Where did that come from?" were typical expressions of fascinated fans who were startled and thrilled by what they had witnessed. One would be watching Robinson and an opponent trading jabs and right crosses, and suddenly Robinson would explode with a series of punches that would send a devastated opponent to the canvas. The punches came so fast, so furiously, and with such complete surprise that opponents were defenseless.

Robinson was, indeed, the great magician of pugilism. His rapid-fire combinations and nimble footwork made him difficult to hit. Rocky would later lament that Robinson was the slipperiest fighter he had fought against. He just couldn't catch him.

Nonetheless, six years before fighting Rocky, on November 6, 1946, Ray's career almost crashed at Cleveland Arena. There, he encountered the man who Ray said had the hardest punch he had ever endured. His name was Artie Levine. He knocked out Robinson in the fourth round, after which the referee slowly walked Levine to a neutral corner. The referee then returned to the fallen figure of an unconscious Robinson and began his count at one. Unfortunately for Levine, 11 seconds had expired by the time the referee finally began his count. Robinson woozily struggled to an upright position as the count reached nine, but he was still unsteady on his feet and somewhat confused. He wasn't sure what had happened.

Years later, Robinson said he began hearing the count at five and couldn't understand why it started at that number. If the count had begun as soon as Ray hit the canvas, he would have been counted out and perhaps his career would have taken a different turn. Robinson almost went down again in the ninth round, but at the beginning of the 10th round, he was told by his corner that he was losing the fight and had to win by taking the fight to Levine, outboxing him and getting the knockout. Ever resourceful and determined, disciplined and talented, Robinson went on to knock out Levine in the 10th. His virtuoso performance was one of the great comebacks in pugilistic history.

Sugar Ray was incomparable, and from 1946 to 1951, he owned the welterweight title, to the frustration of a series of beaten challengers. In 1951, moving up to middleweight, he took the title as if it had been waiting for him. Having proven himself as the king of his division and the "greatest" (before Ali borrowed that epithet), Robinson retired. He owned a block of stores on 125th Street in Harlem. His nightclub was visited by the flashiest celebrities of the era—movie stars, singers, baseball players, boxers, and politicians, among others. He drove around in a custom-made pink Cadillac convertible, which attracted smiles and admiration wherever it appeared. Although rolling in money and drawing in large sums of cash from his stores and real estate holdings, Robinson was an absentee businessman, and others took advantage of his absence, and his generosity and kindness. Money evaporated as if it had been nothing more than a mirage on a hot desert highway.

Yet, for as long as possible, Robinson enjoyed the benefits of his hard-earned wealth; however, those benefits only lasted for a mere two and a half years, as he had lived expensively, traveled the world, and paid for an entourage of men and women with uneven and opportunistic devotion to the king. He then decided he had to remind the world (and his bank account) he was still tops. Thus, in 1955, Robinson negotiated a contract for another fight. He always negotiated his own contracts and was considered the toughest negotiator of any boxer. On the day of a match, he might refuse to enter the ring unless a clause was changed in a contract. He always made sure he got top dollar. Now he once again taped his fists and tied on his gloves, taking the title fans thought still belonged to the great ring dazzler.

While Robinson's fight with Rocky would attract an enormous number of onlookers, it was his series of six battles with Jake LaMotta that captured the attention of fans, much like Rocky's series of fights with Tony Zale. They were some of the bloodiest battles ever seen in professional boxing. In their sixth encounter, on February 14, 1951, Robinson beat LaMotta so badly the fight became known as the St. Valentine's Day Massacre. Sugar Ray was obviously the more skillful boxer, and he easily outboxed LaMotta during the first 10 rounds; unsatisfied with merely outboxing LaMotta, Robinson became a far more ferocious opponent in the 11th round, unleashing a barrage of devastating rapid-fire combinations that left viewers wondering how LaMotta was still on his feet. In the 13th round, LaMotta finally succumbed, a beaten and bloody victim. Robinson was awarded a win by TKO. It was LaMotta's first loss by knockout; he had ostensibly been knocked out in an earlier bout with Billy Fox, but that was subsequently revealed to have been a fixed fight, and LaMotta's loss was easily perceived by fans and sportswriters to have been faked. But when it came to Sugar Ray, the "Raging Bull" had been gored by boxing's greatest fleet of foot matadors.

While Rocky was a brawler with a devastating right hand who always relied on that punch to win his bouts, Robinson was a chameleon, able to change styles at will. He could outbox anyone; he could brawl; he could counterpunch; and he could deliver jabs, hooks, uppercuts, and bolos—and do so with both fists. And if necessary, he could do so while swiftly backing away from another fighter's assault. He was a man of all styles, so well-trained and experienced he was able to do it all by intuition.

On April 16, 1952, eight months before Robinson's short-lived retirement from boxing, he and Rocky met for a title fight at Chicago Stadium, where 22,264 fans paid top dollar to see what some sportswriters, with their normal inclination and usual flare for journalistic hyperbole, stated would be the fight of the century. Throughout the city were posters touting the matchup. It was a command performance. Mob guys from the Outfit showed up in droves with fur-draped babes on their arms. Movie stars flew in from Hollywood and posed for photos for the local papers. Sportswriters from every major newspaper and wire service were in attendance. Photographers parked their big cameras along the apron of the ring. They had been promised this fight for seven long years, and now it was finally about to take place. The excitement was palpable. Ringside seats, reserved for the rich and well-connected, were unattainable for the average fan. Scalpers were able to sell every ticket they could get their hands on. Counterfeit tickets changed hands like wildfire and caused disruptions during the seating of fans.

It was Rocky's 82nd fight, his penultimate one in an 11-year career that had begun in March 1942. For Robinson, it was his 131st fight, and he would go on to fight in 200 bouts, winning 173. Of those fights, he won 108 by knockout. His career in the ring would span from 1940 to 1965.

Typical of many championship bouts, the ring announcer began the evening by introducing legendary former champs and promising new ones: Joe Louis, Barney Ross, Lew Tendler, Joey Maxim, and Chuck Davey were some of the better-known figures who entered the ring to receive the applause, cheers, and whistles of their fans and say hello to the two contenders. The fight, which was broadcast on CBS-TV, was sponsored by Pabst Blue Ribbon beer, and each of the introduced boxing luminaries was referred to as a Blue Ribbon fighter.

The fight was an opportunity for Rocky to regain the middleweight title; he desperately wanted another middleweight belt. But he was no longer the hot, hungry, angry, scrappy young street thug who had thrilled fight fans throughout the 1940s. The flames of anger that had once fired his killer instincts were simmering. Where there had been flashing flames of fury, there was now the golden-red glow of hot coals. The desire to kill an opponent, rip off his head, and teach the bum a lesson he would never forget was gone. Rocky had been living a life of ease and comfort, free of the restraints and commitments of a boxer on the make; he looked to be in excellent shape, but his mood seemed subdued. His understanding of who he had been and what had motivated him to become a boxer was clear in his mind. He was no longer that ferociously angry young man.

The evening began with the words of an ingratiating announcer named Steve Ellis, who would provide punch-by-punch descriptions of the action. There was 33-year-old Rocky in his corner, doing a little shadow-boxing, a little bit of bobbing and weaving, and then letting his trainer, Whitey Bimstein, rub his back and shoulders. Time hadn't softened his body, just his heart and his outlook on life.

In the opposite corner, 31-year-old Sugar Ray Robinson seemed to dance on his long, agile legs. He bounced up and down, and nodded to his cornermen. He was sprightly, a wily fox of a fighter, supremely self-confident and ready to go like a racehorse at the gate. He was so graceful in his appearance he looked as if he could emerge from his corner and do a tap dance or a soft-shoe routine just as easily as he could come out punching.

The referee was Tommy Gilmore, much respected for his ability to ensure good fights. The ring announcer, who kept pronouncing Graziano as if it ended with the letter "a," told spectators Rocky weighed 159¾ pounds. He then informed spectators Robinson weighed 157¼ pounds. Rocky was 5-foot-7, and Robinson was 5-foot-11, which meant Rocky would have to fight from a crouch and attempt to come in under the taller man's fists. In addition, Rocky's reach was 68½ inches, while Ray's was 72 inches. The come-from-under crouch was an approach that was being used to devastating effect by another hard-hitting Rocky named Marciano, who fought opponents who were taller than he was and had longer reaches, although none were as talented as Sugar Ray

Rocky and Sugar Ray acknowledged the applause from their fans, each raising his arms in a salute of recognition, then nodding and briefly smiling at the crowd in the arena. The fighters met in the center of the ring, where Gilmore gave the men their pro forma instructions: no hitting below the belt, no rabbit punches, go to a neutral corner in the event that your opponent is knocked down for a count, separate in clinches. And have a good, clean fight. The fighters perfunctorily touched gloves, almost imperceptibly nodded at one another, and then turned and walked back to their respective corners. Robinson bounced up and down some more, like an impatient runner on a street corner, waiting for the traffic light to change from red to green; his impatience was apparent. Like most fighters just before the sounding of the first bell, he was keyed up and ready to go. Rocky, too, was hot-wired to start the fight, ready to test himself against the reigning middleweight king.

In the first minute of the first round, Robinson's punches came fast and furious. The combinations—for which he was famous—were swift and dazzling. His timing was perfect. Not only were his fists flying faster than Rocky's, but also his fancy footwork. Rocky tried to hold off Robinson with an extended left arm, delivering ineffective jabs. The problem was, of course, that Sugar Ray's arms were longer than his. Yet, Rocky drove the fight; he was often the aggressor, driving Robinson to one side of the ring and then the other. At one point, Rocky swung his powerful right, but his opponent quickly ducked. Had that right connected with Robinson's skull, he surely would have gone down, but the magician was faster at ducking and slipping punches than Rocky was at throwing his right crosses.

But Rocky would not give up; he kept throwing those punches, relentlessly, unsparingly, like a machine that never stops. And a few of those punches began hitting their target. Some were severe enough to leave Robinson momentarily stung and stunned. With 30 seconds left in the round, Sugar Ray launched a counterattack with a series of brilliantly executed combinations that drove Rocky against the ropes. Rocky responded with his own combinations, followed by a few rabbit and kidney punches while in a clinch. Gilmore repeatedly warned Rocky not to throw rabbit and kidney punches, but to little avail. Rocky had to rely on whatever techniques were at his disposal to hold off his foe's combinations, his flurry of blows. A warning by the referee in this fight would not be declared a foul and would not lead to a loss. Clinches offered Rocky the opportunity to slow the pace of the fight, to inflict minor damage.

He knew Robinson was outboxing him, and it made him mad. Although no longer an angry young thug, he was no loser. He would not be a pushover. You don't enter the ring with the expectation of losing. You always want to win, and winning sometimes requires desperate measures. And when you're in a clinch, tying up your opponent and trying to diminish him, you will do whatever is necessary to get an advantage. A few hard-hitting rabbit punches had the possibility of mentally slowing down an otherwise quick-thinking opponent. Never give up; always keep punching. That was Rocky's modus operandi.

The action in the second round was much as it had been in the first, although Rocky seemed to be the more intense aggressor, and Robinson defended himself with brilliant counterpunches. While nimbly backing away from Rocky, Sugar Ray continued to throw punches that served as defensive obstacles Rocky could not penetrate. Watching the fight, one could see that Sugar Ray was luring Rocky into a trap where an explosion of punches would devastate the challenger. It was a round where the aggressor seemed to be the one on the verge of losing. And that's precisely what the mongoose was doing to the snake.

The bell sounded, ending the roles of the pursuer and the pursued. The fighters retired to their respective corners and sat on their stools, where their trainers briefly refreshed them with gulps of water, wiping their faces, applying Vaseline around their eyes, and encouraging them to keep on the attack. Just before the bell announcing the third round sounded, cornerman Al Silvani could be seen giving Rocky some final advice. Rocky gave a small, quick nod of understanding before springing to his feet.

While Robinson was using his left jab to set up Rocky for a knockout combination, Rocky would not be sucker punched; he went on the attack and delivered an unexpected blow to Sugar Ray's head, briefly toppling the dazzler, although the announcer said it wasn't an official knockdown. Again being the aggressor, Rocky was setting the pace, forcing Sugar Ray to backpedal and counterpunch. Rocky, from a crouching position, unremittingly, relentlessly drove his fists at his opponent's head and body. In his book *Somebody Up There Likes Me*, Rocky wrote, "I saw him open there, waiting for it, in the split second that I should have smashed him. But my arms and my hands and my feet would not do what they had to do."[3]

To make matters worse for Rocky, the magical mongoose he had been fighting was as slippery as a wet lemon seed and managed to slip Rocky's punches. Sugar Ray was a genius at avoiding being hit. Perhaps Rocky had become overconfident in his ability to drive the fight on his terms, to be the hard-driving aggressor, but he also must have been frustrated that only a few of his punches were hitting their targets. Robinson chose to affect a different style: He became the aggressor. With their roles suddenly reversed, the scenario dramatically altered. Robinson dominated, driving Rocky against the ropes, feinting with his left, and hitting his opponent with a series of wicked right hand that sent Rocky to the canvas. Rocky's mouthpiece flew from his mouth like a fleeing animal.

The referee counted like a metronome—one, two, three, four—and Rocky, while lying on his side, jerked and bent and unbent his right leg at the knee, as if to see if it was still working. The leg seemed to move back and forth as if it didn't belong to him. It looked like a dying animal in the final throes of death. Within a few seconds, Rocky gained control of his leg and stumbled to an upright position, but it was too late. He had been counted out. Like a drowning man, he hung one arm over the ropes for support, and one of his cornermen rushed out to swab his head with a sponge of cool water.

The king of pugilistic magicians proudly raised his right arm in recognition of his stunning win, still middleweight champion of the world. Like a royal personage being pampered by a retinue of servants, he had the sweat of his body toweled off and his hair finger-brushed, smoothed, and patted into place. He had always traveled with a devoted entourage, and there they were attending to the champ, a money-generating asset that paid off fight after fight.

Rocky's cornermen attempted to calm him down and console the obviously frustrated, angry, and disappointed former champ, now a failed challenger, who would no longer be a title contender. He raised his arms in defeat and frustration before letting them fall; the strong, muscled arms that had once carried him to a championship were now his defeated arsenal, strained and spent. He muttered a few curses and shook his head in disgust. It was over. Whitey Bimstein whispered into one of Rocky's ears, attempting to console him and telling him he had waged a good fight and should feel nothing but pride in his performance. After all, he had come close to knocking out Robinson. They were nice words but hardly compensation for such a major loss.

Regaining his poise, Rocky's sense of honor took over, and as one who always observed postfight decorum, he walked to Sugar Ray's corner and congratulated him, injecting a note of humor by pretending to complain that the mongoose never stood still long enough to take a good punch. The ring announcer told the fans that Sugar Ray Robinson was still world middleweight champion and that the fight had officially ended at one minute and 53 seconds of the third round.

In his dressing room, Robinson was asked if Rocky had hurt him during the fight; he responded that Rocky's hard right landed on the back of his head with such force that it knocked him down. He had been lucky to turn his head away from a direct hit to his chin.

When Rocky was asked about Robinson after the fight, he said Sugar Ray was the greatest boxer he had ever fought and maybe the greatest middleweight of all time. And yet the disappointment on his face looked as if it had been etched in with a razor. His face, like the faces of all fighters who have engaged in brutal ring contests year after year, was an autobiography of wins and defeats, glory and sadness. Each fighter wears his scars like a badge of courage, an announcement to the world of a worker in a tough profession that few others would want to venture into.

The respect Rocky and Sugar Ray felt for one another was obvious during their joint appearances on sports television programs, where the fighters would reminisce about their encounter. They would tell reporters how much they liked one another, how they admired one another's skills and determination as worthy opponents. During one joint interview, Robinson acknowledged that although Rocky had one of the hardest right-hand punches of any boxer, it was Artie Levine who truly had the hardest punch he had ever endured, and it was that punch that nearly derailed his unbroken series of victories. He thought Levine had a fist of steel. Rocky agreed and said he was glad not to have felt it. The two former combatants laughed and kidded one another, and Robinson claimed Rocky was the nicest guy you could ever meet. Inside or outside the ring, he was a fine guy.

On October 20, 1974, the fighters were interviewed by Curt Gowdy and Don Dunphy on a PBS show entitled *The Way It Was*. The two old pugilists, looking back more than 20 years, were reliving and enjoying their memories of that encounter in Chicago. They were like a pair of old drinking buddies who enjoyed kidding one another as much as they admired one another for their courage and skills.

"Why didn't you stand still, so I could've given you a couple of shots," said Rocky, laughing.

" What would you have done differently, Rocky?" asked Gowdy.

Rocky responded, "I woulda grabbed him by the throat or something. This guy was like Vaseline. He was slippin' all over the ring. You couldn't hit him." And with that Rocky reached over and patted Sugar Ray's shoulder.

" When you fight a guy like Rocky, you either C Sharp or you B Flat," laughed Robinson. "You had better keep your eyes on his right fist or you would be looking up at the stars."

" Ray was such a great fighter, it was a pleasure getting knocked out by him," Rocky said as he smiled at his old opponent.

Don Dunphy summed up by stating, "Rocky was probably one of the biggest drawing cards in the history of Madison Square Garden, which was the Mecca of boxing. A fine champion who came along when there were real good middleweights. Rocky has to rate right up there with the best. As for Sugar Ray, if you took every possible ingredient that could possibly be used to make a great fighter, Ray could box, he could punch, he could take a punch. He was as game as they come. He had plenty of heart, and above all he had great desire, the desire of any champion. Any ingredient that any great fighter had, Ray Robinson had them all." [4]

The two would be celebrated throughout the world well beyond the end of their pugilistic careers, for they were superstars of the sweet science, two of the brightest and most charismatic fighters to enter the ring and put on gloves to prove themselves to themselves and relieve the pain of their deep-seated hurts, pain that could only be mitigated by hurting others. But before Rocky could let go of what remained of his anger and hurt, the two emotions that had self-destructively plagued his youth, he would have to endure one more loss, a loss to a man Rocky could have met nowhere other than in a boxing ring. He was the self-assured, college-educated Chuck Davey, the last person one would have thought would have wanted to undertake the grueling punishment that was being a professional boxer.

10

THE LAST RUMBLE

By the time Rocky had been knocked out by Sugar Ray Robinson at Chicago Stadium, he would have been pleased never to the return to the Windy City. He had nothing against Chicago; it just wasn't New York. It wasn't his city, and the streets weren't filled with his people. Chicago was the city that cheered for its midwestern champs and contenders. Rocky never felt welcome there. But if he had to punch and pound his way through one more bout at Chicago Stadium, he would resignedly go there, ignoring the city's infamous stockyards and the nauseating odors emanating from its slaughter houses, but not necessarily the mob guys with the broad shoulders. Many of them regarded Rocky as one of their own, an ex-con, a paisan.

Chicago was the city where Irving Cohen could get the best deal for Rocky. Chicago offered Rocky an opportunity to put the financial icing on a cake of growing savings. For Rocky, one more fight would represent the unremarkable conclusion to his career, during which he could earn $50,000. He knew he could take a punch: He had been taking punches for years. His head was still clear, and he didn't think he ran a risk of being hurt, even if he lost the fight. One more fight, another $50,000. He might as well draw the last bit of money he could out of the fight game.

When he signed the contract, he felt the money was on its way into his bank account. After that payday, Rocky figured he would have enough to retire and live out the rest of his days as a Brooklyn squire, hanging out with his pals and enjoying the company of Norma and taking her on vacations to Florida or just dining at fancy restaurants. And, of course, he looked forward to watching his daughters grow into beautiful young women. It would be a life without the most basic worries about money. What a change it had been from his deprived boyhood.

With so much money at his disposal, Rocky spent it freely—too freely, thought Norma. Thus, she put the brakes on Rocky's spending; she would no longer permit money to fly out of his pockets on wings of generosity, as if being sucked out by a vacuum cleaner. Norma warned Rocky that although he had enough money to retire, he could just as easily become bankrupt. It happened to a lot of free-spending athletes. She warned him he could no longer spend it on anything that caught his fancy. At least Rocky didn't spend it on women. He was strictly in the luxury goods market: fancy cars, expensive vacations, fur coats for Norma, private schools for the kids, and expensive presents for his relatives during the holidays. But he was also an easy touch, so money went to old friends who had fallen on hard times, former boxers trying to make ends meet on paycheck-to-paycheck incomes, and relatives to help pay the rent. He was not a mark or a sucker, just a generous guy whose compassion seemed as big as his bank account. If a boyhood friend contacted Rocky and was desperate for a loan, Rocky sent him a check. Chances are it was never repaid. Norma feared that her husband's generous instincts and ready compassion would have led directly to the deprivations of the Lower East Side. Hence her allowance, and Rocky didn't seem to mind. He loved Norma and regarded her as the more sensible one in their marriage.

The upcoming fight meant not only more money in the bank, but also recognition of Rocky's market value to the world of pugilism. In any case, the bout, he was sure, would not be one of his important ones. It would be no big deal. Bing, bang, boom and it would be over. And then there would be the continuing recognition and respect the money symbolized. It was like severance pay or a golden parachute for a long, hard-fought career.

Rocky's opponent for that fight would be the estimable Chuck Davey, a fighter like no other Rocky had ever fought. Rocky's opponents had been guys much like himself—guys who had come up the hard way, having tough childhoods, living in poverty, experiencing delinquency, and learning to fight to survive on the mean streets of their poor slum neighborhoods. For them, boxing was not just a sport; it was a means to make as much money as quickly as possible, to shoot themselves on rockets of ambition out of their ghetto neighborhoods and into the rarified atmosphere of wealth and security. Few would make it; few had the makings of champions. But they all had the necessary determination to withstand countless blows to their heads, bodies, and egos. They might not make it to the top of their divisions, but if they had to go down for the count, they would go down fighting for a chance to be champs.

And then there was Charles Pierce Davey. The name sounded like that of a senator born to govern, a member of the upper classes, or an investment banker, or a proud and pompous member of the diplomatic corps. One could imagine the name being signed to a Supreme Court decision. The name conjured up an image of a man in a tuxedo with a carnation pinned to his lapel. Many people wondered why Charles Pierce Davey, a child of wealth and privilege, became a boxer. He had the education and means to follow the life of an upwardly mobile corporate executive. His parents were well-to-do Midwesterners. His mother's family, the Pierces, had large and valuable landholdings on Lake Van Etten in Michigan. The family was more land rich than cash rich during the Great Depression. To raise money during that period, the family sold a considerable portion of their land at a handsome profit to real estate developers.

The Pierce property included a highly valued spot of prime real estate known as Loud Island. On the land the Pierces chose not to sell, they used much of their profits to build a colony of cottages, plus several substantial houses. It seemed to be the style at that time: exclusive gated compounds for the rich who did not want to mingle with hoi polloi. The Pierce's property jutted into Lake Van Etten and became known as Pierce's Point. From it, one could watch sailboats gracefully gliding on sun-speckled water and hear the put-put-put of small outboard motorboats. It was idyllic and so were the summers Chuck Davey spent on the lake. It was a far cry from the poor, stinking tenements of Rocky's garbage-strewn neighborhood. The air on the lake was fresh and clean, and the children played without wondering where their next meal would come from or which streets they should avoid so as not to tangle with a local gang. There were no pool halls on the lake, no gangs of young muggers, no kids stealing food from grocers and peddlers, no one peddling nickel bags of heroin. Pierce's Point was safe and salubrious; good food and comfort were taken for granted. It was an ideal place for the young Chuck Davey to spend his summers. Every day, he could go boating, swimming, and water skiing.

By summer's end, he was a tanned, young, athletic-looking boy with an easy and welcoming grin.

During the school year, Chuck lived a happy and productive life with his parents and three siblings in Detroit, where he proved to be a good student who rarely got into trouble. He was a handsome boy who loved athletics; in fact, he seemed to have the grace, endurance, and strength of a natural athlete, someone born to compete and excel. It was no surprise to his family and coaches that he regularly won awards for running track. He found running to be exhilarating; he felt as free as an animal in the wild. Running took his mind off of homework, social obligations, and plans for the future. It gave him a natural high. He would always love running. Nearly every day of his life, he would tie on a pair of running shoes and take off, feeling blissfully free of life's constraints. In fact, he so loved running he continued doing so well into his 70s. With a smile on his face, he would be one of the oldest runners crossing finish lines year after year in marathons, where he had no intention of surpassing women and men in their 20s. His was simply the joy of running. Although he no longer ran like the wind, as he had as a young man, he could still feel the wind at his back.

Unlike Rocky the truant, who had quit school at a young age, Chuck not only earned an undergraduate college degree, but also went on to get a master's degree, both from Michigan State University. College degrees were not normally associated with professional boxers. One surely didn't expect to see a pair of degrees framed and proudly hanging on the walls of a boxer's home. But Davey was not your average boxer. At age 17, he discovered boxing, first as an exercise, then as a sport. He loved it and proved to be as good at it as he was at running. As a boxer, he was a southpaw, rapidly jabbing with his right fist and delivering powerful left crosses to devastating effect. Look at most boxers and you'll see they invariably jab with their left fists. A fighter who jabs with his right is unexpected and not something most fighters train against. Chuck's southpaw attacks frequently frustrated his opponents; they would have to fight at a slight angle, which could diminish the power of their punches.

In addition to being a southpaw, Chuck danced around the ring, both defensively and offensively, like a wild barnyard chicken. His feet and right jab were always in motion. It was hard for most fighters to nail him. He always seemed to dance just out of range, as elusive as a ghost. He proved to be an outstanding competitor for the Michigan State boxing team, where his star performances were applauded by admiring students, teachers, coaches, and deans. Not unexpectedly, he went on to win the National Collegiate Athletic Association's (NCAA) welterweight title. He kept getting better and better.

Coaches at Michigan State encouraged Chuck to try out for the Olympics. He ruminated before agreeing to give it a shot. His tryout proved as successful as his coaches had estimated it would. Chuck became a top-ranked member of Team USA at the 1948 Summer Olympics; however, he did not win a medal. Only one American boxer achieved that goal, when Horace "Hank" Herring, from Chicago, won a silver medal. Prior to entering the Olympic games, Herring had won the Senior Navy welterweight title in 1946, as well as the All-Navy welterweight crown in 1947. He had a brief professional career that began in January 1949, and concluded in July 1950; his modest record consisted of 5 wins, 7 losses, and 1 draw. Although he, and not Chuck Davey, had won the medal, it was Davey who would go on to have an outstanding professional career.

Following his unexpectedly disappointing performance in the Olympics, Chuck served in the military and, upon his discharge, again entered NCAA bouts, winning three more championships. His amateur record was impressive: 93 wins in 94 bouts. But for some inexplicable reason, promoters did not have their eyes on young Davey; none seemed to regard him as championship material. Was he too clean-cut to attract a typical boxing crowd? Certainly the well-groomed and self-educated Gene Tunney had been a favorite of many fans, but he, too, was an anomaly in the fraternity of boxers. (In fact, he was such an anomaly and voracious reader of Shakespeare that following his retirement from boxing, he lectured about the bard to 200 Yale students.) But fans much preferred the hard-hitting model of a tough guy, Jack Dempsey, to the supposedly well-read, articulate, and elegant Gene Tunney, who had beaten Dempsey for the heavyweight title in 1926. Was Davey just another Tunney, albeit in a lower weight class? Promoters weren't sure. And compared to Rocky, he was no big draw, no celebrity, nothing of the colorful bad boy in his past. Rocky, with his "dees, dems, and dos" speech and brutal slugger style of fighting, was one of the biggest draws in the history of Madison Square Garden. In fact, he was responsible for making the welterweight and middleweight divisions as exciting as Joe Louis had made the heavyweight division. Rocky was credited with having breathed new life into boxing.

Rocky and Davey represented different blocks of fans: Rocky's good looks were entirely ethnic; Davey's good looks were white, Protestant, Midwestern. He appeared as nonthreatening as your local banker, doctor, lawyer, or dentist. The young Rocky, by contrast, looked and acted as if he would take your head off, especially if you looked askance at him or, even worse, insulted him. Boxing fans expected their heroes to be tough and look tough, to come from tough backgrounds. If they had criminal backgrounds, even better. Rocky was the original "rebel without a cause" years before the world heard of James Dean. He was the "wild one" before Marlon Brando starred as the rebellious motorcycle gang leader in the movie *The Wild One*.

From another world came Davey. With his modestly handsome looks, articulate diction, and good manners, he could attract new fans to boxing, those who did not like to watch a sport dominated by Italians, Jews, blacks, and Latinos. People who would normally feel uncomfortable and out of place in a boxing gym could feel at ease in the presence of Davey. While Chuck would have been easily accepted as a member in their country clubs, Rocky would have been lucky if he was hired to wash dishes and enter through the service entrance. Rocky was the champ of the common man, of the many ethnics, of the people whose only clubs were their local pool halls, YMCAs, and inner-city boxing gyms.

Davey was not hampered by the lack of professional interest in his career. He was determined to make a name for himself, ascend to the throne of champion, and wear the crown of a titleholder. He fought on, believing his dream was within his grasp and that one day he would be a star in the eyes of the big-time promoters, and once that happened, he felt he could go on dazzling them with his footwork, snappy jabs, and ability to tear up the record book with an unbroken series of winning decisions and knockouts. He would be a professional's professional, a boxer's boxer, a sure thing at the box office, and his career would pay off like an annuity.

So, he fought on, an unstoppable force, taking down one opponent after another. After a while, promoters could no longer avoid taking notice of the young, well-kept fighter with two college degrees. The degrees were good for publicity, but his boxing ability would put fans on their fannies in seats. By 1952, Davey (as he was now called by ring announcers) had a record of 30 wins, 0 losses, and 1 draw. He had reached a plateau above where many of his former competitors stood or had fallen. He was finally being looked up to as a fighter who could attract a sizeable number of fans, many of whom were new to the world of boxing.

In addition, television had begun to play an important role in boxing. Television sets, in the early 1950s, were fast becoming standard items of furniture in living rooms throughout the country. With a wealth of ads after each three-minute round, the money coming in would be far greater than what had previously emanated just from the sale of arena tickets. Fighters, managers, and promoters were eager to partake of that new source of income. And many of the smarter fighters, for example, Sugar Ray Robinson, demanded a percentage of the money that television generated. Thus, fight promoters were eagerly offering more bouts than television producers could accommodate. Contenders refused to get into a ring unless there were several television cameras pointed at it.

Friday and Saturday televised bouts were rapidly becoming rituals for fans. Many of the bars that had catered to boxing fans with their radios tuned to the fights suffered a loss of drinking customers until they, too, installed televisions. The money from advertising was reported in the advertising and broadcasting trade magazines. Sales of razors, shaving creams, and beer skyrocketed. It was a bonanza that enriched not only the boxers, managers, and promoters, but also advertising and television executives and those who performed in commercials. And if you became a popular champ, you could sign a highly remunerative contract to be a product spokesman.

Into this rich, new world entered Chuck Davey. Suddenly, he was looked upon as a natural on the little black-and-white television screen, with its flickering images and sometimes-impetuous lack of vertical and horizontal self-control. He looked like he could have been a quiz show announcer or local newscaster. He had the perfectly bland face and pitch-perfect diction to be a panelist on one of the era's popular quiz shows: *I've Got a Secret*, *To Tell the Truth*, or *What's My Line?* One advertising agency art director believed Davey had the kind of face advertisers would love: It was so completely inoffensive and sincere in expression it could have sold a wide variety of consumer products. A television producer said Davey would not set hearts on fire but that he had the face of a believable political candidate or pitchman. In other words, he was made for television, and as such, he could increase the viewership for boxing and raise its prominence.

And then, of course, there was his record. Sports fans love statistics, and Davey had an impressive resume, something that could be touted in bars throughout the United States, where men could argue about who were the best boxers. His resume and bland good looks were the necessary ingredients for attracting hundreds of thousands of viewers to well-hyped television bouts. And the television flacks went overboard in plugging the clean-cut, midwestern gladiator.

And what could be better and more exciting than a match pitting the articulate, young, college-educated WASP against the slugging ethnic from one of New York's poorer neighborhoods? Davey versus Rocky: It was class warfare with an ethnic component.

(While Davey was being hyped as the bright light of boxing on television, those doing the billing had evidenced no foresight that Rocky Graziano would become one of the most popular television personalities in the United States throughout the 1950s and 1960s. And where would Chuck Davey reside in that pantheon of colorful television characters? Dismissed, barely remembered, another has-been. The best-laid plans of television executives would, like so many other brilliant plans, end in the wastebasket of unfulfilled dreams. Davey was not the ratings sensation television executives had envisioned.)

While the two boxers were being evaluated within the accepted advertising standards of the *Mad Men* era, the more important circumstance was their upcoming bout. Who would emerge the winner? Fans, regardless of whether they would watch the match on television or at Chicago Stadium, looked forward to a brawl between what some called the tough "Italian Stallion" and the likeable Midwesterner, "Mr. Nice Guy," the skillful Olympian.

But before Davey could get his much-anticipated shot at the great Rocky Graziano, he would have to go up against the talented Ike Williams, a former lightweight champion who had moved up to the welterweight division. Davey would have to prove he was worthy of a bout with Rocky, the legendary brawler and crowd-pleaser. If Davey were to fall to Williams's gloves, he would not be a magnet for attracting the dollars of fans. But if he could dazzle the fans with a big win over Williams, it would fuel the burning desire of fans to see if he could go punch-to-punch with Rocky.

Davey went into the Williams fight with the intensity and determination of an unremitting laser; he fought as if he wanted to crush his opponent, with the ferocious diligence and tenacity one would associate with a wild animal. He was a hungry predator. He threw punches round after round without tiring. Most fans and sportswriters had figured Davey would probably win on points, he was such a good boxer. Points were not enough for the determined Davey. He surprised the fraternal order of pugilists by knocking out Williams in the fifth round. That was all he needed. His fans rose to their feet and cheered their hero.

Davey had accomplished the mission he had set himself, and now, overnight, he had become a celebrity, not just in the world of boxing, but also the greater world of sports. Almost immediately after the fight, the well-oiled publicity machinery was set in motion and operated in high gear. Sportswriters and sportscasters on both television and radio let fans know Davey was a great athlete, as well as an exemplary guy: He was every mother's ideal son—honest, thoughtful, decent. He even called his mother after every fight to let her know that he was unharmed.

Sports fans further learned Davey was a regular churchgoer and that he neither drank nor smoked. He was the all-American boy as gladiator. His appeal extended beyond male fight fans, as women admired him too. They would have been pleased to have him as a guest at a family dinner. He could have said grace and spoken about his fine family values rather than bragging about his boxing career. The media played along and even went a little overboard, for they seemed to present Davey as an overaged Eagle Scout or perhaps a scoutmaster, a figure in a Norman Rockwell painting on the cover of the *Saturday Evening Post*. Some cynics thought he might show up on the cover of *Farm Journal*, barefoot and wearing denim overalls and a straw hat, while smiling good-naturedly and holding a corncob pipe in one hand. Others said he could have been on the cover of popular business trade magazines, as he also looked like a young entrepreneur who was about to take over the presidency of a small Midwestern insurance agency.

Regardless of who was offering an opinion, no one thought young Chuck Davey was in the mold of a beer-swigging, street-spitting boxer or an ex-convict-turned-pugilist, both of whom were types the public associated with hordes of boxers. Davey was new and different; he was a Mr. Clean in a dirty business where mobsters fixed fights and broke the knees of those who refused to cooperate with them.

Once Davey defeated Ike Williams, his fans looked forward to him making fast work of a certain once-formidable middleweight, the Rock from New York. They envisioned Davey taking his career to new heights.

On September 17, 1952, the college-educated pugilist with the flat Midwestern accent and polished manners would meet the original dead-end kid, whose accent was pure New Yawkeese, at Chicago Stadium, for a fight that would be a signpost for both fighters. Although Davey was two inches taller than Rocky (Davey was 5-foot-9 and Rocky 5-foot-7), it would be Davey's southpaw style that would be a frustrating obstacle for the Rock to overcome. In addition, Davey bounced and danced around the ring, and wouldn't stand still to take a punch. He was not as hard to catch as Sugar Ray Robinson had been, but he was still as slippery as a fish in water.

Davey was primed and psyched to go on the attack against the man who had once seemed indestructible for his ability to take punch after punch, unfazed and upright, and then deliver a devastating right cross that would send an opponent to sleep on the canvas. Prior to matching skills with Davey, Rocky had built a reputation for slamming another upright, clean-cut Midwesterner, the powerful "Man of Steel," Tony Zale. Fans speculated whether there would be another trilogy in the offing. Fans and promoters loved such trilogies, for it ramped up communal excitement and swelled the gate and the books of bookies; trilogies were made in matchmaker heaven.

As the day of the fight approached, Rocky, Irving, and Whitey knew there would be no trilogy. Rocky knew that win or lose, this would probably be his last fight. He was ready to hang up his gloves. He was no longer the same Rocky who had set the world of boxing on fire. He had lost his last fight with Tony Zale and fell like a bag of wet cement to the powerful combinations of Sugar Ray Robinson.

Still, fans asked if the Rock would batter the college boy with his powerful right cross? Or would he be outsmarted by the quick-thinking, fleet-footed Chuck Davey? The golden boy of the Midwest had proven his prowess prior to his bout with Rocky, not just with Ike Williams, but also with his unexpected win in a bout against the hard-as-nails Carmen Basilio, who would go on to beat Sugar Ray Robinson in 1957, and then lose to him in 1958.

The bell beginning the first rounded clanged, and the fighters drew the rapt attention of their fans. Coming into the center of the ring, Rocky assumed his regular crouch when pursuing a taller opponent, and Davey danced away and out of reach of Rocky's right crosses and left jabs. It went on like that round after round: Davey was fleet of foot as Rocky aggressively plodded on in pursuit of his elusive target. Then, in the seventh round, Davey opened a cut at the corner Rocky's right eye, which was surprising, as many of Davey's punches seemed to land with pillow softness, doing no damage and having no effect on the Rock's aggressiveness. Just before the bell sounded to end the seventh round, Rocky connected with a right cross that briefly stunned and stumbled Davey. His fans erupted with cheers of enthusiasm. And then the bell silenced them, ending Rocky's opportunity to deliver a fateful follow-up punch.

During the eighth round, Rocky was unable to deliver any blows that could stun Davey, and so the round was a repetition of previous tactics. By the ninth round, rather than having tired arms, Davey's arms seemed to possess new power. His right jabs were straight as spears and landed with such power that one could see the effect on Rocky. Never one to let himself be pushed around or pummeled without purpose, Rocky threw a number of wild left and right crosses, none of which connected, as Davey either ducked or danced beyond the range of those flying fists. Unlike the seventh round, it was Davey who connected, sending a hard left uppercut to Rocky's jaw; yet, the Rock barely stumbled and went on punching.

In the 10th round, Rocky seemed energized and went after Davey with a barrage of right and left crosses. Again, Davey danced around like a kangaroo, with springs on his feet. Suddenly, he let loose with a combination that caused Rocky's mouthpiece to fly from his mouth. Then Davey opened the cut on Rocky's right eye, which bled profusely. Twice Rocky lunged at his foe, intending to deliver a right cross that would end the fight, but that legendary right cross swished through the air, missing Davey's bobbing chin. Rocky had thrown that punch with such force that when it missed its target, he—losing his balance—nearly collided with the ropes. Finally, after repeated attempts to land his famous right cross, he landed one on Davey's chin. Rocky's fans again erupted with a cheer, and they could see Davey was stunned by the blow. Yet, Davey simply shook his head like a dog discharging water and managed to dance away from Rocky, but not fast enough to avoid a second right cross. Now, Davey was obviously hurt, and the crowd anticipated his imminent demise.

Again, Rocky went after Davey with a barrage of rapid-fire punches, and Davey seemed on the verge of going down, of leaving the world of the conscious. He had a new cut on his nose. Davey then exhibited two characteristics that always drew the admiration of his fans: resilience and determination. He came back at Rocky and knocked him down. Unwilling to accept such an act as the final verdict of his career, Rocky leapt up as if on springs, in one rapid motion. The two fighters then swiftly, desperately traded punches, winding up in a rabbit-punching clinch.

The bell sounded, and the fight was over. The fighters were exhausted. They returned to their respective corners to await the verdict. Speaking into his dangling microphone, in the same gravelly, sandpaper voice that was once the standard for all ring announcers, the announcer voiced that Chuck Davey had won by a unanimous decision.

And so ended Rocky's boxing career. He had won 67 bouts, 52 by knockout, and suffered 10 losses and endured 6 draws. His career lasted from March 31, 1942, to September 17, 1952. He had been one of the biggest and most exciting draws in boxing, especially at Madison Square Garden, and even—much to his surprise—a top draw at Chicago Stadium. Regardless of where he fought, he was celebrated for his determination and ability to take three punches just so he could deliver his one powerful, well-aimed right cross. His face was a memoir of 11 years of being punched, cut, and broken. But he was not a defeated man. He had proven long ago that his mother's bad boy could become middleweight boxing champion and earn the respect and love of his fans. And those fans included not only his mother, but also his father, the man Rocky hated and loved.

Chuck Davey would go on to have 12 more fights, winning seven and losing five. He suffered a devastating loss against the amazing Kid Gavilan on November 2, 1953, at Chicago Stadium, the site of his exciting win over the far more famous Rocky Graziano. Davey's humiliating defeat by the fists of Kid Gavilan came as a surprise to him and his fans, for he had won 39 consecutive bouts, interrupted by two draws, before entering the ring against the Kid. Yet, the Kid was the 14-to-5 favorite among the bookies.

For the first two rounds, Davey had managed to dance around the Kid and stay out of range of being hit, much as he had done in his bout with Rocky. But in the third round, the Kid figured out Davey's tactics and mounted an effective attack; he pummeled Davey, who went down for a count of nine. It was the first time in his boxing career Davey had been knocked down. In the fourth and fifth rounds, Davey stayed out of range of the Kid's powerful punches, but he was also unable to land any hard counterblows. In the ninth round, Davey was knocked down three times, getting to his feet as the count reached nine. He couldn't come out of his corner at the outset of the 10th round, and the Kid won by a TKO.

That fight haunted Davey and fueled reassessments of his once-sterling reputation. He had never suffered such an overpowering and humiliating loss. His professional career lasted from October 10, 1949, to October 15, 1955. He was fortunate that his brain had not been scrambled during his six-year career, and he had the intelligence to be grateful and the ambition to become a highly successful businessman. After leaving boxing, he was appointed Michigan's boxing commissioner and then president of the United States Boxing Association, before devoting himself to making his fortune in the insurance industry. He became a multi-millionaire and was widely admired for his business acumen. He died on December 4, 2002, at age 77, as a result of a swimming accident. He had been body surfing when he was suddenly picked up by a powerful wave and slammed onto the beach. The force of that slam broke a vertebra in his neck. He was left paralyzed from his neck to his toes. When he died, he left behind a wife and nine children. He was also known as the man who had defeated one of the greatest middleweight champions of the twentieth century.

Of his bout with Chuck Davey, Rocky wrote,

> The next fall they talked me into this television fight with Chuck Davey [by promising me $50,000 for this fight]. I couldn't get near him and I lost, but that was no fight in my book. Sugar Ray was the last one. He threw the last real punch at me, and it was right to my jaw and that was the end of what begun 30 years before when my brother Joe pushed the big, soft glove in my face and I fell over backwards and my father laughed. . . .
>
> I knew that I didn't have to fight again—in the ring, or against the rest of the world, or against myself. It had finally sunk in. I was the winner now and forever, and nobody could ever take this title away from me. . . .
>
> Now, after 30 years, I knew that Rocky Bob Barbella had exploded for the last time.[1]

Rocky would never have to raise his fists in anger again. He would be able to laugh at himself, the world, and even his past. For him, the past was no longer prologue. He felt like a new man—reborn and relieved that his war with the world was over. And he had won.

Speaking of boxing years later, Rocky said,

> To be a fighter you can't be a smart guy. To get in the ring with anybody to fight you got to be a little wacky. Fighters are guys that, mostly all the fighters are guys of no education, with nothing, and the fight for survival is the fight. To be a fighter, that's the worst business. . . . I wouldn't recommend fighting anymore because it's a tough business, and it's a million-to-one shot you can make it. . . . Every time a guy fights he gets three or four stitches on his eyes, his mouth. Then the day after the fight you're all swollen, your head is swollen, your eyes are swollen, your body's swollen. It's a tough business man. It's a tough business.[2]

11

MR. SHOW BUSINESS

By the time Chuck Davey's boxing (and television) career ended in 1955, Rocky had emerged as a popular television personality. He began appearing on ABC-TV, following its broadcast of *Wednesday Night Fights*. In a program called *The Henny and Rocky Show*, professional comedian Henny Youngman and the professional boxer, now an amateur jokester, traded jests and spoke about the evening's bouts. Comedian Buddy Hackett occasionally appeared on the show, which also showcased popular singers. The show could last anywhere from five to 30 minutes, depending on how long the earlier fights had lasted, although most nights it was scheduled to air from 10:45 p.m. to 11:00 p.m. and was followed by a local news program.

On a regular basis, *The Henny and Rocky Show* featured a singer named Marion Colby as part of its lineup and a jazz combo with Buddy Weed on piano and Bobby Hackett on trumpet, both of whom provided a hip musical background to the jests of the eponymous hosts. Typical of the comic dialogues Henny and Rocky executed was this one: Henny asked Rocky how his friend, a man in prison, feels about being away from his girlfriend, who is one of the most beautiful, sexiest, and hottest women in the world. He questioned whether the friend can be certain she is being faithful to him. Isn't he worried she's fooling around with other men while he's locked up? Rocky replied no, because she's in prison too!

Another joke initiated by Rocky went as follows: A woman meets a guy at a singles weekend at a resort hotel in the Catskills. She asks him what he does for a living. He says he just got out of the joint. She asks what the joint is, and he responds it's prison. She asks what he was in for, and he says he killed his wife. She excitedly replies, "Oh, so now you're single!"

Other times, they traded one-liners built around a recap of each night's fight. In addition, for a few minutes, Henny would make fun of the day's news in a segment called "Ribber's Digest." The show was sponsored by Pabst Blue Ribbon beer and Mennen, a manufacturer of men's shaving products, deodorants, and colognes. Fighters, including Rocky, were referred to as Blue Ribbon pugilists.

Henny Youngman was an ideal partner for Rocky, who, in turn, was the ideal comic foil for Henny. Each of them loved one-liner jokes that ended with a quick uppercut punch line.

Henry "Henny" Youngman, whose jokes can be heard in the movie *Goodfellas*, was a comedian-cum-violinist who made one-liners famous in an era when lengthy jokes told as stories were the norm for stand-up comedians. His style has been used by many other comics, for example, Bob Hope, Rodney Dangerfield, and Johnny Carson in his monologues, as well as by other late-night comedic hosts of such shows as *The Tonight Show*, *Late Night*, *The Late Show*, *The Late Late Show*, *Last Call*, and so forth.

Walter Winchell, the most popular gossip columnist of the 1940s and 1950s, called Henny the "King of One-Liners," for he never depended on elaborate jokes to make his audiences laugh. The lines came quick and were delivered in a rapid-fire fashion in a raspy New York-accented voice. A joke rarely took longer than a few seconds. Thus, a series of one-liners could keep audiences guffawing minute after minute after minute, often for as long as a half-hour.

Henny's one-liners were direct and declaratory, as if his jokes were examples of the Euclidian principle that the shortest distance between two points is a straight (punch) line. Zing: his setups went right to unexpected punch lines. Because the punch lines were unexpected, audiences were invariably surprised, and they guffawed with gusto. Oftentimes listeners didn't even get a chance to pause in their laughter as one joke ended and another shot out of Henny's mouth. Typical jokes included the following: "My friend went to the doctor. The doctor gave him six months to live, then presented him with the bill. The patient said he couldn't pay the bill. The doctor gave him another six months!" Before the crowd could stop laughing at that one, Henny would hit them with another one, for instance, "My grandmother is over 80 and still doesn't need glasses. Drinks right out of the bottle." One more: "Some people ask the secret of our long marriage. We take time to go to a restaurant two times a week. A little candlelight, dinner, soft music, and dancing. She goes Tuesdays, I go Fridays."[1]

Henny, like Rocky, had a strong work ethic and would rather perform than do anything else. He regularly appeared in front of audiences, large and small, in theaters and nightclubs, more than 200 times in a single year. He regularly performed in nightclubs in New York City, Las Vegas, Los Angeles, Montreal, and Chicago. In addition to appearing in nightclubs and theaters, Henny took advantage of opportunities to perform at trade shows, sales meetings, corporate gatherings, and banquets, as well as on cruise ships and college campuses—anywhere there was an opportunity. He was relentless in taking advantage of opportunities presented to him and creating opportunities where few others would think to look.

For example, once when in a hotel elevator, he engaged his fellow passenger, a middle-aged man and father, in a brief conversation. Henny learned his companion was the proud father of a boy about to have his bar mitzvah in a ballroom on the second floor of the hotel. The comedian quickly offered a deal: If the father paid him $100, Henny would entertain the guests for 10 minutes; for $150, he would extend his engagement to 15 minutes. The father happily accepted the $150 offer, saying how thrilled his son and his guests would be to have Henny Youngman, the King of One-Liners, spritzing the audience with his famous repertoire of jokes.

If Henny could have worked every day, he would have welcomed the opportunity with delight. If he could have fit in brief engagements, like the one that emerged from the elevator conversation, he would have been doubly delighted.

With such a full schedule, Henny had been considered unavailable by producers to appear on a regular live television show; however, that was before being invited to cohost a show with the great Rocky Graziano. When the offer was made to Henny to appear on his own weekly show with Rocky, who, at the time, was more famous than Henny, Henny found himself unable to resist the opportunity. Rocky was one of the best-known former boxing champions. A number of sports reporters and Broadway columnists even claimed Rocky was more famous than many top-grossing movie stars and *Billboard*-topping popular singers. The hyperbole was typical of such columnists, whose opinions could change on a dime. To give their judgments a patina of credibility, they would often name a movie star, for instance, Clark Gable, or a popular singer, such as Frank Sinatra, as being more popular than Rocky. But grandiose comments were their stock in trade. And what they traded for those opinions could only be viewed from under a table.

Regardless of the accuracy of the judgment of hired commentators, Rocky's fame could not be denied, and it was certainly an advantage to Henny's reputation; indeed, some of that celebrity would rub off on Henny and help drive up his fees.

When working with Rocky on the show, which was broadcast live, Henny would arrive from a previous engagement and sometimes go to another one after the show, if such opportunities arose. Henny could never say no. Rocky had nothing but admiration for Henny's devotion to making a buck. The two got along like partners in crime.

The show not only made Rocky a bigger celebrity, but also increased demand for both performers. Calls from booking agents flooded Henny's apartment-based office and Rocky's home, where Norma jotted down every offer. Henny, not wanting to share his hard-earned fees with an agent, always negotiated deals himself. Unfortunately for Rocky, Henny became too popular. His out-of-town opportunities multiplied so rapidly and came so unexpectedly that Henny reluctantly decided he could no longer perform with Rocky; Henny's engagement on *The Henny and Rocky Show* turned out to be brief. Rocky was deeply disappointed; he had loved working with Henny and thought they made a great team. Although disappointed, Rocky thought the producers would find another partner for him. He knew he was sufficiently popular that his television career was not about to fizzle out.

The Henny and Rocky Show had premiered to positive reviews on June 1, 1955. Soon thereafter, reviewers lamented Henny's premature departure on June 29, for the show hardly had time to become a national treasure. Henny had galloped into the sunset to pursue other opportunities, leaving Rocky with no one but himself to banter with. Rocky wondered what would happen if the producers did not quickly find a replacement for Henny. Would the program go on? Would it be cancelled?

The producers did not have an immediate answer. Rocky obviously needed another comic to play against, but the producers procrastinated before deciding to take a chance and go without another comedian. They figured they could always change their minds, and without Henny on the show, they had reduced their production costs. They renamed the show *Rocky's Corner* and decided to periodically cast other comedians to see how they worked with Rocky, or even if a comedic partner was necessary. Buddy Hackett, for example, appeared a few times to fill the void, but the show was not the same without a steady counterpart for Rocky. He also needed someone who was a master of one-liners. The show had to have a quick-moving format. There was little time for drawn-out anecdotes. In addition, the audience wanted to see the same characters exchanging jests week after week. They found it unsettling that Rocky didn't have a steady counterpart. Sitcoms are built on a foundation of regularly occurring characters, as on the *Lucy-Desi Comedy Hour* of that era and later shows, for instance, *Seinfeld* and *The Mary Tyler Moore Show*. Thus, *Rocky's Corner* lost much of its original audience.

Rocky was obviously a talented and endearing jokester, but he needed to play against another person, someone who was more quick-witted than he. Rocky could be an ideal comic foil—like Lou Costello to another's Bud Abbott, but as a solo act, he was miscast. In the tried and true formula for comedic duos, Rocky was an ideal second banana, the perfect foil for a predominant comedian. With Henny, Rocky had been the slightly dim second to a brighter, quick-minded, fast-talking professional comedian. As the ratings slid, ABC decided to cancel the show, and it breathed its last laugh on August 10, 1955. It lasted for two months and 10 days, and then was gone, barely making a dent in the annals of television sitcoms.

Rocky thought a new show would come along, but he worried it might take years rather than months. Would his short-lived television career go on hiatus? Television and advertising executives had not counted out the Rock. They thought he was a unique character. His brief television career had caught the attention of not only television and advertising executives, but also producers and creators of numerous shows. He was a distinctive working-class personality whose appeal extended beyond blue-collar workers. Eclectic audiences enjoyed hearing his mangled syntax and Noo Yawkeese accent. Rocky had said that when he heard himself speaking in front of an audience, he sounded as if he had marbles in his mouth. Audiences, consisting of both the educated and uneducated, thought he was naturally funny. If teamed with the right comedian, he could be charmingly and endearingly funny. But who was that comedian?

A television writer, producer, and songwriter named Nat Hiken had been hired to write a new television show starring the inimitable Martha Raye. Hiken envisioned a character Rocky could play while essentially being himself. Hiken alone awakened Rocky from his briefly hibernating television career.

Rocky recounted to W. C. Heinz what had occurred:

> [Martha Raye] didn't discover me. . . . It was her writer, Nat Hiken. A guy calls my manager. I was at Stillman's [Gym], and the guy comes over. He says, "My name is Nat Hiken. You got an agent?" I said, "I got a friggin' manager named Irving Cohen." He says, "We're looking to maybe put you on *The Martha Raye Show*. We're looking for a boyfriend for Martha Raye."
>
> What Nat Hiken told me was some guy says, "Get some stupid guy like Rocky Graziano." Nat says, "Why not get Rocky Graziano?" The guy says, "He can't talk. He can't read." Hiken says, "I'll go see him."
>
> I go to this office. I meet Marlon Brando, and they give me a friggin' stupid script. Big words I can't pronounce. Hiken says, "Don't worry. The public doesn't know what the script is." I go on and the guys are sayin', "Great! Great!" I was playin' myself.[2]

And that's what the public loved: the real Rocky, playing himself—no frills, no phony façade, no actor's mask. He proved to be the perfect foil for Martha Raye. And her career benefited from her association with him. They worked together as smoothly as aerial acrobats catching one another without a net and enjoyed one another's company. The show was not taped; it was performed live every week. There were no re-dos. Rocky, although nervous at the outset, proved to be a true professional, never missing a beat, never missing a cue, never flubbing a line.

When it came to learning his lines, the Rock had wondered if he had the ability to memorize dialog for each of his skits. He was told not to worry. If he forgot a line, he was to stay in character and just say what would be natural for him. It was not flubbing lines; it was ad-libbing. The audience would never know the difference. He was encouraged to just be himself, and he was. In or out a costume, Rocky was always Rocky. When he appeared as a Boy Scout on *What's My Line?* he was Rocky. He couldn't be anything else, even if he tried. He was a natural ham and enjoyed being in front of a camera and getting laughs. He had quickly mastered the requirements of each of the characters he played, for each one was essentially him.

Raye and Hiken were impressed Rocky proved so adept at doing whatever the skits demanded of him. In addition, he was being handsomely paid without being punched. His weekly salary started at $500 but was soon increased to $2,500, once producers realized he was essential to the success of the show. Raye needed him as much as he needed her, and the producers needed both of them together. The show was proving to be a champion in the heavyweight ratings wars and a bonanza for advertisers.

It was obvious to everyone that Martha Raye had turned out to be a much better partner for Rocky than Henny Youngman. Nicknamed the "Big Mouth" because of her large, rubbery lips, Raye was considered one of the greatest female television comedians of her time—maybe one of the best of either sex. She was even considered funnier than Lucille Ball, her primary comedic rival on television. Both *TV Guide* and *Variety* thought she was the funniest lady on the tube. When on camera, she dominated the environment. No one, not even the most brilliant actors or comedians, could steal a scene from her. To miss seeing Raye on television was to miss a comedic genius at work. She was loud, sassy, boisterous, and capable of spitting out the best of slapstick routines on television. Moreover, she could sing beautifully and had numerous hit records. "What an amazing talent!" gushed television critics.

Raye had been a professional entertainer since her parents put her on a vaudeville stage at age three. Spending her childhood singing, dancing, and telling jokes, she was not given a formal education. Reading, writing, and arithmetic were not in her syllabus. No one ever took the time to teach her to read. What she learned came offhandedly from her parents, backstage hands, directors, producers, booking agents, and fellow performers. As she got older, her informal educators were men who seduced her or wanted to take advantage of her celebrity. They were like pilot fish clinging to a fast-moving shark. By the time Martha was an adult, she understood with considerable disappointment and embarrassment that she was considered illiterate by friends and colleagues. She carried the burden of her illiteracy with angry insecurity but did nothing to remedy her shortcoming. She was embarrassed she couldn't read the scripts Nat Hiken had written for her, so he had to read each one to her. At Martha's insistence, those readings occurred in private. How embarrassing it would have been for her if others witnessed her being read to because she was unable to read her own scripts.

By contrast, Rocky, the grade-school dropout, was able to read his own scripts, although he was often flummoxed by multisyllabic words he could not pronounce. While Rocky made self-deprecating jokes about his limited abilities and miserable education, Raye was so insecure about the manifestations of her lack of education that she was frequently fearful of being ridiculed by those with whom she worked. She would no more make a self-deprecating joke about her lack of education than she would have expected to have been cast as the female lead in *Gone with the Wind*. She sought to mitigate her anxieties and often erase them by seeking solace, approval, and adoration in the applause and laughter of her fans. If she could make people laugh and keep them laughing, and then keep them laughing some more, they would never know how uneducated she was. In fact, she could forget about her own ignorance at such times. For her, the best remedy was not remedial education, but being honored for her superb comedic talents. And because her show was broadcast live, the applause that fed her sense of self was real.

There was no canned laughter on *The Martha Raye Show*. Raye never doubted that she was a great comedian and that she was what brought her audiences to feverish pitches of hilarity, sometimes even doubled over, if not convulsed. Her loyal audiences confirmed and reconfirmed, week after week, that she was a superb comedian. Raye believed her audiences loved her. And she took immense pride in the fact that she never disappointed them. She never failed to make them laugh; her jokes and skits never fell flat, as they often do for other comedians. Her audiences arrived expecting to laugh and would have been surprised if it had turned out they were watching a sentimental soap opera.

In addition to the esteem her audiences bestowed upon her, Raye relied on the affection of men to bolster her self-image. There were many who wanted to be her lover and many she accepted. There were others who wanted to marry her, and she accepted numerous proposals (as if each one was an accolade) before dropping them into a wastebasket of fond memories. While she could show the face of a circus clown to her fans, her big mouth and rubbery lips were no obstacle for those who wanted to share her bed. Yet, while her sexual affairs and the laughter of audiences were a tonic for her inadequate sense of self, they were not enough.

When not performing, rehearsing, or having sex, Raye would drink excessively. Alcohol in enormous quantities became her self-hypnotizing weapon to keep reality at bay. It extinguished the fires of her low self-esteem, while fueling visions of inebriated grandiosity. In time, the grandiose visions would fade and be replaced by repellent self-appraisals. She loved being in front of the camera but not mirrors, with their honest evaluations. When the mirror's harsh reality became too much for her to bear and her exaggerated visions turned into satirical cartoons, Raye would fly into violent rages, throwing lamps, ashtrays, plates, glasses, and anything at hand. Sometimes her target would be the surrounding walls and other times the face of a man who she suspected had been sneering at her. Although she presented the laughing face of a clown to the public, her reputation for having an impetuous, violent, hair-trigger temper was escaping beyond the anodyne words of television publicists. Her instability and anger, which increasingly couldn't be assuaged, resulted in six miserably acrimonious divorces; her seventh marriage, which concluded with her death, was a trial with nightmare dimensions.

Raye's anger even extended to one of her greatest benefactors, Nat Hiken, who conceived and wrote episode after episode of *The Martha Raye Show*. Like many insecure stars with hungry egos who needed to impress the world with their manifold talents, Raye resented Hiken's creative role and made his life difficult. She wanted all the credit for herself and attempted to diminish Hiken's contributions when talking to the television reporters who had always written so enthusiastically of her talents. Her resentment of Hiken was regularly inflamed every time she had to sit through his readings of the scripts. She felt like an ignorant child and decided it was Hiken who made her feel that way. He had imprisoned her, and it was only in front of an audience that she felt free to display her extraordinary talents.

And though the television critics regularly praised her, they also praised Hiken as the genius behind the curtains. Raye resented the fact that although she was the one who got the laughs, the critics wrote that Hiken had engineered it all. They sang their praises for Hiken's ability to write wild comedy sketches. They also credited him with writing skits that showed the softer side of Raye and Rocky, giving them the kind of vulnerability audiences responded to with affection. Raye felt such comments cast doubt on the authenticity of her emotions. She further resented that Hiken took credit for coming up with a nickname Rocky hadn't heard except in the company of his Lower East Side pals. He became Raye's "Goombah," a word that refers to an Italian who is a criminal and/or an associate of criminals. For *The Godfather* , Mario Puzo wrote the famous line, "I don't care how many guinea Mafia goombahs come out of the woodwork."[3]

Raye couldn't bear the idea that the public and the critics thought Hiken might be pulling her strings. For her, Hiken was no puppet master. She would yell at him, curse him, challenge his masculinity, and, in fact, do almost anything to make his life miserable.

Hiken finally cut ties with the show and left to conceive, produce, and write other sitcoms, all of which were highly successful and generated multiple Emmy Awards. Raye had Hiken replaced by Norman Lear, the virtuoso creator of *All in the Family, The Jeffersons, Maude, Sanford and Son*, and *Good Times*, as well as other television comedies. Meanwhile, much to Raye's annoyance, Hiken's career took off like a rocket. Raye claimed he owed it all to her, for without his work on her show, he never would have achieved the success that made him one of television's most celebrated creators. He is perhaps most widely known today for his award-winning comedic plots for *The Phil Silvers Show* (aka *Sergeant Bilko*) and *Car 54, Where Are You?*

Although disliking scriptwriters, Martha was not an insecure prima donna when it came to sharing the stage and spotlight with other performers. In fact, she seemed to relish their presence, playing opposite them and even letting them perform solo on her show. She invited some of the best-known stars to be her guests, including such talents as Zsa Zsa Gabor, Art Carney, Buddy Ebsen, Errol Flynn, Buster Keaton, Harpo Marx, Vincent Price, Edward G. Robinson, and many others. And while Raye gave them free rein to use their talents to entertain her audiences, none of them could equal her comedic skills. She was the reigning champ of television comedy, and her steadfast sidekick was the most colorful middleweight boxer of the twentieth century, another kind of champ in his own right.

In the company of the greatest luminaries of show business, Rocky managed to hold his own. Producers and directors were surprised, for he had no theatrical training. Yet, he often proved the focal point of many of the comedic skits they cast him in. Nonetheless, when the baton was passed to Raye, she dominated the television screen with the fireworks of her routines, casting everyone else in her shadow. No matter how funny and charming Rocky could be, he was still a second banana, the perfect role for him. While he could say funny lines in his marbles-in-the-mouth style, he could not match his costar's natural ability to be a clown. He could not mug for the camera as she did by crossing her eyes, sticking out her tongue, contorting her eyebrows, opening her mouth wider than any human thought possible, and twisting her lips as if made of rubber bands. In addition, Raye could sing like a lark, and audiences loved the sound of her melodious voice. Rocky was happy just to be part of it, and he would often look at Raye with a proud smile on his face, the proud smile of not only her devoted goombah boyfriend, but also a man thrilled to be given the opportunity to be her second banana and have a highly regarded career in show business. His face beamed gratitude.

Hiken had written Rocky's part as someone who was a gentleman, slow to anger but always ready to pummel anyone who threatened or was about to take advantage of Raye. One such villain who regularly appeared on the show was smooth-talking, elegantly dressed actor Cesar Romero. Rocky's "dees," "dems," and "dos" diction was a comedic counterpoint to Romero's debonair use of seductive words stated with perfect diction. Audiences howled at the distinctions in how the two performers expressed themselves. They came from different worlds, if not different universes.

For viewers, it was apparent that Raye and Rocky were so good together they wondered if the two were off-screen lovers. In fact, they were good friends. Rocky was devoted to Norma, and as Paul Newman (who would portray Rocky in the movie version of *Somebody Up There Likes Me*) once said about why he didn't cheat on his wife, "I have steak at home. Why should I go out for hamburger?"[4]

Rocky and Raye were a team as much as Abbott and Costello, Laurel and Hardy, or Martin and Lewis, and although Raye had angered many with whom she worked, Rocky was not one of them. He was never the target of the harsh criticism she had frequently aimed at Hiken. For Rocky, Raye was the source of his television success, and so he held her in the highest regard. He told Irving Cohen that Raye had been instrumental in his achieving the success he enjoyed as an entertainer. Hiken had chosen him, and Raye elevated him to celebrity status. He would never say a bad word about either of them.

Of Martha, Rocky wrote,

> During the Second World War, nobody put out more than this chick, traveling all over the world entertaining servicemen in an outa hospitals. . . .
>
> She ain't a big girl, but she got more pepper in her ass than any 10 women t'rown together. When she opens her gapper you could see Brooklyn and hear her all the way back in Butte, Montana, where she was born, but her voice is pure gold.

Of Martha, Hiken, and others on the show, Rocky wrote, "I never in my life believed these great people could treat me like a king. Me, a poor fuckin' ex-hood from 10th Street and First Avenue."[5]

Rocky felt as if he were on top of the world and had it on a string. He loved the Frank Sinatra song "I've Got the World on a String." He felt he had earned not only fair remuneration for his part on the show, but also the respect and affection of people who had never seen him box, even the people who had no interest in boxing or perhaps even disliked the sport. And Rocky was no Pollyanna.

As a street kid and a boxer, he had learned early on that all good things must eventually come to an end, just as his middleweight crown had been placed on the head of another king of boxing, Tony Zale. And so for Raye and Rocky, their show had a short lifespan, although not as short as *The Henny and Rocky Show*. *The Martha Raye Show* had been a ratings bonanza for two seasons, making it a surefire ticket for high-priced ads. The incident that terminated the show was an event that ignited flames of anger in racist viewers, who were determined to burn down the source of their outrage.

A 12-year-old black girl named Gloria Lockerman had been a winner on the popular quiz show *The $64,000 Question*. She appeared as a guest, along with Tallulah Bankhead, on *The Martha Raye Show*. At the end of the show, Raye and Bankhead hugged and kissed the young girl. Thousands of people in the South and other conservative regions of the country sent vituperative letters of outrage, demanding the show be cancelled. How dare two white women hug and kiss a black child. The show's sponsors proved to be melting towers of wax for whom the word *backbone* was either a pejorative or something that had long ago become extinct. The ad agencies that made and placed the show's ads were mere sieves that believed in going along to get along. Spinelessness was the order of day. And so the show was cancelled, and neither Rocky nor Raye would ever again have a weekly comedy variety show on television.

At the time of the show's cancellation, Raye was devastated by her sense of failure. Her fifth marriage was heading for the sewer into which all failed marriages are flushed: divorce court. And to make matters worse, she was sued by her lover's 20-year-old pregnant wife for alienation of affection. The publicity was humiliating. She felt she was living in a nightmare that was getting louder, more intense, and prolonged. It was driving her to the edge of an abyss, and so she attempted suicide by taking an overdose of sleeping pills. She did not sleep the sleep of the dead, but her life had lost its mercurial spirit.

The clown princess of television was left with her collection of clowns. Rocky wrote, "Martha loves clowns, an she got them made outa glass, porcelain, stuffed, shaped like pillows, outa wood, little dolls, you name 'em, but nothing but clowns."[6]

The clowns and her patriotic devotion to the U.S. military and the soldiers it comprised were the only constants in her life. In her last years, her legs had to be amputated as a result of poor circulation. She also suffered from Alzheimer's disease. For her untiring work benefiting the USO and ministrations to wounded troops, she was buried as an honorary colonel in a military ceremony at Fort Bragg, North Carolina. She is the only civilian buried there, and each year, she receives military honors on Veterans Day.

And one of those who never failed to honor her was her second banana, the former middleweight boxing champion who had gone AWOL from the army, received a dishonorable discharge, and served a prison term at Leavenworth. Raye never remonstrated against Rocky for his delinquent military career.

While disappointed when the show was cancelled, Rocky was not about to go down for the count and lie on the canvas of a cancelled television career. He was more popular and better known than he had ever been. As a fighter, he had never given up, and now he would prove as tireless in pursuing opportunities as his former partner, Henny Youngman.

Rocky proved to be one of the most effective pitchmen advertising agencies could hire. For Post Raisin Bran cereal, he did a series of television ads in which he pretended to be a cowboy, tugboat captain, mountain climber, and zookeeper. His opposite in the commercials was an innocent young boy or a group of enthusiastic kids, along with a cartoon character who would count the number of raisins in each box of cereal. Each character Rocky played was obviously him in a ridiculous costume, and that was the joke: No matter which costume he wore, Rocky was always Rocky, the character beloved by millions of television watchers. He was the same lovable guy millions of people had seen for two years on *The Martha Raye Show*. Audiences were charmed, and the sales of Post Raisin Bran skyrocketed. It was another unanimous decision for Rocky. He was unstoppable—the undisputed champ.

When not performing in national ads, Rocky was in demand for many local products and services. In local business ads, he sang the praises of his clients. In one for Shell Barn Discount Beverage Center, Rocky is seen holding a mug of cold beer as he advises viewers to get their beer and soda at Shell Barn. Lenny's Clam Bar, another local business, which consisted of a group of Italian seafood restaurants located in and around New York, featured Rocky touting its culinary delights, naming a mouth-watering array of delicious seafood specials and then mixing happily with restaurant patrons. When New York legalized off-track betting on horse races, Rocky proved to be a natural, doing commercials for the Off-Track Betting Corporation. He was also the spokesperson for Lee Myles Transmissions. He could be seen and heard talking about the taste sensations afforded by a local fruit juice company. And who better than Rocky, Raye's goombah, to tout a chain of pizzerias?

Years later, on the *Tonight Show Starring Johnny Carson*, he would joke about the money he made doing commercials. When asked how many commercials he had made, he responded, "More than 5,000!" He had an extraordinary run, the ex-hood from 10th Street and First Avenue. But there was more to come, much more.

Rocky wrote,

> I love bein a TV salesman almost more than anything I ever done. I got so good at it I could sell some of those Texas oil millionaires the Pacific Ocean and make 'em believe they was buying the biggest swimming pool you ever seen.
>
> Lately, I even started producing my own commercials for some pretty good companies, I'm doing great at it.[7]

Indeed, he was great at it. Rocky became a multimillionaire, and he was a million figurative miles from where he had started out.

12

ON THE BIG SCREEN

Rocky's career gained legendary status with the publication of his auto-biography, *Somebody Up There Likes Me*, written with Rowland Barber and published in 1955. After a brilliant PR campaign and countless posi-tive reviews, the book shot up on the *New York Times* best-seller list and made Rocky Graziano a household name. Riding on a New York subway or bus, there were always numerous people reading the book. Italy was another story altogether: *Somebody Up There Likes Me* was a smashing success, not only on mass transit, but also in homes and libraries through-out the country, as the book took off like a rocket and orbited as a number-one Italian best seller for months.

Rocky was celebrated as a formerly poor paisan who had made it big in the land of immigrants. He was a hero, a role model, an icon as popular as another paisan who had made a success of his life, Frank Sinatra. People in the United States who had never watched a boxing match, never read the sports pages of newspapers, or never heard of *Ring* magazine suddenly knew the name of the former middleweight fighter. The book was so popular one of the author's neighbors, an Italian cop and boxing fan, named his dog Rocky. The dog just happened to be a boxer.

Somebody Up There Likes Me was reviewed in book pages, as well as sports pages. Rocky was a guest on numerous television and radio inter-view shows, where he played the part of a palooka to the hilt, complete with marbles-in-his-mouth diction (he sounded as if he had taken diction lessons from former light heavyweight champion and actor Slapsie Maxie Rosenbloom). Audiences loved Rocky, for he was charming, self-deprecating, witty, and seemingly fun-loving. He no longer showed signs of being an angry, vicious street hoodlum who would beat the crap out of someone, belting, gouging, and kicking his opponent into pathetic submission. The young man's anger was long gone, cooled or evaporated and replaced with an easygoing, warm, good-humored nature inhabiting the soul of a guy who was grateful boxing had saved him from a life of crime, as well as a life sentence and perhaps even the electric chair. Boxing had opened a door to a new life, and Rocky had raced through that open doorway as if hot on the trail of an elusive dream. Unlike many others, he had caught the dream, and the dream became him. He wore it as if it had been tailor-made for him.

Boxing, while the most violent of sports, had taught Rocky compassion and respect for others less fortunate than he was. He had developed an ability to empathize with the plights of those struggling to survive, especially old, forgotten boxers, some of whom had been permanently damaged while trying to attain fame and fortune. They had failed, their dreams were shattered, their futures were without hope, and they now lived poor, hand-to-mouth existences, for there are no unions for boxers, no pensions. Some became taxi drivers, some bartenders, and others construction workers—whatever was necessary to keep a roof over one's head and food on the table. Theirs had been a tough life, tougher than most. They had been society's disposable gladiators. They not only finished out of the money, but also had scars and misshapen bones in their hands and noses—borne as signs of the profession by even the most successful boxers.

Rocky knew that if you're not a champ or a contender, you exist in the shadows of those who are. His father, Fighting Nick Bob, was a sad example of the failed and bitter boxer. And while the history of boxing celebrates the champions, there is a much larger history of the broken men who never made it to the top. Rocky didn't have to read history books to know the fate of most of his brethren. He merely had to look at the fading phantom of success that existed in his father's dreams.

In the fraternity of boxers, whether champs or has-beens, there was no one more generous than Rocky, for he had manifested his empathy in his financial generosity. Rather than trumpeting his financial generosity to those in need, Rocky's autobiography serves as an inspiration and a challenge to others, whether aspiring boxers or otherwise, to enter life's arenas and fight to realize one's dreams—to never give up, never give in to despair. Never settle for feeling that you're a loser. When you feel as if you've been backed against the ropes, keep punching. Rocky's story, after all, is a classic American rags-to-riches tale, one of almost Dickensian dimensions, where a scrappy, tough street urchin goes from dire, bleak poverty to the comforts of wealth, from blinding, burning anger to having a warm, clear-eyed understanding of those he once hated; it is a story of how boxing started out as a vehicle for expressing anger and bitterness but became a form of therapy for extinguishing the flames of anger and diluting the acid of bitterness. Boxing had been the natural occupation for a thug, and once the thug realized he was no longer a hoodlum, no longer needed to be a thug, he found himself a new man, redeemed and at one with himself and the world around him. Rocky's life became an extraordinary odyssey of personal growth. Boxing made Rocky, and Rocky made boxing into one of the most popular sports during the years he boxed. The two came together like a clenched fist in a boxing glove.

The following appeared in a review of Rocky's autobiography in the *New York Times*, written by Orville Prescott:

> These are the words of an honest man who won a harder battle than most people ever face, the battle with himself. A rough diamond still and hardly a drawing-room type is the man Rocky Graziano. But, with the aid of Mr. Barber he is the author of a book with a kick like his own Sunday punch.[1]

The book sold more than one million copies and made Rocky a rich man. His life had taken him from the Lower East Side of poverty and deprivation to the Upper East Side of affluence, comfort, and eminence. While the Upper East Side of Manhattan and the Lower East Side are two neighborhoods only a few miles apart, for the residents of each the separation can seem like the distance between stars in the heavens. Rocky's uptown journey was one only the most ambitious, talented, and determined are fated to take.

Such a story was perfect for the movies. It would have audiences cheering in their hearts for the dead-end kid as he made his way to the top of the boxing world. Hollywood would not have to spend millions of dollars promoting the movie, for the book had already created a ready and welcoming audience.

In the spring of 1955, the hottest young movie star was James Dean. Producers thought he would be dynamite in the role of Rocky Graziano, although some had reservations and thought the slender, blonde, Aryan-looking actor would be miscast as a swarthy, muscular Italian. Nevertheless, he signed to play the role and agreed to spend hours daily in a gym to build a muscular physique. But in September of that year, Dean was killed in an automobile crash when his 1955 Porsche Spyder was rammed by a Ford sedan, whose driver could not see the low-slung silver sports car racing down a rural California highway. In death, Dean went on to be a bigger star than in life.

The part of Rocky was then offered to Montgomery Clift, who had played a conscience-driven, reluctant boxer in the movie *From Here to Eternity*. Clift turned down the part, as he had turned down the leads in *Sunset Boulevard* and *On the Waterfront*, a pair of misguided career decisions if ever there were ones. James Darren and Rod Taylor were also considered for the part and given screen tests but were ultimately rejected. Next among the aspirants was relative newcomer Paul Newman, who had screen tested with James Dean for a part in *East of Eden* but was passed over. (That screen test, if you're interested, can be viewed on YouTube.) A number of Hollywood executives thought Newman should not be given the part because he had been critically derided for his acting in the 1954 movie *The Silver Chalice*, a box-office failure that was dismissed by the critics, who devoted paragraphs to the hiss of their snidely scoffing sniggers. The final decision to have Newman play the part was reached after he received plaudits for his critically acclaimed portrayal of a boxer in the television drama *The Battler*. He had surprised directors and producers with the extraordinary authenticity he brought to the role. Many viewers thought Newman must have been a boxer-turned-actor.

For the part of Norma, Eva Marie Saint was considered because of her role as the girlfriend of former boxing character Terry Malloy, portrayed by Marlon Brando in *On the Waterfront* (Brando had studied Rocky, watched films of his fights, and copied his walk and speech patterns not only for the role of Terry Malloy, but also for that of Stanley Kowalski in *A Street Car Named Desire*). If Dean had gotten the part of Rocky, the team of Dean and Saint would have given the film two northern European blondes playing the roles of an Italian and a Jew. Instead of casting Eva Marie Saint in the part of Rocky's wife Norma, the part went to dark-eyed, brunette beauty Pier Angeli, who proved ideal: She was sweet, reticent, warm, and loving, not one of Alfred Hitchcock's "calm, cool, collected blondes."

Eileen Heckart, who was six years older than Paul Newman, was cast as Rocky's mother and delivered a sympathetic and credible performance. This was only her second movie, but she would go on to act in films for the next 40 years.

Harold J. Stone, who was often called upon to play tough, urban ethnics, was cast as Rocky's father, Fighting Nick Bob. His character appeared to be only slightly better off than a street bum, and that portrayal annoyed Rocky. He wrote, "I tell them [the director, star, and producer] I don't like . . . how brutal and dirty they make my old man. They never once show him with a fresh shave, and always in a torn, beat-up, dirty undershirt."[2]

Everett Sloane plays the part of Rocky's patient and paternalistic manager, Irving Cohen. Sloane's first movie role was in the celebrated classic *Citizen Kane*, and he would appear as one of Hollywood's premier character actors in more than 25 films.

Romolo, Rocky's closest pal and a member of his gang, is played by Sal Mineo, who had become a star after his performance in *Rebel without a Cause* with James Dean. Mineo told Rocky why he so loved the part of Romolo, saying, "You know something, Rocky, this is one pitcha I don't have to act in. Down here on the East Side is just like the Italian neighborhood I came from in the Bronx. We useta do all these things up there too."[3]

Another member of Rocky's gang is Steve McQueen, whose role is uncredited. Years later, Newman and McQueen would argue about which one of them should receive top billing in *The Towering Inferno*. In addition to ultimately sharing top billing, it was agreed that both actors would receive the same amount of money and same number of lines (the egotism of movie stars may be unmatched by mere mortals).

Another uncredited role is performed by Angela Cartwright as Rocky's daughter Audrey. Cartwright made six more movies after *Somebody Up There Likes Me* and was credited in each one.

Other actors who debuted in the movie but are uncredited for their roles are Frank Campanella and Dean Jones, both of whom went on to have successful big-screen and television careers.

Al Silvani, who worked with Rocky's trainer, Whitey Bimstein, and was often in Rocky's corner during his fights, plays the part of Rocky's unnamed cutman. He played the same part in 1976, as Rocky Balboa's cutman in the first of the *Rocky* movies.

The movie was directed by Robert Wise, whose list of directorial credits includes the 1949 critically acclaimed boxing movie *The Set-Up*, starring Robert Ryan and Audrey Totter. It is considered one of the best noir boxing movies and was one of Wise's favorites. Based on Wise's success directing that movie and its positive critical reception, producers thought he would be an ideal director for *Somebody Up There Likes Me*. Wise is also known for such hits as *West Side Story*, *The Sound of Music*, *I Want to Live*, *Star Trek: The Motion Picture*, and many other award-winning movies. Earlier in his career he was nominated for an Academy Award for editing *Citizen Kane*, which is considered one of the most influential and admired American movies of the twentieth century.

The movie adaptation of Rocky's autobiography was written by Ernest Lehman, who had previously written the screenplay for *Sabrina* and would go on to write such award winners as *The King and I*, *The Sweet Smell of Success*, *North by Northwest*, *The Sound of Music*, *Who's Afraid of Virginia Woolf?*, and *Hello, Dolly*, among many others.

Robert Wise was a stickler for gritty realism and decided to film at Manhattan locations that figured in Rocky's life. The scenes that take place at Stillman's Gym are some of the rare cinematic views of what was once the most prominent boxing gym in the United States. Other locales include Rikers Island prison in the East River; the Tombs jail in Lower Manhattan; the Brooklyn Bridge; and a number of tenements, bars, and pool halls. The movie was filmed in black and white, which heightens its grittiness. Most of the daytime scenes were shot on location, while nighttime ones were filmed in studios, where the darkness would not reveal the artificiality of sets.

The movie compresses the life of Rocky, but it is accurate in dealing with the low points and high points of his life. One sees that Rocco has a hard-bitten, poverty-stricken childhood. He frequently endures beatings delivered by his father. He becomes the leader of a wild street gang of young criminals. He is caught committing crimes and sent to prison. After his release, he is drafted into the army and goes AWOL. Desperate for money, he takes up boxing and proves to be a natural at it; however, before his career can take off, he is arrested by military police and sent to prison for a year. Upon his release, he returns to boxing and meets Norma Unger; they fall in love and marry. Rocky loses a title fight to Tony Zale.

A gangster attempts to blackmail him about his having gone AWOL and served time in prison so that he will take a dive in his next fight. Rocky fakes an injury to avoid the fight. He is investigated by a district attorney and refuses to name the blackmailer, so his license to box is revoked. His manager gets him a rematch with Tony Zale in Chicago, and after taking a terrible pounding, Rocky wins the bout and is now a world champion. He returns to New York and is feted by the cheers of friends and neighbors in his old neighborhood, and the movie ends as Rocky, Norma, and Irving are being driven in an open convertible through the streets of the Lower East Side, as if they are returning war heroes. As the credits roll, Perry Como sings the title song, "Somebody Up There Likes Me." The movie was an enormous hit, winning the plaudits of critics immediately after its openings in San Francisco and New York.

But before filming could begin, the alumnus of the Yale School of Drama and the Actors Studio had to learn to become Rocky Graziano, which was no easy achievement. To give a convincing portrayal, Newman moved in with Rocky. He learned to walk like Rocky, slouch like Rocky, speak like Rocky, hunch his shoulders like Rocky, and be wary of strangers like Rocky—and be inarticulately tender to Pier Angeli. He even learned to spit like Rocky. He is filled with Rocky's nervous energy and restlessness. He seems always on the move, jittery and anxiously aware of his surroundings and about to take off like a startled deer hearing the discharge of a hunter's gun. Together, they returned to Rocky's old haunts. They played pool together on the Lower East Side. They drank beer together in neighborhood bars. They ate their meals together in Rocky's favorite local Italian restaurants. They had egg creams together in the candy store where Norma and Rocky's sister used to hang out. The two guys even smoked the same kinds of cigarettes.

Newman got to meet several of Rocky's former gang members, at least those who were not in prison or dead. Rocky gave Newman precise boxing lessons, teaching him how to jab with his left, deliver a right cross, slip punches, feint with one fist and deliver with the other, bob and weave, and fake being hurt to draw in your opponent and then wallop him on the jaw. He taught Newman how to use the speed bag and heavy bag, and the proper way to skip rope.

Like the great acting student he was, Newman proved to be a natural, and Rocky was duly impressed. Newman had been athletic since his teenage years, when he worked in his father's sporting goods store. He had been an excellent tennis, baseball, and basketball player. He was an adept, skillful skier. To learn the necessary skills of a boxer and develop the well-muscled body of a fighter, Newman trained for six hours a day at Stillman's Gym. He was not yet a star, so no one paid attention to him. During the long, arduous hours he spent at the gym, he was able to transform his lithe, long, lean muscles into bulging, rock-like ones. He developed strong biceps and a washboard of stomach muscles. At the conclusion of his training, he had a hard body that looked as convincing as Rocky's was. Newman was able to imitate the moves of a boxer and seemed to have inhaled the aura of a pugilist. Rocky said that, other than Newman's handsome face (which no boxer had), the actor had the physique of a well-trained and disciplined boxer, and although Newman could never be a boxer, he could certainly portray one.

Newman stated, "I tried to find universal physical things that he did . . . or emotional responses that he had to certain things, that would allow me to create not the Rocky Graziano, but a Graziano. . . . There were two things that I discovered about him. One was that there was very little thought connected with his responses; they were immediate and emotional. Another was that there was a terrific restlessness about him, a kind of urgency and thrust."[4]

After meeting Newman, Rocky was smitten, saying,

> He makes everybody laugh, and even though he kids me I could see right off there ain't one thing phony about this guy. Maybe there was. He was too good lookin. In fact, the guy is pretty. That didn't matter because I knew they could fix up an flatten his nose for the part, an if they couldn't I could do it for them. I could see in the guy's eyes that he was a fighter. He's got bright blue eyes, but when you look in 'em you see a hard look dancing around inside. Only one other guy I ever see these same eyes on an that was Frank Sinatra. When their blue eyes spot a wiseguy, the eyes say, "Don't fuck with me, man!"[5]

Newman and Wise wanted to know more about Rocky's early family life and inner emotional life than what was portrayed in the autobiography and the script for the movie. For Newman, it would be a means of developing a greater understanding of the character he was determined to play as honestly as possible. For Wise, it meant being able to film Rocky with the greatest possible intimacy, understanding, and empathy. Hence, one night, in an effort to get Rocky to elaborate on his life story and reveal some previously hidden emotional core, Newman and Wise took him to a local bar and attempted to get him inebriated. Rocky kept ordering drinks for his two interlocutors, who proceeded to get tipsy and then completely drunk.

Instead of hearing an amplified version of Rocky's life, the star and the director poured out their own life stories. Rocky, like a brilliant psychoanalyst, kept asking gently probing questions. He learned all about Newman and Wise, from their childhoods to the present. By the end of the evening, Rocky was the only one who was sober. When the stories had been completed and the bar was about to close, Rocky suggested they all leave. He had to guide his two wobbly, shuffling compatriots to a taxi. He opened the door for them and seemed to pour their thoroughly relaxed and slackened bodies onto the back seat. The actor and director, in slurred voices, bid Rocky a good night. Rocky laughed, shut the taxi door, wished his friends a safe voyage home, and strode to his own home, a big grin on his face. He and Norma would laugh about it later that night.

A less humorous event occurred when Tony Zale was hired to play himself in the movie. Wise thought it would add a great sense of gritty verisimilitude to have Rocky's most formidable opponent appear as himself. It was a decision made without consideration for the consequences. No one, including the director and his star, considered that Newman wasn't a real boxer. Yet, he would be put in the ring with a tough world champion whose first instinct would be to slug anyone who landed a hard punch on him. It's what professional boxers do. And the Man of Steel was no exception, never mind that a boxer's hands are considered lethal weapons, especially when brought to bear against someone who isn't a boxer.

Rocky describes what occurred as follows:

> Paul is in top shape, and he learnt how to t'row a pretty good punch himself, but he ain't no match for an ex-middleweight champ, let alone any pro.
>
> They tell Zale to let Newman get in punches, that Newman's gonna pull head punches but not the body punches. But then, if you know Zale, anything Newman can't t'row is gonna feel like powder puffs against "The Man of Steel," as the sportswriters call Zale.
>
> They warm up in the ring, doing some footwork and shadowboxing, getting useta each other being there. . . . All of a sudden, Newman

grabs his side, doubles up a little, and yells, "Whoa, man! You trying to fucking kill me?"

I jump up in the ring and grab the Polack. I yell at 'im. "What the fuck you doin?"

"I didn't mean it Rock."[6]

A production conference, which included Newman and Zale, took place. After several minutes of apologizing, acting as if he finally understood what was expected of him, Zale insisted he would pull his punches. He would avoid hurting the star. Everyone agreed they should go on with the scene.

Newman and Zale resumed their performance, attempting to recreate one of the most famous bouts in boxing history, and also the bloodiest of the Graziano–Zale trilogy of fights—maybe even one of the bloodiest fights of the 1940s. Rocky quickly noticed Zale had begun taking a professional stance. "This is trouble," he muttered. Rocky could see it about to happen. Zale initially threw a couple of easy right hooks to Newman's head, following up with a powerful right punch to Newman's gut, sending him to the canvas, where he sprawled and wriggled in pain, gasping for air. Newman overcame the initial pain and stood and yelled at Zale, letting him know he had had enough and was leaving the set. That was the end of Zale's part in the movie.

The producer paid Zale what was owed to him and sent him away. His movie career was short-lived and inconsequential. Newman was relieved he wouldn't have to face Zale in the ring again, but he still had to nurse his sore ribs for a month. Whoever would replace Zale would have to avoid landing anything harder than a powder-puff blow to Newman's midsection. And who would that replacement be? The producer and director scurried to find their guy; it had to be someone who resembled Zale.

They spoke with casting agents, looked at photos of dozens of actors, and held a series of open auditions, but no one fit the requirements. Finally, they discovered someone who wasn't an actor. He was a local bartender with a broken nose who had been a successful college and amateur boxer, thus the broken nose. He was eager to be in the picture and get away from mixing drinks. He not only proved to be adept at mimicking the style of Zale, but also looked enough like him to convince audiences he was the genuine article.

Following completion of the movie, Newman was interviewed by the press and stated no one should attempt to follow in Rocky's path. Few people are tough enough to survive such a life and then write a book about it and have a movie made of it. He hoped young men would be inspired by the movie but not look upon it as a road map.

Of Rocky as a friend and source for understanding what was necessary for the role of portraying him, Newman explained Rocky never took offense at his jokes and jests. Rocky was actually amused by the way Newman mumbled, spoke with a New York accent, and bounced and shuffled along like a second incarnation of the fighter. In fact, Rocky thought Newman had so mastered the role that he did it better than Rocky had ever done it. Newman admitted, of course, that it was acting. Rocky's life had been a brutal one devoted to surviving. Newman could portray that, but he never had to live it.

And what did Rocky think of Newman's performance? "All the news-paper guys was sayin the same about him [Newman] as they said about Jimmy Dean, that he was copyin Brando, but me for one, I knew, watcha saw was watcha got. If ya ask me, I say all three of them, Brando, Dean, and Newman, were copyin me," he said.[7]

In addition to the image of his father in the movie that Rocky found insulting, one other thing about the movie disturbed him. He wrote that his home was not the dump portrayed in the movie:

> The thing I don't like is the apartment they made out to be where I lived as a kid. Sure, the tenement house was a broken-down rat and roach trap, but inside the apartment we lived in was always clean. In the movie they made it out a scurvy, dirty hole that wasn't fit for animals. I gotta say, that even though my mom was sick a lot, and they never had any good furniture because we were so poor, she still kept the house always neat 'n clean, an the curtains an sheets, torn an sewed I don't know how many times, were still always washed 'n ironed.[8]

The movie proved a great success, making Paul Newman a star who could choose whatever roles he wanted to play and presenting Rocky Graziano as a real-life rebel and reformed criminal. As a rebel, he certain-ly was the real deal compared with James Dean and Marlon Brando, whose rebel images were manufactured by Hollywood's hype machinery. The character Newman portrayed was appealing to not just impression-able teenage boys who were experimenting with their own roles as rebels, but also millions of moviegoers of all ages who saw dedication, spunk, and decency overcoming sloth, anger, and criminality. Nevertheless, Bosley Crowther, in the *New York Times*, headlined his review "Hate Worked for Him." His review continues,

> In this asserted biography of Rocky Graziano, who rose from reform school and penitentiary to the middleweight championship of the world, the prize ring is highly recommended as a fine place to vent his spleen and gain for himself not only money, but also public applause and respect.
>
> If this broad-minded commendation seems a little too kindly disposed, not only toward public attitudes, let it be noted that this picture is essentially a hard-boiled romance, more sentimental than censorial and more forgiving than stern.[9]

Crowther goes on to provide a synopsis of the plot. He concludes his review by writing, "Robert Wise's direction is fast, aggressive, and bright, and the picture is edited to give it a tremendous crispness and pace. The representation of the big fight of Graziano and Tony Zale is one the whoppingest slugfests we've ever seen on the screen."[10]

The friendship between Rocky and Newman continued well beyond the making of the movie. They continued to get together on a regular basis to drink beer and gossip about movies and boxing. Rocky said the thing he learned from Newman was how to guzzle beer, a pastime they both enjoyed. While Rocky put on considerable weight from beer drinking and a love of pasta after his boxing career concluded, Newman would regularly go on crash diets to slim down for his movie roles. Although they enjoyed getting together, Newman refrained from beer drinking while acting. He did claim that one of the things he learned from Rocky that never left him was his ability to spit.

Rocky embraced fame and fortune, and Norma and his kids. Anyone who knew him in the old days and had lost track of him in the ensuing years would not have recognized the happy, affluent man-about-town he had become. But Rocky wore his fame lightly; he was neither arrogant nor standoffish. He was always happy to say hello to those who recognized and greeted him on the street or in bars and restaurants. If someone asked for his autograph, he readily signed whatever they put in front of him. He helped friends in need. In fact, he never forgot a friend. He had left his old life, but its characters still played a part in his new one.

Reflecting on where he had come from and where he landed, he was amazed at his good fortune. His had fought his way through a tough passage, but he now had a good life. And when he grinned, you could almost miss the scars on his face, which served as a map of that daunting passage.

13

THE MAN AND THE ICON

Famous and wealthy, the subject of many admiring stories in newspapers and magazines, Rocky felt he could be true to his new disarmed self. There was nothing left for him to fight against. He was one of life's winners, and he wore that mantel with modesty and charm, and expressed it through his many acts of munificence. If there was ever a picture of a man redeemed and transformed, it was Rocky Graziano. His old friend, the great sportswriter W. C. Heinz, was as much impressed by the new Rocky as he had been by the old battling pugilist. The earlier incarnation of Rocky was of a man who wanted to tear the heads off his opponents; the transformed Rocky wanted to help those in need.

The early Rocky offered occasional instances of the thoughtful generosity that would become a larger part of his later life. Heinz relates a story that had not been previously publicized:

> The Christmas of the first year that he had made any real money he bought a six-year-old Cadillac and loaded it with $1,500 worth of toys. He drove it down to his old East Side neighborhood, and he handed out the toys to the kids and another $1,500 to their parents. He never mentioned it, but it came out because a trainer at Stillman's [Gym] who lived in the neighborhood had seen it. [1]

While such acts stimulated deep feelings of admiration and friendship in not only Heinz, but also in Irving Cohen, it made Irving worry that Rocky was so generous he would not look after his own financial well-being. In fact, Irving was so concerned he thought Rocky was in jeopardy of giving away such a large portion of his hard-earned money that he would not have sufficient funds to support his family after he had retired from boxing. He asked Rocky to have dinner with him one night at P. J. Clarke's, a favorite Third Avenue hangout for Rocky, where he had a table permanently reserved for himself and his friends. Heinz reported the following conversation between Rocky and Irving:

> "Look, Rocky," Irving Cohen said to him, "It's nice to do things like that, but you haven't got that kind of money, and you've got to save money. You won't be fighting forever."
> "Sure thing," Graziano said, "but those are poor people. They're good people. They never done no wrong. They never hurt nobody. They never got a break."[2]

Still not satisfied Rocky would do the right thing for himself and his family, Irving refused to give up until he got Rocky to at least consider an option he was about to propose. As they ate dinner, Irving suggested that Rocky invest large sums of his money in annuities, for they would pay regular monthly dividends throughout his retirement. Rocky silently listened, occasionally nodding along, and when Irving had finished talking, Rocky smiled at his paternalistic manager and said, "Sure. Sign me up. Good idea."

Another example of Rocky's concern for others and generosity was evidenced in his treatment of a destitute harmonica player who hung around Rocky and his entourage. Less for Rocky's entertainment than for Rocky's amusement, the harmonica player performed idiosyncratic renditions of his three favorite tunes: "Bugle Call Rag," "Beer Barrel Polka," and "Darktown Strutters' Ball." The poor guy knew no other tunes. What made his renditions so uniquely idiosyncratic was that he played the three tunes by pressing the harmonica to his nostrils. He claimed it had taken years of practice to develop that virtuoso ability, and he was not about to abandon it so he could play like any other harmonicist. He would never be considered a typical French harpist, he said. Rocky tried every which way to find the old tunesmith a job, but no one wanted to hire him. Rocky, an easy touch, would give the poor guy some money on a regular basis. Rocky pretended the money was payment for the tunes the harmonicist played.

Regardless of such acts of friendship, Rocky told a reporter that he only associated with millionaires because they never asked to borrow money. The irony of his statement was not lost on the reporter, who smiled and shook his head as if he was in on the joke. The comment, when reported to readers, only served to reinforce the image of Rocky as a man of wealth.

The image of Rocky as a man of wealth started immediately after newspapers reported how much he had earned from his bouts with Tony Zale. His money attracted those who came out of the darkness and shadows, and into the light of Rocky's world. They wanted some of Rocky's money. They came ever closer to him like moths to a brilliantly lit dollar sign. Had Rocky been a flame of pure selfishness, he would have incinerated the moths or they would have flown away. But that was not Rocky's way. It wasn't only that he was an easy touch. He was more than that. To those who wanted to cash in on their association with Rocky, he was a walking, talking bank balance. In the gun sights of the avaricious, Rocky was a broad target; he was perceived as sustenance by those hunters of wealth who stalk the land looking for likely victims. Rocky gloried in his affluence. And why not—he had come from the bottom of the barrel of poverty into a fertile land where everything was available to him. But, of course, such pride in one's affluence ignites flames of envy in those who feel fate has kicked out their teeth.

And so it happened. That a former thief would become the target of thieves was not an irony Rocky had ever conceived. He could readily admit that in his teenage years and early 20s, he had been a member in good standing of a fraternity of thieves. But he had always been a stand-up guy, never snitched on anyone, never traded his safety for theirs, never cheated a member of his gang. Yes, he had gone straight, but he never gave up on his old pals. Nevertheless, the unexpected happened: a brazen theft of the symbols of Rocky's affluence. It was like a left to the gut, a right to the chin.

Rocky soon realized he was being seen through the wrong end of a telescope. In the distance, he was simply seen as just another wealthy celebrity. He was no longer viewed close-up, as an honest-to-God Noo Yawk character. Those with larceny on their brains and greed in their hearts could not see a human being with whom they could relate to on a one-to-one basis. For them, Rocky was not a guy beloved by many, loyal to a fault, and generous to friends and relatives. He was a "Mr. Money Bags," to be ripped off and treated with contempt. The distorted view from the hellhole inhabited by thieves was worse than myopic: It was vile and unreal. It had been reported throughout town that Rocky had a closet filled with the most expensive suits and sports jackets, many of which were custom made. For a guy who primarily wore sweaters and polo shirts, the suits and sports jackets were a sign of superfluous, conspicuous consumption.

A headline on an inside page in the *New York Times* told of the result: "20 Graziano Suits Loot of Burglars."[3] Rocky and Norma had returned to their home in Brooklyn to find the front door ajar. Lights that had been off were now on. Rocky immediately knew it was a break-in and told Norma to wait outside. After he had inspected the premises and realized no one was lurking in the shadows or hiding under the beds or in the closets, he asked Norma to come inside. While her closets were bountiful, his were destitute. Not one suit, not one sports jacket remained. The thieves even took the hangers.

Rocky and Irving tried to keep news of the burglary quiet, for such acts only attracted more villainous actors and made the victim look vulnerable; however, a neighbor who lived in the same two-family house as the Grazianos discovered, much to her dismay, that her husband's suits had been stolen too. Did the thieves think those suits might also have belonged to Rocky? She later said she didn't know what the thieves thought. How could she?

When she discovered the burglary, she immediately called the police. She didn't spend time wondering who the thieves might be. Her call to the police was like a starter's pistol being fired, and reporters—who hang around local precincts and listen to police radios—raced from their starting lines to the scene, their pens and pads at the ready, and then spread their stories far and wide. Some of those reporters, having grown cynical covering crime, laughingly speculated that one of Rocky's former opponents had stolen his suits. Which of his opponents was the same size as Rocky? Others speculated that perhaps it was a haberdasher intent on replenishing his inventory. What better sales pitch was there than announcing that Rocky Graziano's suits were for sale? Of course, all the suits were the same size, so the buyers would have to be of the same measurements as the middleweight champion. Others pondered the irony that a former prince of thieves had been deposed and was now the victim of anonymous thieves.

Years later, Rocky would not be portrayed as the victim of thieves, but as an associate of thieves of a different kind—life-threatening extortionists. The news stories that followed were an embarrassment to Rocky and his family, but there was nothing he could do to counter the fabrications. It happened in the 1960s, years after Rocky had retired and become a television celebrity. Rocky became headline news as a result of the trial of Thomas Kaiser, who had been indicted for extorting a jukebox distributor, Irving Holzman. Rocky had been subpoenaed to testify at the trial and was reluctant to do so. He was told that if he didn't testify, he could find himself in jeopardy, or as a prosecutor said, in hot water. Although Rocky laughed and said he preferred a cold shower, he retained the services of an attorney, who devoted his considerable efforts to making sure Rocky's career would not be tainted by the trial.

According to a June 23, 1966, article in *Newsday*,

> Jurors in the extortion trial of Thomas R. Kaiser listened yesterday to a series of tape recordings, in one of which a suspect in the case suggests that ex-middleweight champion Rocky Graziano knew of the plot to take down jukebox distributor Irving Holzman.
>
> In one of the tapes, which Holzman said was a conversation between him and (Salvatore) Granello, Graziano was pictured as knowing about the extortion scheme. Holzman is represented as telling Granello that Graziano met a man on the street and that the "guy in the street told him (Graziano) that somebody is looking to take a piece of Irving's (Holzman) business." The tape continued, "So Rocky says, 'I told the guy in the street if anybody gets a piece, my cousin (Joey Albino, a Holzman associate) gets a piece. He's been with him for 23 years.'"
>
> The recording further represents Holzman as saying that Graziano went to Albino's house later "with a whole story about, about how Irving is going to get himself killed, and this and that, you know?"[4]

During the trial of Kaiser, the prosecutor wanted Rocky declared a hostile witness. Rocky had annoyed the prosecutor, whose name was Doolittle, by referring to him as Mr. Doodle. The angry prosecutor then stated Rocky was attempting to use his time on the witness stand to grandstand for an audience. The prosecutor said Rocky should not have a forum. The judge told the prosecutor Rocky did not need a forum, nor was he grandstanding. He didn't need a forum because he was on television every day, several times a day, selling a yogurt product to millions of consumers. That was certainly forum enough for him. So once the prosecutor's claim of high-flying grandstanding had been shot down by the

judge, Rocky admitted from the witness stand that he had known Holzman for six years and been introduced to him by Joe Albino, a close
friend and the godson of Graziano's uncle. Graziano then testified that he
had introduced Holzman to Salvatore Granello (aka Sally Burns), who he
had known for 40 years. Although Kaiser was found guilty at that trial,
there were no negative effects on the ongoing show business career of
Rocky Graziano, who was not only doing a series of televised yogurt
commercials, but also performing in commercials for Lee Myles Transmissions and Post cereals. As Rocky told the judge, he was making more
money doing television commercials than he had as a boxer.

If anything, the trial revealed that Rocky had not abandoned his old
friends. While he associated with mob guys, some of whom were close
friends from his childhood, he never participated in criminal activities
once he became a boxer. Following the trial, Rocky left the courtroom.
He exited like a man whom the court had never laid a glove on. He
walked out like a champ.

Rocky was also the subject of a less-serious complaint. A story appeared in the *New York Times* with the headline, "No Punches Pulled."
The subhead was, "Murtagh Gives Graziano Choice of $250 Fine or 10
Days in Jail." Apparently, always the carefree motorist, oblivious of rules
and regulations, Rocky had accumulated five parking summonses and
never paid the fines. The summonses may have been mislaid after being
deposited in either a desk drawer or an unused bread box. When Rocky
told the judge he didn't have the $250 with him, the judge told him to
come back to court with the money. Chief Magistrate John M. Murtagh,
presiding in New York City's Traffic Court, was a stern, no-nonsense
judge who had listened to the most unlikely excuses from motorists asking or begging to be treated leniently, often promising that if let off, they
would never repeat the actions that had driven them into traffic court.
Rocky did not offer any excuses. He simply said he would return with the
$250. That, however, did not hinder Murtagh from issuing one of his
typical stern warnings: "It's high time I started giving out straight jail
sentences on all motorists who fail to come in on time to answer summonses."[5]

Neither the Kaiser trial nor the traffic court reprimand and fine did
anything to tarnish Rocky's reputation. He was still king, sitting on his
throne, his crown tilted at a rakish angle, a smirk on his face. The city
loved him. And advertising agencies flocked to him.

At the very worst, Rocky was perceived by the public and the media as a lovable, charming rogue. People got a kick out of his Noo Yawk marbles-in-his-mouth accent. He was invited to speak at trade shows and conventions, and even to college and university audiences. Fordham University, for example, paid Rocky to lecture on the dangers of delinquency. He also spoke to Police Athletic League groups and at expensive private schools, where hard-core juvenile delinquency was not thought to exist in epidemic proportion or even at all.

Students at colleges and private schools attended Rocky's lectures not to be forewarned about the dangers of delinquency, for few of them were headed down that path, but to be entertained by a sui generis celebrity. Rocky was a charming exotic. He had been one of the real-life dead-end kids, and he was now a millionaire. They laughed at his jokes and "anec-jokes," and applauded the retelling of his famous bouts. They were fascinated by the famous people who were his friends. Best of all, he seemed like a redeemed sinner, and such people, if they have a self-deprecating sense of humor about themselves, draw crowds of admirers. There he was without polish, entirely himself, a lovable, good-humored guy who had turned his life around with a pair of hard-pounding fists. The dangerous, menacing thug of old seemed like the kind of guy you wanted to have a couple of beers with as you listened to his tales.

In fact, Rocky's image as a lovable, redeemed rogue had such allure, even among the rich and famous, that Edward G. Robinson, the formidable Hollywood star, asked Rocky to take him downtown to Little Italy and introduce him to some real-life mobsters. Rocky was only too happy to oblige, and he gave Robinson an evening that would provide enough amusing stories for both of them to dine out on for years to come. Rocky's friends were induced to join the two men and delighted to have drinks and dinner in an old-fashioned ristorante on Mulberry Street in New York's Little Italy, where they regaled the movie star with exaggerated or apocryphal tales of their illicit pasts. To be in the company of the man who had played gangsters in such movies as *Little Caesar* and *Key Largo* was a thrill for Rocky and his pals. They didn't seem to realize that Robinson, who was also raised on the Lower East Side, was a sensitive, educated, bookish man who was one of Hollywood's most prominent art collectors.

As an actor, Robinson had appeared in many Broadway plays before making a name for himself on the silver screen. As a result of his acclaimed screen roles, he is rated 24th in a list of the 25 greatest male stars of the classic American cinema compiled by the American Film Institute. That information, no doubt, would have caused a whistle of appreciation from Rocky, who came to admire many movie stars, for instance, Frank Sinatra, especially if they came from backgrounds almost as poor as his own. For years, Rocky told friends about his wonderful dinner with Edward G. Robinson, who had played the part of gangsters and wanted to meet the real deal.

The real deal, of course, was Rocky Graziano, and his name was known throughout the world. And the name Rocky, without a surname, developed a life of its own. Until the emergence of Rocky Marciano as a top-ranked heavyweight boxer, the single name Rocky was associated with only one man: Rocky Graziano. Many ads could use just his first name, and everyone knew to whom it referred. The name Rocky implied toughness and fearlessness. By the 1950s, teenage delinquents wearing black leather motorcycle jackets and regularly combing their greased hair into ducktails often referred to themselves as Rocks. Some even took on the name Rocky or it became a nickname. Some had the name tattooed on their forearms. If a gang member lost his temper and started punching and kicking his opponent, his friends would shout, "Let him have it Rocky. Kill him Rocky. Knock him on his ass, Rocky."

And to add to the toughness, fearlessness, and ferocity implied by the name Rocky, there came on the scene a second pugilistic celebrity named Rocky. The combination of Rocky Graziano and Rocky Marciano solidified the iconic status of the name Rocky, so much so that Sylvester Stallone didn't need a surname in the title of his first *Rocky* movie. Everyone knew what the name stood for, and, of course, it had to be a movie about a boxer.

Would such movies have been so titled if there had never been a Rocky Graziano? If his life hadn't been celebrated in the movie *Somebody Up There Likes Me*? If he hadn't done hundreds of commercials on television? If he hadn't been the costar on *The Martha Raye Show*? His name naturally led to the name Rocky Marciano, and the two Rocky's coalesced into one name with the same meaning: championship boxing. It's no wonder the two Rockys often appeared together on speaking tours throughout the United States and on television interview shows. Today, there are many athletes named Rocky on the Internet. Younger generations may not know of Rocky Graziano's great skills as a brawling boxing champion of the 1940s. But when they hear the name Rocky, they know it refers to a prizefighter, and in the case of Rocky Graziano, one of the most colorful and endearing fighters of all time.

APPENDIX

Rocky Graziano's Boxing Record

Bouts: 83
Rounds: 410
Wins: 67 (52 by knockout)
Losses: 10 (3 by knockout)
Draws: 6

The result of each bout is noted as follows:

W: win
L: loss
D: draw
PTS: points
KO: knockout
TKO: technical knockout
UD: unanimous decision
SP: split decision
MD: majority decision
DQ: disqualification
RTD: corner retirement

Date	Opponent	Location	Result
September 17, 1952	Chuck Davey	Chicago Stadium, Chicago, IL	L-UD
April 16, 1952	Sugar Ray Robinson	Chicago Stadium, Chicago, IL	L-KO
March 27, 1952	Roy Wouters	Auditorium, Minneapolis, MN	W-TKO
February 18, 1952	Eddie O'Neill	Jefferson County Armory, Louisville, KY	W-TKO
September 19, 1951	Tony Janiro	Olympia Stadium, Detroit, MI	W-TKO
August 6, 1951	Chuck Hunter	Boston Garden, Boston, MA	W-DQ
July 10, 1951	Cecil Hudson	Municipal Auditorium, Kansas City, MO	W-TKO
June 18, 1951	Freddie Lott	Coliseum, Baltimore, MD	W-KO
May 21, 1951	Johnny Greco	Forum, Montreal, Quebec, Canada	W-KO
March 19, 1951	Reuben Jones	Miami Stadium, Miami, FL	W-KO
November 27, 1950	Honeychile Johnson	Convention Hall, Philadelphia, PA	W-KO
October 27, 1950	Tony Janiro	Madison Square Garden, New York City	W-KO
October 16, 1950	Pete Mead	Arena, Milwaukee, WI	W-KO
October 4, 1950	Gene Burton	Chicago Stadium, Chicago, IL	W-KO
May 16, 1950	Henry Brimm	Memorial Auditorium, Buffalo, NY	W-KO
May 9, 1950	Vinnie Cidone	Arena, Milwaukee, WI	W-TKO
April 24, 1950	Danny Williams	Arena, New Haven, CT	W-KO
March 31, 1950	Tony Janiro	Madison Square Garden, New York City	D-SD

March 6, 1950	Joe Curcio	Miami Stadium, Miami, FL	W-KO
December 6, 1949	George "Sonny" Horne	Arena, Cleveland, OH	W-MD
September 14, 1949	Charley Fusari	Polo Grounds, New York City	W-TKO
July 18, 1949	Joe Agosta	Century Stadium, West Springfield, MA	W-KO
June 21, 1949	Bobby Claus	Wilmington Park, Wilmington, DE	W-KO
June 10, 1948	Tony Zale	Ruppert Stadium, Newark, NJ	L-KO
April 5, 1948	George "Sonny" Horne	Uline Arena, Washington, DC	W-UD
July 16, 1947	Tony Zale	Chicago Stadium, Chicago, IL	W-TKO
June 16, 1947	Jerry Fiorello	Swayne Field, Toledo, OH	W-TKO
June 10, 1947	Eddie Finazzo	Fairgrounds Arena, Memphis, TN	W-TKO
September 27, 1946	Tony Zale	Yankee Stadium, Bronx, NY	L-KO
March 29, 1946	Marty Servo	Madison Square Garden, New York City	W-TKO
January 18, 1946	George "Sonny" Horne	Madison Square Garden, New York City	W-UD
September 28, 1945	Harold Green	Madison Square Garden, New York City	W-KO
August 24, 1945	Freddie "Red" Cochrane	Madison Square Garden, New York City	W-KO
June 29, 1945	Freddie "Red" Cochrane	Madison Square Garden, New York City	W-KO
May 25, 1945	Al "Bummy" Davis	Madison Square Garden, New York City	W-TKO
March 9, 1945	Billy Arnold	Madison Square Garden, New York City	W-TKO

December 22, 1944	Harold Green	Madison Square Garden, New York City	L-MD
November 3, 1944	Harold Green	Madison Square Garden, New York City	L-UD
October 24, 1944	Bernie Miller	Brooklyn Arena, Brooklyn, NY	W-TKO
October 6, 1944	Danny Kapilow	St. Nicholas Arena, New York City	D-PTS
September 15, 1944	Frankie Terry	St. Nicholas Arena, New York City	D-PTS
August 14, 1944	Jerry Fiorello	Queensboro Arena, Long Island City, NY	W-SD
July 21, 1944	Tony Reno	Fort Hamilton Arena, Brooklyn, NY	W-PTS
June 27, 1944	Frankie Terry	Dexter Park Arena, Woodhaven, Queens, NY	W-TKO
June 7, 1944	Larney Moore	MacArthur Stadium, Brooklyn, NY	W-TKO
May 29, 1944	Tommy Mollis	Griffith Stadium, Washington, DC	W-TKO
May 9, 1944	Freddie Graham	Turner's Arena, Washington, DC	W-KO
April 10, 1944	Bobby Brown	Turner's Arena, Washington, DC	W-KO
March 14, 1944	Ray Rovelli	Brooklyn Arena, Brooklyn, NY	W-PTS
March 8, 1944	Harold Gray	Scott Hall, Elizabeth, NJ	W-PTS
March 4, 1944	Leon Anthony	Ridgewood Grove, Brooklyn, NY	W-KO
February 24, 1944	Nick Calder	Masonic Hall, Highland Park, NJ	W-KO
February 9, 1944	Steve Riggio	Madison Square Garden, New York City	L-PTS
January 18, 1944	Paul Enzenga	Westchester County Center, White Plains, NY	W-TKO

January 7, 1944	Jerry Pittro	Madison Square Garden, New York City	W-TKO
January 4, 1944	Harold Gray	Grotto Auditorium, Jersey City, NJ	W-PTS
December 27, 1943	Milo Theodorescu	Laurel Green, Newark, NJ	W-TKO
December 6, 1943	Charley McPherson	St. Nicholas Arena, New York City	W-PTS
November 12, 1943	Steve Riggio	Madison Square Garden, New York City	L-PTS
October 13, 1943	Jimmy Williams	Scott Hall, Elizabeth, NJ	W-TKO
October 5, 1943	Freddie Graham	Broadway Arena, Brooklyn, NY	W-KO
September 21, 1943	George Wilson	Broadway Arena, Brooklyn, NY	W-PTS
September 10, 1943	Joe Agosta	Madison Square Garden, New York City	L-PTS
August 24, 1943	Tony Grey	Queensboro Arena, Long Island City, NY	W-KO
August 20, 1943	Ted Apostoli	Madison Square Garden, New York City	W-PTS
August 12, 1943	Charley McPherson	Fort Hamilton Arena, Brooklyn, NY	W-PTS
July 27, 1943	Randy Drew	Queensboro Arena, Long Island City, NY	W-KO
July 22, 1943	George Stevens	Fort Hamilton Arena, Brooklyn, NY	W-TKO
July 8, 1943	John Atteley	Fort Hamilton Arena, Brooklyn, NY	W-RTD
June 24, 1943	Frankie Falco	Fort Hamilton Arena, Brooklyn, NY	W-KO
June 16, 1943	Joe Curcio	Twin City Bowl, Elizabeth, NJ	W-TKO
June 11, 1943	Gilberto Ramir Vasquez	Fort Hamilton Arena, Brooklyn, NY	W-KO

May 25, 1942	Lou Miller	St. Nicholas Arena, New York City	D-PTS
May 12, 1942	Godfrey Howell	Broadway Arena, Brooklyn, NY	W-KO
May 4, 1942	Eddie Lee	St. Nicholas Arena, New York City	W-KO
April 28, 1942	Charlie Ferguson	Broadway Arena, Brooklyn, NY	L-PTS
April 20, 1942	Godfrey Howell	St. Nicholas Arena, New York City	D-PTS
April 14, 1942	Kenny Blackmar	Broadway Arena, Brooklyn, NY	W-KO
April 6, 1942	Mike Mastandrea	St. Nicholas Arena, New York City	W-KO
March 31, 1942	Curtis Hightower	Broadway Arena, Brooklyn, NY	W-TKO

*Statistics were compiled from BoxRec, http://boxrec.com/boxer/9016.

NOTES

INTRODUCTION

1. W. C. Heinz, *The Top of His Game: The Best Sportswriting of W. C. Heinz*, ed. Bill Littlefield (New York: Library of America, 2015), 541.
2. Phil Berger, "Rocky Graziano, Ex-Ring Champion, Dead at 71," *New York Times*, 23 May 1990, B7.
3. Berger, "Rocky Graziano, Ex-Ring Champion, Dead at 71," B7.

I. THE BAD BOY DID IT!

1. Rocky Graziano, with Rowland Barber, *Somebody Up There Likes Me* (New York: Simon & Schuster, 1955), 1.
2. Graziano, with Barber, *Somebody Up There Likes Me*, 88.
3. Graziano, with Barber, *Somebody Up There Likes Me*, 147, 148.
4. Graziano, with Barber, *Somebody Up There Likes Me*, 206.
5. Graziano, with Barber, *Somebody Up There Likes Me*, 215, 252.
6. W. C. Heinz, *The Top of His Game: The Best Sportswriting of W. C. Heinz*, ed. Bill Littlefield (New York: Library of America, 2015), 537.

2. THE TRAINERS AND THE GYM

1. Robert K. Fried, *Corner Men: Great Boxing Trainers* (New York: Four Walls Eight Windows, 1991), 191.

2. A. J. Liebling, *The Sweet Science* (New York: North Point Press, 2004), 139.

3. Fried, *Corner Men*, 201, 207.

4. Fried, *Corner Men*, 298.

5. Angelo Dundee, with Bert Randolph Sugar, *My View from the Corner: A Life in Boxing* (New York: McGraw-Hill, 2009), 27.

3. THE GIRL FROM OCEAN PARKWAY

1. Rocky Graziano, with Rowland Barber, *Somebody Up There Likes Me* (New York: Simon & Schuster, 1955), 257–58.

2. Graziano, with Barber, *Somebody Up There Likes Me*, 261–62.

3. W. C. Heinz, *The Top of His Game: The Best Sportswriting of W. C. Heinz*, ed. Bill Littlefield (New York: Library of America, 2015), 143.

4. Heinz, *The Top of His Game*, 138.

5. Joe Morella and Edward Z. Epstein, *Paul and Joanne: A Biography of Paul Newman and Joanne Woodward* (New York: Delacorte, 1988), 157.

4. ROCKY MAKES A NAME FOR HIMSELF

1. Descriptions of fights are taken from old newsreels, many of which are available on YouTube.

5. MEETING THE MAN OF STEEL

1. John Devaney, "Great Rivalries: Rocky Graziano vs. Tony Zale," in *The Italian Stallions: Heroes of Boxing's Glory Days*, ed. Thomas Hauser and Stephen Brunt (Toronto: Sport Media Publishing, 2003), 101.

2. Rocky Graziano, with Rowland Barber, *Somebody Up There Likes Me* (New York: Simon & Schuster, 1955).

3. W. C. Heinz, *The Top of His Game: The Best Sportswriting of W. C. Heinz*, ed. Bill Littlefield (New York: Library of America, 2015), 522.

6. HUNG OUT TO DRY

1. James P. Dawson, "Graziano Loses His License; Censured for Silence on 'Fix,'" *New York Times*, 8 February 1947, 1.
2. Rocky Graziano, with Rowland Barber, *Somebody Up There Likes Me* (New York: Simon & Schuster, 1955), 323.
3. Graziano, with Barber, *Somebody Up There Likes Me*, 333.
4. W. C. Heinz, *The Top of His Game: The Best Sportswriting of W. C. Heinz*, ed. Bill Littlefield (New York: Library of America, 2015), 524.
5. Heinz, *The Top of His Game*, 526.

7. THE BAD-BOY CHAMP

1. Rocky Graziano, with Rowland Barber, *Somebody Up There Likes Me* (New York: Simon and Schuster, 1955), 334.
2. Graziano, with Barber, *Somebody Up There Likes Me*, 335.
3. Graziano, with Barber, *Somebody Up There Likes Me*, 342.
4. W. C. Heinz, *The Top of His Game: The Best Sportswriting of W. C. Heinz*, ed. Bill Littlefield (New York: Library of America, 2015), 529.
5. John Devaney, "Great Rivalries: Rocky Graziano vs. Tony Zale," in *The Italian Stallions: Heroes of Boxing's Glory Days*, ed. Thomas Hauser and Stephen Brunt (Toronto: Sport Media Publishing, 2003), 106.

8. THE END OF THE TRILOGY

1. John Devaney, "Great Rivalries: Rocky Graziano vs. Tony Zale," in *The Italian Stallions: Heroes of Boxing's Glory Days*, ed. Thomas Hauser and Stephen Brunt (Toronto: Sport Media Publishing, 2003), 106.

9. FIGHTING THE SWEETEST OF THE SWEET SCIENTISTS

1. John Rendel, "Graziano Reinstated by New York Boxing Board after Two-Year Suspension," *New York Times*, 7 May 1949, Sports section, 18.
2. Rendel, "Graziano Reinstated by New York Boxing Board after Two-Year Suspension," 18.

3. Rocky Graziano, with Rowland Barber, *Somebody Up There Likes Me* (New York: Simon & Schuster, 1955), 361.

4. Curt Gowdy and Don Dunphy, *The Way It Was* , "Ray Robinson vs. Rocky Graziano," *PBS* , 20 October 1974, https://www.youtube.com/watch?v=NT-DgrGDWxQ (accessed 30 May 2017).

10. THE LAST RUMBLE

1. Rocky Graziano, with Rowland Barber, *Somebody Up There Likes Me* (New York: Simon & Schuster, 1955), 362.

2. Peter Heller, *In This Corner!* (New York: Dell, 1973), 285.

11. MR. SHOW BUSINESS

1. BrainyQuote, "Henny Youngman Quotes," http://www.brainyquote.com/quotes/authors/h/henny_youngman.html (accessed 20 February 2017).

2. W. C. Heinz, *The Top of His Game: The Best Sportswriting of W. C. Heinz*, ed. Bill Littlefield (New York: Library of America, 2015), 541.

3. The Mavens' Word of the Day Collection, "goombah," *Words@Random*, https://www.bookdepository.com/Mavens-Word-Day-Collection-Random-House/9780375719769 (accessed 4 April 2017).

4. Joe Morella and Edward Z. Epstein, *Paul and Joanne: A Biography of Paul Newman and Joanne Woodward* (New York: Delacorte, 1988), 157.

5. Rocky Graziano, with Ralph Corsel, *Somebody Down Here Likes Me Too* (New York: Stein and Day, 1981), 92–95.

6. Graziano, with Corsel, *Somebody Down Here Likes Me Too*, 150.

7. Graziano, with Corsel, *Somebody Down Here Likes Me Too*, 205–12.

12. ON THE BIG SCREEN

1. Orville Prescott, "Books of the Times," *New York Times*, 21 March 1955, 23.

2. Rocky Graziano, with Ralph Corsel, *Somebody Down Here Likes Me Too* (New York: Stein and Day, 1981), 132.

3. Graziano, with Corsel, *Somebody Down Here Likes Me Too*, 131.

4. Shawn Levy and Paul Newman, *Paul Newman: A Life* (New York: Harmony Books, 2009), 111.

5. Graziano, with Corsel, *Somebody Down Here Likes Me Too*, 128–29.

6. Graziano, with Corsel, *Somebody Down Here Likes Me Too,* 133–34.

7. Graziano, with Corsel, *Somebody Down Here Likes Me Too*, 137.

8. Graziano, with Corsel, *Somebody Down Here Likes Me Too*, 132.

9. Bosley Crowther, "The Screen: Hate Worked for Him," *New York Times*, 6 July 1956, 6.

10. Crowther, "The Screen," 16.

13. THE MAN AND THE ICON

1. W. C. Heinz, *The Top of His Game: The Best Sportswriting of W. C. Heinz*, ed. Bill Littlefield (New York: Library of America, 2015), 523.

2. Heinz, *The Top of His Game*, 523.

3. "20 Graziano Suits Loot of Burglars," *New York Times*, 20 July 1947, 7.

4. Adrian J. Meppen and Ronald Howorth, "Graziano Said to Know of Plot on Holzman," *Newsday*, 23 June 1966, 11.

5. "No Punches Pulled," *New York Times*, 19 May 1954, 34.

BIBLIOGRAPHY

BOOKS

Anderson, Dave. *In the Corner*. New York: William Morrow & Company, 1991.

Dundee, Angelo, with Bert Randolph Sugar. *My View from the Corner: A Life in Boxing*. New York: McGraw-Hill, 2009.

Fernandez, Robert F., Sr. *Boxing in New Jersey, 1900–1999*. Jefferson, NC: McFarland, 2014.

Fried, Ronald K. *Corner Men: Great Boxing Trainers*. New York: Four Walls Eight Windows, 1991.

Graziano, Rocky, with Rowland Barber. *Somebody Up There Likes Me*. New York: Simon & Schuster, 1955.

———, with Ralph Corsel. *Somebody Down Here Likes Me Too*. New York: Stein and Day, 1981.

Hauser, Thomas, and Stephen Brunt. *The Italian Stallions: Heroes of Boxing's Glory Days*. Toronto: Sport Media Publishing, 2003.

Heinz, W. C. *The Top of His Game: The Best Sportswriting of W. C. Heinz*. Ed. Bill Littlefield. New York: Library of America, 2015.

Heller, Peter. *In This Corner . . .!* New York: Dell, 1973.

Levy, Shawn, and Paul Newman. *Paul Newman: A Life*. New York: Harmony Books, 2009.

Liebling, A. J. *A Neutral Corner*. New York: Fireside/Simon & Schuster, 1992.

———. *The Sweet Science*. New York: North Point Press, 2004.

Manzello, Nick. *Legacy of the Gladiators: Italian Americans in Sports*. Worcester, MA: Ambassador Books, 2002.

Morella, Joe, and Edward Z. Epstein. *Paul and Joanne: A Biography of Paul Newman and Joanne Woodward*. New York: Delacorte, 1988.

Sugar, Bert. *The 100 Greatest Boxers of All Time*. New York: Routledge, 1984.

———. *100 Years of Boxing*. Ed. editors of *Ring Magazine*. New York: Galley Press, 1982.

Sussman, Jeffrey. *Max Baer and Barney Ross: Jewish Heroes of Boxing*. Lanham, MD: Rowman & Littlefield, 2016.

Vitale, Rolando. *The Real Rockys*. London: RV Publishing, 2014.

NEWSPAPERS

Chicago Daily News

Chicago Tribune
New York Daily Mirror
New York Daily News
New York Journal-American
New York Post
New York Times
Newark Star-Ledger

MOVIES

Somebody Up There Likes Me. Directed by Robert Wise. Metro-Goldwyn-Mayer, 1956. 113 min.
Tony Rome. Directed by Gordon Douglas. Arcola Pictures, 1957. 110 min.

INDEX

ABOUT THE AUTHOR

Jeffrey Sussman is the author of 12 nonfiction books. In addition, he is president of Jeffrey Sussman, Inc. (www.powerpublicity.com), a marketing/PR firm based in New York City. He has been a boxing fan since the age of 12, when his father taught him the elements of boxing and signed him up for 10 boxing lessons at the legendary Stillman's Gym. Sussman writes for several boxing websites, one of which is www.boxing.com. His latest book is *Max Baer and Barney Ross: Jewish Heroes of Boxing* (2016).